Elections and Voters i

CONTEMPORARY POLITICAL STUDIES SERIES

Series Editor: John Benyon, *University of Leicester*

Published

DAVID BROUGHTON
Public Opinion and Political Polling in Britain

JANE BURNHAM and ROBERT PYPER
Britain's Modernised Civil Service

CLYDE CHITTY
Education Policy in Britain: 2nd edn

ALISTAIR CLARK
Political Parties in the UK

MICHAEL CONNOLLY
Politics and Policy Making in Northern Ireland

DAVID DENVER, CHRISTOPHER CARMAN
and ROBERT JOHNS
Elections and Voters in Britain: 3rd edn

ROBERT GARNER
Environmental Politics: Britain, Europe and the
Global Environment: 2nd edn

ANDREW GEDDES
The European Union and British Politics

WYN GRANT
Economic Policy in Britain

WYN GRANT
Pressure Groups and British Politics

DEREK HEATER and GEOFFREY BERRIDGE
Introduction to International Politics

DILYS M. HILL
Urban Policy and Politics in Britain

RAYMOND KUHN
Politics and the Media in Britain

ROBERT LEACH
Political Ideology in Britain: 2nd edn

ROBERT LEACH and JANIE PERCY-SMITH
Local Governance in Britain

PETER MADGWICK
British Government: The Central Executive
Territory

ANDREW MASSEY and ROBERT PYPER
Public Management and Modernisation in Britain

PHILIP NORTON
Parliament and British Politics

MALCOLM PUNNETT
Selecting the Party Leader

PAUL WHITELEY
Political Participation in Britain

Elections and Voters in Britain

Third Edition

David Denver
Christopher Carman
and
Robert Johns

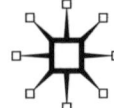

First edition 2003
Second edition 2007
Third edition 2012

Published by
PALGRAVE MACMILLAN

Palgrave Macmillan in the UK is an imprint of Macmillan Publishers Limited, registered in England, company number 785998, of Houndmills, Basingstoke, Hampshire RG21 6XS.

Palgrave Macmillan in the US is a division of St Martin's Press LLC, 175 Fifth Avenue, New York, NY 10010.

Palgrave Macmillan is the global academic imprint of the above companies and has companies and representatives throughout the world.

Palgrave® and Macmillan® are registered trademarks in the United States, the United Kingdom, Europe and other countries.

ISBN 978–0–230–24160–2   hardback
ISBN 978–0–230–24161–9   paperback

This book is printed on paper suitable for recycling and made from fully managed and sustained forest sources. Logging, pulping and manufacturing processes are expected to conform to the environmental regulations of the country of origin.

A catalogue record for this book is available from the British Library.

A catalog record for this book is available from the Library of Congress.

10   9   8   7   6   5   4   3   2   1
21   20   19   18   17   16   15   14   13   12

Printed and bound in China

Contents

List of Tables and Figures

Tables

Figures

Preface to the Third Edition

When it was suggested by the publishers that a new edition of *Elections and Voters in Britain* would be a good idea, David Denver – the single author of the previous versions – decided that in order to prevent staleness (and allow more time for golf) it would be advantageous to bring in new co-authors. Chris Carman and Rob Johns, rated by Denver as 'two of the brightest younger stars in the British electoral studies field', agreed to participate and have borne most of the burden of updating the material as well as contributing their own insights and arguments. They will take increasing responsibility for any future editions.

In this edition, reflecting developments in electoral research, the sections on social class and voting have been abridged while coverage of a number of topics has been expanded – the images that parties project, their perceived competence, and evaluations of their leaders. These are all central to the 'Performance Politics' agenda set by Harold Clarke and colleagues in the latest book based on the British Election Study (Clarke *et al.*, 2009). In addition, results and survey data from the 2010 elections have been fully incorporated into the discussion as well as relevant tables and figures.

As noted in the Preface to the first edition, this book is not primarily for colleagues actively researching and writing about elections. Although we hope that they find it a useful overview which can be recommended to their students, specialists in electoral analysis will already know, more or less, most of what is written in the following pages. Rather, our intention is to summarize and simplify the work of these colleagues for non-specialists and students in both schools and universities (as well as, perhaps, people who just happen to be interested in elections). One consequence of this focus is that we have tried to keep tables as clear and uncluttered as possible. In many cases this has meant not showing in tables the raw numbers on which calculations are based. This would be unforgivable in a research paper, of course, but seems, on balance, to be a sensible strategy in this case.

As before, we have included a glossary of statistical terms, and items appearing in the glossary are printed in **bold** when they first appear in the text. The explanations and descriptions of various statistical measures and techniques in the text are intended to be non-technical. They attempt to enable readers to understand why various techniques are used and what the results can tell us.

Everyone writing about electoral behaviour in Britain has to acknowledge a debt to the successive teams which, from 1963 onwards, have undertaken the burden of directing the BES surveys. In particular, the team involved in 2001, 2005 and 2010 (Harold Clarke, David Sanders, Marianne Stewart and Paul Whiteley) have made the survey data available to colleagues with unprecedented speed, often within days of polling. Given how heavily we draw on BES data in the book, this speed is all the more appreciated. Since we have not always shown the same promptness, we are grateful for the patience showed by our publishers, Steven Kennedy and Stephen Wenham.

The first edition of the book began with the words 'Elections are fun'. Almost twenty years later we still think that and hope that this book will start to develop in at least some readers the same interest and enthusiasm that we have for the subject.

DAVID DENVER
CHRISTOPHER CARMAN
ROBERT JOHNS

Acknowledgement: the screenshots used in Figure 6.7 are reproduced with permission from the Conservative Party, the Green Party and the UK Independence Party.

1

Studying British Elections

The British general election of 1950 was the first 'normal' general election after the Second World War. Due to the war, the previous election in 1945 was the first to be held for ten years and it had taken place while the war with Japan was still in progress. Many electors were still serving overseas with the armed forces, with about three million being registered as 'service voters'. By 1950 things had settled down and the election of that year is an appropriate point of departure when surveying electoral developments in Britain over the post-war period.

A simple comparison of the results in 1950 with those of the most recent election in 2010 illustrates some of the major changes that have occurred during these years (see Table 1.1). These data suggest that in many respects there were very marked differences – as might be

Table 1.1   Results of the 1950 and 2010 general elections in Great Britain

	1950			2010		
	% of votes	Candidates	Seats	% of votes	Candidates	Seats
Conservative	43.0	607	288	36.9	631	306
Labour	46.8	612	315	29.7	631	258
Liberal (Democrats)	9.3	475	9	23.6	631	57
SNP	0.0	3	0	1.7	59	6
Plaid Cymru	0.1	7	0	0.6	40	3
Communist	0.3	100	0	0.0	6	0
Others	0.5	41	1	7.6	2,132	2
Turnout	84.1%			65.3%		

Note: The figures shown exclude Northern Ireland. The Speaker was not opposed by Labour or the Liberal Democrats and is counted as an 'other'.

Sources: Data from Rallings and Thrasher (2000); authors' calculations (2010 election).

expected – between these two general elections held sixty years apart and in different centuries. Indeed, the only similarities relate to the position of the Conservative and Labour parties. In both elections they were the largest parties in terms of share of the votes obtained and seats won. Even so, their dominance was not nearly as overwhelming in 2010 as it had been in 1950. In the earlier election, together they obtained 89.8 per cent of the votes and 98.4 per cent of the seats; by 2010 their share had declined to 69.4 per cent of the votes and 89.2 per cent of the seats. As will be seen later, it was the operation of the electoral system which ensured that the decline in seats won was much smaller than the decline in votes.

Some of the other changes between 1950 and 2010 are even more striking. First, the old Liberal Party emerged from the 1950 election with less than 10 per cent of the votes and only nine Members of Parliament (MPs). By 2010 they had been transformed into the Liberal Democrats, more than doubled their vote share and won 57 seats, slightly down from the 62 won in 2005 which had been their largest tally since 1923. Second, in Scotland and Wales the part played in elections by the nationalist parties was much more significant in 2010 than it was in 1950. In the early 1950s the Scottish National Party (SNP) and Plaid Cymru were generally regarded as rather peculiar parties, supported by eccentric individuals and on the fringes of politics. Few candidates were put forward in 1950 and, within Scotland, the SNP won just 0.4 per cent of the votes, while in Wales Plaid Cymru took 1.2 per cent. In 2010, however, both contested all seats in their respective countries; the SNP won 19.9 per cent of the Scottish vote while 11.3 per cent of Welsh voters opted for Plaid. Although these were somewhat disappointing results for both parties, they are now major players in the electoral and political game in their respective countries.

Third, there has been a massive increase in the number and variety of 'others' participating as candidates in British elections. In 1950 there were 100 candidates representing the Communist Party (who totalled more than 90,000 votes) but in 2010 there were just six Communist Party of Britain candidates who managed only 947 votes between them. These Communists have been joined, however, by an abundance of new parties. In 2010 there were 572 United Kingdom Independence Party (UKIP) candidates, 338 representing the British National Party (BNP), 310 for the Green Party, 107 English Democrats and around 700 others representing a bewildering variety of other parties and groups, or simply themselves. Why has there been this explosion in the number of candidates from small parties? One reason is that the deposit required for candidacy (retained by the authorities if the candidate does not obtain 5 per cent of the votes in the relevant constituency) is no longer a serious barrier. In 1950 the deposit required was £150. This was equivalent to about £3,500 in 2010 but in fact the deposit in 2010 was only £500. Moreover, small parties and some individuals have realized that the deposit buys a lot of publicity. Every nominated candidate is entitled to a free postal delivery to every household in the relevant constituency; 50 candidates nominated nationwide by a party guarantees it a free national radio and television broadcast.

Finally, the figures in the table show that the turnout of electors in 2010 was much lower – by around 20 percentage points – than in 1950. The gap would have been even wider had we compared 1950 with 2001, the latter election having seen a post-war low of 59 per cent. It should be noted, however, that the figures for 1950 and 2010 are not exactly comparable. The voting age was lowered from 21 to 18 just before the 1970 general election so that the 2010 percentage turnout is based on a larger electorate, containing a much larger proportion of young people (a group which has a poor turnout record), than the 1950 figure. Nonetheless, the declining turnout in general elections has provoked much discussion in recent years and is a subject to which we return in the next chapter.

To younger people, the election of 1950 probably seems like ancient history, but it firmly established the broad pattern of two-party politics that was to dominate in Britain for most of the rest of the century, and it acts as a sort of benchmark against which later developments can be measured. The 1950 election is also important to students of voting behaviour since it was in that election that the first-ever election survey of British voters was carried out. Before discussing this and subsequent surveys, however, it is worth considering why we should study elections.

Why study elections?

One good reason for studying elections is that they are fun events. In the first half of the nineteenth century, part of the fun involved the voters getting roaring drunk at the candidates' expense (being 'treated', as this was known), pelting them with rotten fruit and brawling in the street with opponents. The practice of candidates treating voters was effectively ended by the Second Reform Act of 1867 which greatly enlarged the electorate. There were now simply too many voters to treat. In addition, in 1872 the Ballot Act made voting secret (previously voters had to declare their choice in public), so that candidates could no longer check that the voters they had treated actually voted for them. Finally, in 1883 the Corrupt Practices Act outlawed treating (much to the disappointment of many voters, one suspects). Despite this, elections continued to be a form of public entertainment until well into the twentieth century. In 1922 a crowd of 10,000 assembled to hear the declaration of the general election result in Dundee and was rewarded with the news that the sitting member, Winston Churchill, had been defeated by a Prohibitionist (in a city notorious for drunkenness).

Popular enthusiasm does not reach those standards today. Nonetheless, even given the relatively low turnouts in the last few elections, general elections are still major national events which precipitate greatly increased political activity, discussion, interest and media coverage. On election night, the attention of a substantial portion of the nation is at least partly engaged by the election. Next day, the front pages of all newspapers are entirely devoted to election news. During the 2010 election, television channels dedicated to news provided almost round-the-clock campaign coverage, well over the top for most electors but certainly a binge for election 'junkies'. And elections continue to be enjoyed by all sorts of people. Candidates and party workers often experience a sense of exhilaration during campaigns; people in the media are caught up in the excitement of reporting a major national event; television presenters get to use all sorts of computer gadgetry; pollsters, analysts and pundits find themselves in great demand. Even the mass of ordinary voters who now largely 'spectate' on election campaigns appear to enjoy the 'horse race', some of them betting on the outcome and many watching campaign reports and party broadcasts on television. Election night parties are not uncommon.

Studying elections is also fun – at least for some people. Others collect stamps, pore over cricket statistics in *Wisden*, or track celebrities as they hurtle into and out of marriages. But there are 'election buffs' around the country who collect, collate and analyse election results. Part of the fascination is the sheer mass of information available. In British general elections there are results for 650 (UK) constituencies to be looked at, but in addition there are elections to the European Parliament, the Scottish Parliament, and the Welsh and Northern Ireland Assemblies as well as local council elections involving many thousands of wards and electoral divisions. Election results are also fascinating because they are numerical in form and numbers can be analysed endlessly. Voting figures can be aggregated, averaged, correlated, graphed and used to construct maps. Some academic studies of electoral behaviour take statistical manipulation so far that they are well-nigh incomprehensible to all but a few specialists, but most require only a basic understanding of some common statistical measures and techniques.

The fact that elections yield masses of quantitative data amenable to statistical analysis, together with the rapid development of computer technology and appropriate software, partly explains the huge growth in the academic literature focusing on elections over the past 40 years or so. There is more to it than that, however. Elections are studied because they are important. Most people would agree that it is the existence of free, competitive elections which distinguishes political systems that we normally call 'democratic' from others. Different versions of democratic theory attach different weights to elections and assign them different functions, but all see elections as central to democracy.

In traditional democratic theory, elections give sovereignty or ultimate power to the citizens. It is through elections that the citizen participates in the political process and ultimately determines the personnel and policies of governments. Only a government which is elected by the people is a legitimate government. Other democratic theorists view elections as only one among a number of channels of citizen influence, stressing the indirect nature of influence through the electoral process, and an influential version of democratic theory suggests that elections simply allow citizens a choice between competing elites. The existence of free elections remains, nonetheless, the essential difference between democratic and non-democratic states. In the 1990s, the extension of voting rights to black people in South Africa and the introduction of free competitive elections into the ex-Communist states of Eastern Europe were widely praised as extending democracy. At a minimum, elections provide a peaceful way of changing governments (and this is not unimportant given the number of governments around the world that are removed by violence). Elections are also the means by which the great mass of citizens can participate directly in the political process, and in Britain millions of citizens do participate in this way. For most, voting is the only overtly political action which is regularly undertaken. Finally, elections make governments accountable to the electorate, at least once every five years in Britain. Voters can pass judgement on the government and either keep it in office or replace it.

These would be reasons enough for studying elections but it is also clear that elections do make a difference to the policies pursued by governments and hence to the lives of most people. Exactly how and how much elections affect what governments do is a matter of some debate. Voters themselves disagree about how much difference it makes when one party rather than another wins an election and it is certainly true that governments of any party are constrained by external events over which they have little control. Nonetheless, it strains credulity to suggest, for example, that the Conservative victory in the 1979 general election had little effect on, say, the status and role of trade unions in Britain or that the results of the 1997 election had nothing to do with the subsequent implementation of devolution to Scotland and Wales. Elections are so central to politics that, as David Butler (1998: 454) observed, 'History used to be marked off by the dates of Kings …Now it is marked by the dates of [general] elections'.

Elections, then, are central to democracy, occasion mass political behaviour, determine who governs and thus affect the lives of all of us. By studying them we seek to deepen our understanding of how a key process of democracy operates, to discover how citizens make their voting decisions and to explain election outcomes.

Studying elections

Unsurprisingly, given their importance and fascination, there is a vast literature dealing with elections and voting in Britain, including specialized academic journals such as the *Journal of Elections, Public Opinion and Parties*. This literature covers every conceivable aspect of elections, but here we focus on the two main ways in which voting has been studied: by means of sample surveys and by analysing election results themselves.

Surveys of the electorate

Sample surveys are commonly used – by a variety of agencies in a variety of fields – to collect information about individuals. They provide, therefore, **individual-level data.** On the basis of the sample figures, generalizations can be made, within limits, about the population from which the sample was taken. Lay people frequently express astonishment or disbelief when it is pointed out that, on the basis of a sample of around 2,000 voters, generalizations can be made about the whole British electorate. To avoid going into sampling theory, we simply assert that this can be done with some accuracy and surveys are among the most important tools of empirical social science.

Academic survey studies of voting behaviour were pioneered in the

1940s in the United States but, as noted above, the first-ever academic survey relating to voting behaviour in Britain was carried out at the time of the 1950 election. This was a local study: some 850 voters in the constituency of Greenwich were interviewed before, during and after the election. Partly because of the rudimentary nature of the technology available to analyse survey returns (there were no computers in those days), the book reporting the results of this study was not published until six years later (Benney, Gray and Pear, 1956). Although the topics covered have remained central concerns for electoral analysts – the role of social class and policy opinions, voters' attention to the local and national campaigns, vote switching, and so on – the report was very much an exploratory and mapping operation and the analysis was confined to what would now be regarded as the elementary technique of **cross-tabulation.**

Further local surveys followed in the 1950s – in Bristol (Milne and Mackenzie, 1954, 1958), Glossop (Birch, 1959) and Newcastle under Lyme (Bealey, Blondel and McCann, 1965) – but the next major development came in 1963. In that year, the first national survey study of the British electorate was undertaken under the direction of David Butler and Donald Stokes. Although 1963 was not an election year (the survey was one of two focusing on the 1964 election), this proved to be the first of a series of national surveys carried out at every general election since 1964 under the auspices of the British Election Study (BES). Butler and Stokes themselves covered the 1964, 1966 and 1970 elections. A team from the University of Essex took over for the elections of 1974 (two) and 1979. From 1983 until 1997 Anthony Heath, Roger Jowell and John Curtice were the principal investigators, while in 2001 the baton passed to – and currently remains with – David Sanders and Paul Whiteley at Essex and two election specialists from the United States (Harold Clarke and Marianne Stewart). These surveys have resulted in a number of major works on voting in Britain and hundreds, possibly thousands, of book chapters, scholarly articles and papers. The major BES reports on the elections from 1964 to 2005 are by Butler and Stokes (1969, 1974), Sarlvik and Crewe (1983), Heath *et al.* (1985, 1991, 1994, 2001), Evans and Norris (1999) and Clarke *et al.* (2004, 2009). In addition, a valuable compendium of the main results of the surveys conducted between 1963 and 1992 can be found in Crewe, Fox and Day (1995).

The basic structure and function of the BES has remained the same over the decades: a survey of a representative sample of British voters, aimed not only at recording but also at explaining whether, how and why they voted. But the scale and complexity of the studies have increased considerably. The 2010 version involved around 20,000 respondents, some interviewed face-to-face and others surveyed online, and multiple 'waves' of data collection beginning many months before and ending many months after polling day. Such endeavours are expensive, however, and there are many examples of more limited surveys. Researchers have surveyed voters in particular localities and also specific groups of voters such as women, affluent workers, young people and members of ethnic minority groups. Others have focused on particular topics, such as voting in local elections or the impact of media coverage on political attitudes.

Other important sources of survey data about individual voters are the regular public opinion polls and election-day exit polls (which involve interviewing voters as they leave the polling station after having voted and are regularly commissioned by the main terrestrial television channels at by-elections and general elections). Poll results are frequently used by commentators and electoral analysts (see, for example, Rose and McAllister, 1986, 1990; Worcester, Mortimore and Baines, 2005; Wring, Mortimore and Atkinson, 2011). In addition, researchers sometimes 'piggy-back' on pollsters by paying them to ask specific questions in their regular monthly surveys (see, for example, Bartle, 2001; Clarke, Stewart and Whiteley, 2001).

The general public usually pay attention to political polls only at election time, when they achieve high visibility by giving almost daily figures for the voting intentions of the electorate. Polls have, indeed, become an important and controversial feature of modern election campaigns (see Chapter 6). In fact, the leading political pollsters (ICM, Ipsos MORI and YouGov) monitor the opinions of the electorate on a regular basis, producing monthly reports which, in addition to current voting intention figures, record details of the voters' perceptions of party leaders, government performance, current issues and much else (see www.icmresearch.co.uk; www.ipsos-mori.com; www.yougov.com). Polling firms are commercial organizations, of course, and carry out political polls on behalf of clients (mainly newspapers and television). Their clients are not particularly interested in obtaining the kind of detailed information about voting choice and the factors affecting it that academics require. Poll interviews tend, therefore, to be much shorter than interviews for major academic surveys. They are mostly conducted by telephone (or, increasingly, via the internet) and the information sought from voters, in addition to their political opinions, is normally confined to a few obvious attributes such as age, education, sex and occupation. Nonetheless, polls constitute a valuable source of individual data. They provide regular monthly data and their results are analysed and published very rapidly. Almost as soon as an election is over, commentators use poll results to analyse voting patterns. In contrast, in the past it has taken many months, if not years, for reports on major academic surveys to become available.

The reliability and accuracy of survey results vary with the type and size of sample used. As a rule of thumb, however, in reputable studies it is usually highly probable (95 per cent certain) that a sample figure will be within about two points either way of the true figure for the population as a whole. For example, in MORI's aggregated election polls for the 2005 election it is reported that 30 per cent of 18 to 24 year olds who voted chose the Conservatives. It is highly probable, therefore, that among all 18 to 24 year olds the proportion voting Conservative was between 28 and 32 per cent (that is, 30 per cent plus or minus two points). The important point to note is that figures derived from surveys should not be regarded as being precise. They are *estimates* of the true situation among the population being studied. Put another way, surveys are liable to sampling error (a fact which authors appear to forget when they report survey results with great precision). For this reason, when presenting data based on sample surveys it is sensible to round the figures to whole numbers rather than report them to one decimal place, as is sometimes done.

Surveys are also liable to other sources of error. Questions may be ambiguous or unclear, lead respondents to give particular answers, be incomprehensible to the respondent or be interpreted in a way that was not intended by the questionnaire designer. Often respondents obligingly answer a question even if they do not understand it or have no opinion on the matter. They may also give the answer that they suspect the interviewer or researcher wants to hear, and avoid admitting to opinions that they perceive as socially unacceptable. More mundanely, mistakes may be made by interviewers in recording answers, whether by hand or on lap-top computers. Even so, sample surveys are generally reliable and powerful research tools. They have become an indispensable part of electoral analysis and have played a crucial role in advancing our understanding of electoral behaviour.

Analysing election results

A quite different approach to studying voting is to analyse election results themselves. This approach has a much longer pedigree than the

use of surveys. There is, for example, a famous analysis of the relationship between votes and seats won in British elections dating from 1905
(Edgeworth, 1905) and the literature on proportional representation
suggests that there certainly were election 'anoraks' in the nineteenth
century, poring over their figures by candlelight (see Hart, 1992). In the
modern era, this approach has been sustained by the series of Nuffield
Studies of British general elections (so-called because of their association with Nuffield College, Oxford). Begun in 1945, the series has
provided a contemporary account of the campaign in every election
since then and also an analysis of the election results. The full list of
Nuffield studies since 1950 is McCallum and Readman (1947); Nicholas
(1951); Butler (1952, 1955); Butler and Rose (1960); Butler and King
(1965, 1966); Butler and Pinto-Duschinsky (1971); Butler and
Kavanagh (1974, 1975, 1980, 1984, 1988, 1992, 1997, 2002); Kavanagh
and Butler (2005); and Kavanagh and Cowley (2010).

A simple first step in this sort of analysis is to fill in the gap between
1950 and 2010 in order to assess trends in party support. The relevant
data are shown in Table 1.2 and the parties' shares of the votes are
graphed in Figure 1.1. Obviously, the picture is rather more complicated
than that suggested by looking at only the first and last elections in the
series. After 1951 Labour's support in general elections fell steadily
(with a slight reversal of the trend in the mid-1960s) to just 28.3 per cent
in 1983. There was something of a recovery in 1987 and 1992 and a
clear victory in 1997. In 2001 and, more noticeably, in 2005, Labour's
vote share declined again. Although Labour won the 2005 election, the
party's vote share was smaller than it had achieved in every election
between 1950 and 1979. Then, in 2010, the party's support plunged to
29.7 per cent, barely above the post-war low of 1983.

Despite easily outpolling Labour in the 1980s and early 1990s,
Conservative support was also on a downward trend over the period as
a whole. However, the 1997 election was an unparalleled catastrophe for
the party and, since then, there has been only limited recovery. The
Conservative vote share in 2010, although enough to return the party to
office, was still only on a par with its showing in the October 1974 election that, until 1997, had marked the low point in the party's fortunes.
The 1950 election marked almost the last gasp of the old Liberal Party
and during the 1950s it was nearly eliminated as a serious force in electoral politics. Under Jo Grimond (party leader 1956–67) the abyss was
avoided, however, and in February 1974 their share of the British vote
increased sharply to almost 20 per cent. The formation of the Social
Democratic Party (SDP) in 1981 revolutionized the politics of the centre

Table 1.2 Party shares of votes in general elections, 1950–2010 (Great Britain)

	1950 %	1951 %	1955 %	1959 %	1964 %	1966 %	1970 %	Feb. 1974 %	Oct. 1974 %	1979 %	1983 %	1987 %	1992 %	1997 %	2001 %	2005 %	2010 %
Conservative	43.0	47.8	49.3	48.8	42.9	41.4	46.2	38.8	36.7	44.9	43.5	43.3	42.8	31.5	32.7	33.2	36.9
Labour	46.8	49.4	47.4	44.6	44.8	48.8	43.9	38.0	40.2	37.8	28.3	31.5	35.2	44.3	42.0	36.2	29.7
Liberal (Democrats)	9.3	2.6	2.8	6.0	11.4	8.6	7.6	19.8	18.8	14.1	26.0	23.1	18.3	17.2	18.8	22.7	23.6
Others	0.9	0.2	0.5	0.6	0.9	1.1	2.3	3.4	4.3	3.2	2.2	2.1	3.7	7.0	6.5	8.0	9.9
Lab.–Con. swing		+1.1	+1.8	+1.2	−3.1	−2.8	+4.9	−0.8	−2.2	+5.3	+4.1	−1.7	−2.1	−10.2	+1.8	+3.2	+5.1
Standard deviation of swing		1.7	1.9*	2.3	2.4	1.7	2.1	2.9*	1.5	3.1	3.0*	3.2	2.8	3.4*	2.6	2.4	3.7*
Pedersen Index		7.4	2.0	3.3	6.7	4.3	6.0	13.3	2.7	8.4	11.8	3.2	5.3	12.4	2.3	5.9	6.5

Notes: The figures for the Liberals in 1983 and 1987 are for the 'Alliance' between the Liberals and the Social Democratic Party (SDP). Standard deviation of swing figures for elections in which there were comprehensive boundary revisions are asterisked. In these cases, except for 1955, constituency swings are based on estimates of voting in the preceding election. The standard deviation for 1955 is calculated on the basis of seats in which there was no major boundary change ($N = 442$).

Sources: Data from Rallings and Thrasher (2000); Electoral Commission (2001b). Swing, standard deviation and Pedersen Index statistics were calculated from the original data.

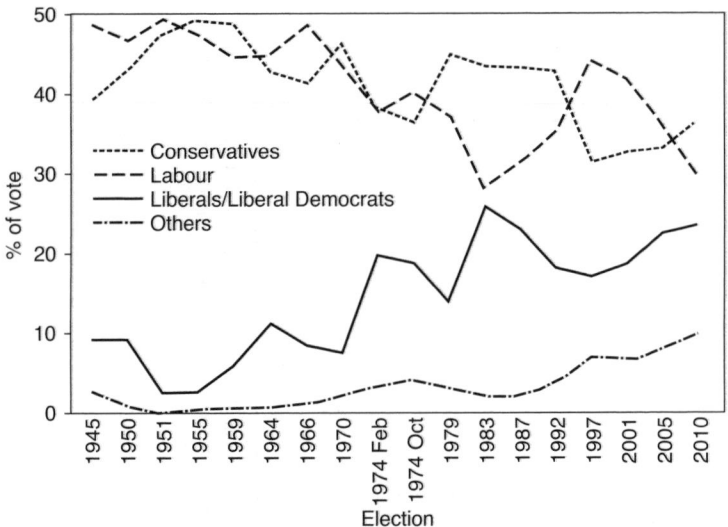

Figure 1.1 Party shares of votes in general elections, 1950–2010 (Great Britain)

and, in 1983, the 'Alliance' between the Liberals and the SDP almost pipped Labour for second place. In 1988 the two parties merged to form what we now know as the Liberal Democrats. In the four elections since then, support for the Liberal Democrats has been relatively steady, with signs of improvement in the last three elections, and the party is now a much more serious contender for votes than the Liberals were at the start of the period. For a couple of days during the 2010 election campaign, the party even took the lead in the opinion polls. Perhaps the most obvious message of Figure 1.1, however, is the fragmentation that has occurred in British electoral politics. Up to 1970 the two big parties were the main players on the stage with the rest being confined to bit parts. From 1974, however, when the Liberals took a leap forward, it would clearly be a mistake to think of elections in terms of a simple two-party system. In addition, the share of votes going to 'others' has steadily increased since 1987.

We can take the analysis of trends in election results a stage further by looking at 'swing' figures. Swing is a measure of the net change in support for two parties in a pair of elections. It was developed by David Butler, is simple to calculate and is defined as follows:

$$\frac{(C_2 - C_1) + (L_1 - L_2)}{2}$$

In this formula, C_1 is the percentage share of the total vote obtained by the Conservatives at the first election and C_2 the percentage at the second; L_1 is Labour's share at the first election and L_2 Labour's percentage at the second. The statistic produced by this formula is known as 'Butler' or 'traditional' swing. By convention the parties are put in the order shown and the effect of this is that a positive figure denotes a swing to the Conservatives and a negative figure a swing to Labour. The parties could appear in any order, however, and any two parties could be substituted for Conservative and Labour. A variant known as 'two-party' or 'Steed' swing (having been devised by Michael Steed) is also commonly used. Here the formula is exactly as above but, when calculating the percentage vote for the two parties concerned, votes for all other parties are excluded, so that the two parties' shares of the vote always total 100 per cent.

Table 1.2 shows the Butler Conservative–Labour swing between successive elections and is calculated on the basis of the national distribution of votes. The last point means that the swing shown is the 'overall' or 'national' swing. This needs to be distinguished from the **mean** swing, which is sometimes used in analysis and refers to the average of swings in individual constituencies (which is usually slightly different from the overall figure). Swings between the parties were very small in the 1950s but more variable thereafter. A new post-war record was set in 1979 with a swing of 5.3 per cent to the Conservatives, but this was dwarfed by the massive swing to Labour (10.2 per cent) in 1997. Compared to that 1997 figure, the swing to the Conservatives in 2010 also looks quite modest but, on a wider comparison, it stands out as one of the bigger electoral turnarounds. (In order to win a majority in the 2010 election, the party would have needed to achieve its biggest swing from Labour since the war.)

The table also shows the **standard deviation** of constituency swings. This gives an indication of the extent to which swing varied across constituencies in each election: whether it was broadly similar (lower score) or varied a good deal (higher score). The figures up to October 1974 suggest that swings tended to be similar across the country; the average standard deviation is 2.1 for that period. From 1979 there was usually greater variation in swings. The average standard deviation in the eight elections over that period was 3.0 and 2010 marked a high point. The increase in standard deviations means that, in more recent elections, the overall shift in support from Conservatives to Labour or – as in 2010 – vice versa has become less uniform across the country. In 2010, then, some parts of the country and even some individual seats will have shown a huge swing to the Conservatives while, in others, the Labour vote held quite steady and the Conservatives made little headway.

In the past, swing was a widely used and very useful measure of electoral change. It provided a simple summary of the extent of change and was used to compare inter-election movements in different parts of the country and different constituencies. In addition, before general elections psephologists could work out the swing needed for any constituency to change hands. Thus, if in a particular constituency the Conservatives had 48 per cent and Labour 44 per cent of the votes at the preceding election, then a swing to Labour of anything over 2 per cent would mean a Labour gain. Since swing tended to be in the same direction and of the same magnitude over the country as a whole, accurate estimates could be made of the number of seats that would change hands given a particular national swing, and of the swing needed for a party to win or lose a majority of seats in the House of Commons. Indeed, once the results in a relatively small number of seats had been declared, a reasonable estimate of the national swing could be made, and the final result of the election could be predicted with some confidence, even to the extent of identifying which seats would change hands. As Crewe (1985a: 101–3) put it, 'To know the swing in Cornwall was to know, within a percentage point or two, the swing in the Highlands; to know the results of the first three constituencies to declare on election night was to know not only which party had won – but by how many seats'. The last point is something of an exaggeration but it is a pardonable one. Significant deviations from the national trend used to be relatively rare.

In the context of more recent elections swing is rather less useful. This is partly because swings between elections have become less uniform across constituencies than they used to be but it is also the case that swing was developed in a situation in which elections were essentially contests between two parties only. Since 1974 patterns of party competition have been more complex and swing cannot tell us about relative change between three parties. There have been attempts to devise three-way swing figures (Miller, 1981) but these are complicated to calculate and lack the elegance and simplicity of traditional swing. The commonest way of measuring aggregate or net electoral change nowadays is simply to use the changes in each party's percentage share of the vote. There is, however, a relatively simple measure of overall electoral change called the Pedersen Index (see Pedersen, 1979). This was designed to measure the amount of electoral volatility revealed by election results and it is calculated by summing the changes in each party's share of the vote in successive elections and dividing by two. The relevant index scores for elections since 1950 are shown in Table 1.2. The figure for 1951 is relatively large, reflecting the steep decline in Liberal support, but thereafter the index suggests only moderate levels of change until February 1974, which saw the biggest turnover in votes of any post-war election. There was also high volatility in 1983 (due to the impact of the Liberal–SDP Alliance) and 1997 (when Labour won its first election in more than twenty years), but the figures for 2005 and 2010 – both of which saw a moderate rather than spectacular swing from Labour to the Conservatives – reflect only moderate volatility.

Until the late 1960s, the analysis of aggregate election statistics was normally confined to the election results themselves (as in the statistical appendices to the Nuffield studies). There were very few examples of analysis systematically relating the distribution of party support or turnout in constituencies to their socio-economic characteristics. The reason for this was that it was not until the sample census of 1966 that census data were made available on a constituency basis. This was continued in subsequent censuses and has given rise to a flourishing industry in the aggregate analysis of election data. This sort of analysis can involve more complicated statistical methods, however, and we will consider some examples in later chapters.

Aggregate and survey data compared

Election results are a form of **aggregate data**: that is, data which relate to an aggregate or collectivity such as a constituency, region or country. We know, for example, that in the Lancaster and Fleetwood constituency at the 2010 general election there was a 61.1 per cent turnout and the distribution of votes was 36.1 per cent Conservative, 35.3 per cent Labour, 19.1 per cent Liberal Democrat, 4.4 per cent Green, 2.4 per cent UKIP and 2.2 per cent BNP. This result was obtained by totting up, or aggregating, the number of people who voted and the party that they voted for. From the final result we do not know whether or how any individual voted but we do know something about the collectivity of voters in the constituency. Other examples of aggregate data are the percentage of council tenants in a ward, the number of people aged 65 and over in a constituency, the percentage of manual workers in the North of

England, and the change in Labour's share of the vote between 2001 and 2005 over the country as a whole. It is an important feature of aggregate data that they cannot be used to infer anything about the behaviour or characteristics of individuals; for that, survey data are required.

This point is well illustrated by returning to the topic of swing. As pointed out above, swing is a summary measure of net electoral change based on aggregate data (namely, election results). It does not tell us anything about how individuals behave but rather describes the net effect of the changes in individuals' voting behaviour between two elections. This can be easily understood if we distinguish the different components of electoral change. Whether over the country as a whole or in individual constituencies or wards (assuming no boundary changes) the differences between two consecutive election results are produced by four sorts of change:

1 *Switching between major parties* (conventionally the Conservatives and Labour). Some people who voted Labour in the first election will vote Conservative in the second, and vice versa. Clearly the outcome of the second election will only be affected if there is some imbalance in these switches.
2 *Minor party traffic.* Here again switching parties is involved but this time from minor parties (such as the Liberal Democrats, Greens, SNP) to one of the major parties, and vice versa. (There may also be some movement between different minor parties but this will not affect the swing calculation.) As with major-party switching, there will be some self-cancelling effect but an imbalance will affect the election outcome.
3 *Non-voting traffic.* Some people who did not vote in the first election will vote in the second; others who voted first time round fail to do so the second time. Clearly, if it is the case that one party's previous supporters stay away from the polls in larger numbers, or if previous non-voters flock to one of the parties, then this will affect the result.
4 *The physical replacement of the electorate.* Every year (although the number fluctuates a bit), around 750,000 people in Britain turn 18 and therefore become eligible to vote, while about 600,000 people die. If one party gets a disproportionate share of the new voters, or if the supporters of one party are dying off in greater numbers, this will affect election outcomes. Immigration to and emigration from the country or a particular constituency can have a similar effect. Population movement can change the character of a constituency or, more quickly, a ward over time.

Aggregate measures of electoral change, such as swing or changes in the parties' shares of the vote, simply summarize the effects of all of these ebbs and flows. For more detailed information about the various components of change we have to turn to individual-level data produced by surveys.

Ideally, a survey study designed to analyse electoral change would interview a sample of voters after one election and then re-interview the same people after a second election. This is a **panel survey**. It is well established that many voters do not accurately recall which party they voted for some years previously and the use of a panel eliminates this problem. Panel surveys have their own problems, however. They suffer from 'attrition' as many respondents – especially those less interested in politics – drop out and the sample becomes unrepresentative; and even this approach is unable to measure the impact of the physical replacement of the electorate. (It is impossible to re-interview people who have died or emigrated between the two elections, and hard to identify those who were too young to vote in the first election but who reach voting age by the time of the second.) Nonetheless, despite these problems, the panel design is an extremely powerful tool for those studying voting behaviour.

Whether through a panel or simply asking voters to recall their earlier behaviour, any survey obtaining the reported votes of respondents at two successive elections allows for a detailed analysis of electoral change. The usual method is to construct a two-way table showing exactly what people did at the two elections concerned. A table of this kind is sometimes called an 'election transition matrix' or, more simply, a 'flow of the vote' table; Table 1.3 is an example of this based on survey respondents in 2010 recalling their vote in 2005. (Fuller examples of election transition matrices for earlier elections, including estimates of the population entering and leaving the electorate, are given in Butler and Stokes, 1974, ch. 12; Sarlvik and Crewe, 1983, ch. 2; and Heath *et al.,* 1991, ch. 2.) The table shows how survey data can provide information about the various elements of electoral change which cannot be derived from election results alone.

In most British elections, switching between the two major parties is relatively rare. Even in an election like 2010 that saw a very large overall swing to the Conservatives, only 11 per cent of 2005 Labour voters actually switched directly to the Conservatives. More predictably, just 4 per cent of 2005 Conservative voters moved in the opposite direction. This represents a considerable net gain for the Conservatives, especially since there were quite a few more Labour than Conservative voters in

2005 (see *N*s at the foot of the table). However, as usual, the gains and losses for the major parties were driven mostly by switching in and out of abstention or voting for the other parties. Liberal Democrat traffic clearly harmed Labour in 2010. Of those who had voted Liberal Democrat in 2005, appreciably more moved to the Conservatives (13 per cent) than to Labour (7 per cent). At the same time, 16 per cent of former Labour voters defected to the Liberal Democrats compared with only 7 per cent of former Conservatives. A similar story can be told about non-voting traffic. The Conservatives gained more previous non-voters than the other major parties (14 per cent) while it was Labour who lost most to abstention (11 per cent). The only positive sign for Labour is among the small group who came of voting age after 2005 (or had otherwise been ineligible to vote in that election). While a large minority of them (44 per cent) did not vote in 2010, Labour was the most popular option among those who did (25 per cent). Taking all respondents together (*N* = 2,517), 62 per cent voted for the same party or did not vote in both elections. Major party switching involved 5 per cent, minor party traffic (including the Liberal Democrats) 14 per cent and non-voting traffic 11 per cent, while new voters comprised 8 per cent. In 2010, therefore, it was the movement of people between major and smaller party voting that was the largest contributor to the net swing of 5.1 per cent from Labour to the Conservatives.

The analysis above concerned the flow of votes between two elections. Provided that the panel survey data are available, the same method can be applied to electoral change between any two points in time. For example, the BES now typically includes a 'pre-post' panel, in which

Table 1.3   The 'flow of the vote' between 2005 and 2010

	2005 vote					
2010 vote	*Ineligible/ too young* %	*Did not vote* %	*Conservative* %	*Labour* %	*Liberal Democrat* %	*Other* %
Did not vote	44	67	6	11	6	9
Conservative	12	14	81	11	13	16
Labour	25	7	4	58	7	5
Liberal Democrat	16	7	7	16	70	18
Other	4	5	2	3	4	52
(*N*)	(105)	(334)	(638)	(913)	(293)	(132)

Source: Data from British Election Study (BES) 2010 face-to-face survey.

voters are asked about their vote intention – and many other things – a few weeks before the election and then, following polling day, asked about how they actually voted. This allows for a flow-of-the-vote table tracking the effects of the campaign. This reveals not only how many people changed their mind but also the patterns of switching, indicating which parties made gains and where these came from.

Clearly, then, aggregate measures of change between elections, while important and necessary, are limited. A fuller understanding of electoral change requires the kind of detailed information about individuals that only surveys can provide. Nonetheless, both aggregate and survey data are extensively used in electoral analysis and both have advantages and drawbacks. The advantages of using aggregate data are as follows:

1 If it is confined to publicly available data, analysing aggregate data is cheap. Whereas it costs many thousands of pounds to employ a firm to undertake a major national survey of the British electorate – and even a modest local survey is expensive – anyone can consult a newspaper, go to a library or access an appropriate website and collect election results, census data and other information. Armed only with a calculator (or, more likely, a personal computer), and a knowledge of some elementary statistical techniques, anyone can embark on analysing all of this freely available data.

2 Aggregate data such as election results reflect real behaviour, or what voters actually did, while surveys only report what voters *say* they have done. There is sometimes a disjunction between these. Surveys always find, for instance, that more people claim to have voted in an election than actually did, according to the election returns.

3 Aggregate data usually refer to the total population being studied and are therefore not susceptible to sampling error in the way that survey data are. Whereas we know from election results the precise percentage of the electorate which voted Conservative, a survey would enable us only to estimate the percentage which did (or intended to).

4 Whereas survey studies of electoral behaviour are of relatively recent origin, lots of relevant aggregate data – in particular, election results – are available going back to the nineteenth century. This has enabled modern techniques to be applied to elections in the distant past (see, for example, Field, 1997; Miller, 1977).

5 Aggregate data are almost always **interval-scale** or **continuous data** and the most powerful statistical techniques can therefore be applied to them.

On the other hand, surveys also have certain important advantages:

1   When using aggregate data the analyst is usually restricted to mate-
    rial that has been collected and published by official bodies. Until an
    appropriate question was included in the 2001 census, for example,
    there were no reliable figures showing the distribution of different
    religions or Christian denominations across constituencies (except in
    Northern Ireland). In surveys, on the other hand, the investigator can
    ask respondents for any information that seems appropriate.
2   More precisely, aggregate statistics refer only to the objective
    characteristics and behaviour of a population. It is only by using
    surveys that the knowledge, beliefs, attitudes and opinions of voters
    can be discovered.
3   Individual data collected by survey permit analysis of individuals
    rather than collectivities. We have already commented on the impor-
    tance of this with respect to electoral change, but it is of more
    general significance in electoral analysis. Without surveys we would
    not know which groups vote for which parties and in what propor-
    tions, how opinions relate to party choice, and so on. Theories about
    why people vote the way they do would remain highly speculative.

Theories of voting

Despite the impression that is sometimes given, the study of elections
and voting behaviour is not just about collecting facts and 'number
crunching' on the basis of complicated statistical analysis. As in all
social sciences, facts have to be selected, collected, ordered, analysed
and interpreted. For that, theory is required. We have never yet seen a
survey study of voting which asked respondents what colour their eyes
are, for the simple reason that there is no theory suggesting that eye
colour may affect a person's choice of party. Theories give guidance as
to which facts should be collected and how they should be organized,
interpreted and explained.

In electoral analysis there is an assortment of theories at different
levels of generality. At a simple level, someone might have a theory that
married people are more likely to vote because they are more likely to
conform to socially approved behaviour. This is better described as a
hypothesis and it could be tested by asking a sample of electors whether
they were married and whether they voted. If the expected association is
found, the hypothesis provides the explanation. At a slightly more

general level, there are various theories which seek to explain why older people tend to be more likely to vote Conservative than younger people, the changing pattern of party choice among women, the effect of newspapers on opinions and so on. These will be considered in later chapters. Here, however, we introduce two even more general theories or approaches which have strongly influenced how voting in Britain has been understood and explained, and which inform much of the rest of the book.

The sociological approach and the Michigan model

The first of these theories suggests that voting is largely a product of the social situation of the voter. The authors of the first-ever survey study of voting behaviour in the USA, *The People's Choice* (Lazarsfeld, Berelson and Gaudet, 1968, first edition 1944), had intended to focus upon short-term factors affecting voting choice in the presidential election of 1940 – the book was subtitled 'How The Voter Makes Up His Mind in a Presidential Campaign' – but in the course of their research they became more impressed by the importance of social characteristics such as class, religion and race in structuring party choice. Lazarsfeld and his colleagues discovered that they could predict a person's vote with considerable accuracy from knowledge of just a few social characteristics. They concluded (p. 27) that 'a person thinks, politically, as he is socially. Social characteristics determine political preference.'

Describing relationships between various social and demographic characteristics and party choice is not in itself very useful, however. It would certainly be interesting if it were found that left-handed people with brown eyes tended to vote in a distinctive way, but it seems unlikely that knowing this will advance our understanding of what motivates voters. What is required is some theory that explains why there *should be* a link between specific social or personal characteristics and voting. We need an answer to the question: 'Why are some social differences associated with political differences whereas others are not?'

In 1948, the authors of *The People's Choice* carried out a second study and, in *Voting* (Berelson, Lazarsfeld and McPhee, 1954), they extended and reinforced their original argument. In particular, they provided an answer to the above question by suggesting (p. 75) that for a social difference to be translated into a political cleavage three conditions need to be fulfilled:

(a) initial social differentiation such that the consequences of political policy are materially or symbolically different for different groups;

(b) conditions of transmittibility from generation to generation; and

(c) conditions of physical and social proximity providing for continued in-group contact in succeeding generations.

The first condition requires that the social groups concerned must have differing material or symbolic interests which are affected by government policy. Thus council tenants and owner-occupiers might have different interests with regard to housing policy. Policy in areas such as abortion or embryo research might not directly affect many people but could be said to be of symbolic importance to some groups (such as Roman Catholics and others). On the other hand, 'groups' such as the left-handed or the brown-eyed are not normally treated differently from the rest of the population in matters of public policy and do not fulfil the first condition. The second and third conditions relate to the processes by which social and political divisions are maintained and reinforced. In Chapter 3, we show how these conditions were fulfilled in the context of social class in Britain.

We have here, then, what might be termed an 'interests plus socialization' theory or model. Different social groups have different interests and hence different needs. They tend, therefore, to vote for different parties which they perceive as representing these interests. Awareness of a group's distinctiveness and of group–party links is sustained by regular contact with fellow group members in the family, among peers and in the community.

This 'interests plus socialization' model is appealingly simple and has played a large part in voting research in Britain. However, it is not without difficulties. One of these is the issue of overlapping group memberships. Everyone belongs to a variety of social groups and the theory offers few clues about which will be decisive in determining an individual's party support, and why. This might explain why the sociological approach is often confounded by 'deviants': that is, the (often large) minorities who do not conform to group voting norms, such as middle-class Labour supporters in the 1950s or ethnic minority Conservatives in the 1990s. Second, it is not self-evident that a large and relatively heterogeneous group of people – such as those belonging to the same class, religious denomination or geographical region – will have the same interests. Who decides what the group's interests are, and in what sense can political parties be said to represent the interests of such diverse groups? Third, the theory tends to give the impression that party choice is a sort of spontaneous effect of social location, voters automatically calculating their interests and finding the party that best serves them. This ignores the active role that political parties play in mobilizing and structuring the electorate. It also neglects the key part played by group identities: the subjective sense of belonging to a distinctive group (being Scottish, for example) which voters may have (see Norris, 1997a).

A number of these difficulties were addressed – at least in part – by an important extension to the sociological model. This, too, derives from the study of voting in the US, and specifically from a book called *The American Voter* (Campbell *et al.,* 1960). In this famous study, Campbell and his colleagues developed a model or theory of voting behaviour that has come to be known as the 'Michigan model', since the original research was directed from the University of Michigan. It shared the same foundations as the sociological model in its suggestion that long-term factors are most important in determining party choice. However, in the Michigan model there is no simple step from social location to voting behaviour. Rather, the social position that an individual occupies affects the kinds of influences that he or she will encounter in interacting with family, friends, neighbours, work colleagues and so on. As a consequence of these interactions – especially within the family – the individual acquires a *party identification.* This means a sense of attachment to a party, a feeling of commitment to it, being a supporter of the party and not just someone who happens to vote for the party from time to time. This sense of identity could act as such a powerful driver of voting behaviour that issues of overlapping group memberships, or differences of interests within groups, are overridden. Party identifiers feel that their party will serve their interests, a belief encouraged by parties for whom such identifications are a very efficient means of retaining and mobilizing support.

When an election comes along, there is an interaction between a voter's long-term party identification and various short-term influences, such as current political issues, campaign events, the personalities of party leaders or candidates and, in the British case, the tactical situation in the local constituency, to produce a vote decision. The Michigan team were at pains to emphasize, however, that it is the long-term factors which are usually decisive. Indeed, a person's party identification will influence how he or she interprets and evaluates issues, party leaders and so on.

The concept of party identification (also referred to as 'party identity' or 'partisanship') is central to the Michigan model and worth exploring in a little more detail. It is analogous to national identity. Most of us think of ourselves as English, Scottish, Welsh, British or whatever (perhaps even as European when the Ryder Cup golf tournament is being played). Similarly, party identity involves people thinking of themselves as Conservatives, Labour supporters, Liberal Democrats and so on. Another analogy, borrowed from marketing, sees party identification as akin to 'brand loyalty'. Just as consumers frequently have a long-lasting preference for a particular make of car, brand of toothpaste or breakfast cereal, so voters develop a loyalty to a party. It is important to grasp that identifying with a party is not the same as voting for it; indeed, it is possible to identify with one party and vote for a different one. For example, in recent years a good deal of attention has been given to the idea of tactical voting, which involves voters who might identify with one party voting for another one because their own party has no chance of winning in the constituency concerned. A Labour supporter living in Bath, for example, might decide to vote Liberal Democrat while still remaining basically a Labour supporter.

There are three clear differences between party identification and voting:

1 Party identification is psychological, while voting is behavioural. This means that identification exists in people's heads; we cannot observe it directly. Voting, however, is a definite action – putting a cross on a piece of paper in the case of British elections – and, in principle, it is observable (although normally done in secret).
2 Voting is time-specific, while party identification is not. Voting can only take place at an election (and general elections occur relatively infrequently in Britain), whereas identification is ongoing and continuous. There does not need to be an election in the offing for people to consider themselves supporters of a party.
3 Party identification varies in intensity, while voting does not. Some people will be very strong party supporters, while others will be not very strong or just weak supporters. All votes count equally, however, whether the voter marks the ballot with a large bold black cross or a tiny faint one.

Conceptually, then, party identification is distinct from voting. This means that it can be used to help explain party choice in an election, as in the Michigan model. According to the theory, party identification serves important functions for the individual, including simplifying the task of understanding the complex world of politics. Once someone decides (or has learned) who are the 'goodies' and who the 'baddies' in the party battle, there is no need to pay great attention to the details of political debate, and no need to bother with the details of party policies or election manifestos. Identification acts as a sort of psychological filter or 'perceptual screen' through which political messages pass to the individual; it provides a framework within which political events are understood and evaluated. For example, if a Labour and Conservative identifier were to sit together and watch the leader's speech at the Labour Party conference, they would probably have very different views not just on the substance of the speech but also on the quality of the performance, the sincerity of the body language and even the calibre of the jokes. The term 'perceptual screen' is rather a polite description for this tendency for identifiers to interpret politics in a manner consistent with their partisan sympathies. A blunter description would be 'bias'.

When party identification is widespread, it has important effects on the political system as a whole. Most obviously it provides an element of stability and continuity. If people identify with a party they are not likely to shoot off in all directions at successive elections (just as people – at least, adults – who identify themselves as Liverpool supporters don't suddenly switch their affections to Manchester United). Rather, they will have a 'normal' vote which, in most cases, will remain stable from election to election and across different types of election.

The way in which party identification has been measured in Britain (although not the concept itself) has come under considerable criticism in recent years (see Bartle, 2001), but the idea is central to the model of party choice in Britain that was developed by Butler and Stokes (1969, 1974) in their pioneering survey studies. Simplifying drastically, the

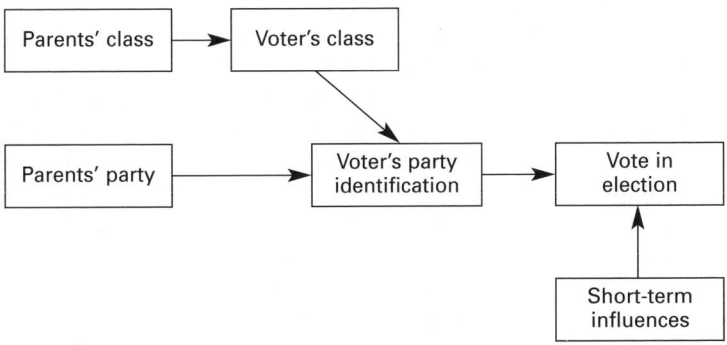

Figure 1.2   Butler–Stokes model of party choice (individual voters)

picture that Butler and Stokes drew of the British voter at this time was as shown in Figure 1.2. The starting point of the model is the class and party of voters' parents and it is underpinned by the theory of political socialization, which suggests that families are particularly important in transmitting political attitudes and beliefs to succeeding generations. Butler and Stokes saw party identification as being inherited to a large extent through the family and leading almost automatically to support for one party or another in elections.

Voting as rational choice

One of the most striking aspects of the sociological approach is that it makes little reference to voters' opinions about the policies or performance of parties. Although the Michigan model does include 'issue orientation' and 'candidate orientation' as short-term influences on party choice, their role is very much downplayed. The two models are largely concerned with voting as a function of social and psychological processes. A quite different broad approach stems from rational choice theory (see McLean, 1982). In its modern form rational choice theory derives from economics but it has been applied in a variety of ways in a large number of fields. In economics, the starting point of the theory is to make an assumption that economic actors (whether firms or individuals as consumers) act rationally: that is, before deciding on a course of action (such as buying a particular product) they weigh up the costs and benefits of the various alternatives and they will take the decision which maximizes the benefits and minimizes the costs to themselves. On the basis of this assumption, economic behaviour can be successfully predicted.

When applied to political activity, this elegant and simple idea – and propositions deduced from it by logical reasoning – has been fruitful in yielding insights in a number of areas, including the behaviour of parties, pressure groups, politicians and voters. As with consumers, it can be hypothesized that voters weigh up the pros and cons of voting for different parties (or of voting at all) and opt for the course of action which they think will bring them the greatest benefit. This apparently simple suggestion has importantly influenced recent electoral analysis, spawning a variety of more specific approaches to understanding party choice – such as issue voting, spatial or proximity voting, economic voting, and valence or 'performance' politics – which focus on the judgements made by voters and which will be explained and discussed in later chapters. Admittedly, it is a broad definition of rational choice that includes all of these approaches. We need to specify how voters evaluate the 'benefits' available from the competing parties; otherwise, saying that voters choose the party that will bring them the greatest benefit is trivial, if not tautological. In this book, we use the term 'rational' largely as a contrast with the sociological or Michigan approach: rational voters, rather than voting according to long-standing attachments, instead make judgements anew at each election on the basis of what the parties are offering at that time. It is also worth noting that 'rational choice' does not imply arduous and complex calculations of the costs and benefits associated with each party. It may well be more rational, especially for those less engaged with politics, to find a quick and simple way of judging the parties.

To summarize this section, then, theories or models are required to provide frameworks within which appropriate data can be collected and understood and also to provide explanations for the empirical relationships that are discovered. Having outlined the most influential general theories of voting behaviour here, we will discuss them again, offering some evaluation of their relative usefulness, in the final chapter. Before examining patterns of party choice, however, it is important to discuss another decision that electors have to make – whether to vote at all – which logically must precede a decision about which party to vote for. The next chapter, therefore, is concerned with turnout in elections.

2

Turnout: Why People Vote (or Don't)

Electoral turnout is a **variable**. The level of turnout varies from country to country and within Britain it varies from one type of election to another and from one election to the next. In any one election turnout varies across constituencies or wards and it also varies from person to person: some people vote and some don't. Variations across different types of election in Britain between 2005 and 2010 are illustrated in Table 2.1.

The interpretation of turnout levels is complicated by the fact that different elections are sometimes held on the same day but even so it is apparent that different types of elections do not attract the same level of interest on the part of the electorate. The lowest turnout was for the 2009 European Parliament elections (34.5 per cent). European elections have consistently held the wooden spoon for participation (although the low level of interest in them has been partially disguised by holding them on

Table 2.1   Turnout in British elections, 2005–2010

	%
General election 2005 (GB)	61.3
English locals 2006	36.6
Scottish Parliament 2007	53.9
Welsh Assembly 2007	46.4
English locals 2007	38.3
English/Welsh locals 2008	35.6
London Mayor 2008	45.3
English locals 2009	39.3
European Parliament 2009	34.5
General election 2010 (GB)	65.3

Sources: Various. For local elections see the *Local Elections Handbook* series by C. Rallings and M. Thrasher.

the same day as local elections in both 2004 and 2009). Turnout in the 2007 Scottish Parliament election was well over 50 per cent but it was significantly lower in the Welsh Assembly elections of the same year. The two general elections at the start and end of the period saw the highest turnouts, even although participation in these was still poor by historical standards.

The electorate, then, differentiates between different levels and types of elections. In general, these variations can be explained by the importance that is attached to the body being elected, which is sometimes referred to as the 'salience' of the election concerned (Franklin, 1996). Thus the European Parliament is seen as remote (its activities being virtually unreported in the British media) and there is a good deal of antipathy to the EU in general. Local councils have steadily lost powers to the central government and voters could be forgiven for thinking that it doesn't really make an enormous difference whichever party controls their local government. By-elections return a Member of Parliament for the constituency concerned but do not determine who forms the government or becomes Prime Minister. The Scottish Parliament has extensive powers, however, and that is reflected in the relatively high turnout, while the Welsh Assembly has been more restricted and, in line with that, elections to it attract a much smaller proportion of the electorate. Now that Wales has voted in favour of expanding its powers (the referendum was held in March 2011), it will be interesting to see if more voters turn out for future Welsh Assembly elections. Despite devolution, general elections are still seen by the voters as the most important elections; they are major national events. Although the idea was first developed in relation to European elections, elections in Britain other than general elections can be described as 'second-order' elections (Reif and Schmitt, 1980): not a great deal appears to be at stake, they attract much less media coverage, and the parties do not campaign as strongly. In general elections, on the other hand, there is saturation media coverage, the parties mount intense national and local campaigns and the electorate usually thinks it important who wins. These are 'first-order' elections, and electors are keener to turn out and vote in them.

There have been three main theoretical approaches to explaining variations in the propensity of people to vote in elections (see Franklin, 1996). Each of these is clearly related to the theoretical approaches – the sociological approach, the Michigan model and rational choice theory – outlined in the previous chapter. The first approach to turnout concentrates on the social locations and circumstances of voters. As we shall see, different social groups tend to have different turnout rates and these differences can be explained in a variety of ways. The second focuses on the connections between parties and voters, and is concerned with how parties mobilize voters and the impact of voters' identification with parties as in the Michigan model. The third derives from rational choice theory, especially the work of Anthony Downs (1957). This directs attention to the costs and benefits of voting and suggests that voters act instrumentally. Turnout will be higher when there are more incentives to vote and costs are kept at a minimum. Where the incentives are less strong and/or costs are higher, turnout will be lower. The patterns shown in Table 2.1, for example, suggest that voters are more willing to turn out when they believe the relevant elections to be more important. Although these three approaches do not exhaust possible lines of explanation, they provide valuable frameworks within which to discuss turnout variations in Britain.

Turnout variations over time

Before discussing the turnout trends in Britain, it is worth remembering what it is that turnout figures measure. When comparing turnout across different countries – and British turnout has not been very high in an international context (see Crewe, 1981a; Franklin, 2002) – it is important to remember that rules about registration and voting vary and this affects the interpretation of comparative figures. In the USA, for example, registering to vote is a fairly complex process while in Australia voting is compulsory. In Britain, official turnout figures report the percentage of people whose names are on the electoral register who put a ballot paper into the ballot box (or vote by post). Compiling the electoral register is the responsibility of local authorities. In February 2001, however, a new system of 'rolling registration' was adopted. There is now no fixed date of registration; instead, once the initial register is drawn up (in October) people can apply to be included and, if eligible, their names will be added up to a short time before an election.

The register cannot possibly be 100 per cent accurate. People are accidentally missed off (most commonly young people who would become 18 before the register lapsed); others are included who should not have been; yet others are registered in two places (students, for example, are often registered at their homes and at their college or university). Official turnout figures do not take account of the problems associated with compiling the electoral register but some electoral analysts have tried to do so. Rose (1974: 494), for example, calculated that the 'real' national turnout figure could be obtained by dividing the reported percentage turnout by 100 plus 2.4 (to take account of those not registered less those registered twice) minus 0.82 for each month from the compilation of the register to the date of the election (to take account of those who have died or moved away in the intervening period), expressing the result as a percentage.

The Rose formula for adjustment is probably not now as accurate as it was originally, but Table 2.2 shows adjusted figures, as well as the overall 'raw' turnout in general elections in Britain since 1950. Again it should be remembered that turnout levels are not exactly comparable over the whole period, since in 1970 the voting age was lowered from 21 to 18 and this added some three million young people to the register. The unadjusted figures show that turnout was very high in 1950 and 1951 and then was always between 70 and 80 per cent until 2001, when it slumped to below 60 per cent with a slight recovery in the two subsequent elections. The adjusted figures suggest that, once the age of the register is taken into account, turnout was actually greater than the 'raw' figures imply, although the trend over time is similar. The trend can be seen more clearly in Figure 2.1, which plots the adjusted turnouts – measured on the y-axis (vertical line) – against the number of years after 1950 that each election was held as measured on the x-axis (horizontal line). Simply looking at the figure suggests that four of the first five elections had relatively high turnouts, then the next eight showed no real trend. The lowest turnout in the series was in 2001 and since then there has been a slight bounce back to 65.3 per cent in 2010 – though turnout levels are still quite some way off their levels in the 1980s and 1990s.

Table 2.2   Turnout in British general elections, 1950–2010 (%)

Election	Turnout	Adjusted	Election	Turnout	Adjusted
1950	84.1	84.8	Oct. 1974	73.0	78.9
1951	82.6	90.0	1979	76.2	79.5
1955	76.9	79.6	1983	72.7	76.5
1959	79.0	85.4	1987	75.5	79.5
1964	77.2	83.4	1992	77.9	79.9
1966	76.1	78.7	1997	71.5	74.0
1970	71.9	75.7	2001	59.1	61.8
Feb. 1974	79.1	80.5	2005	61.4	63.5
			2010	65.3	67.6

Note: For details of the 'adjustment' made, see text.

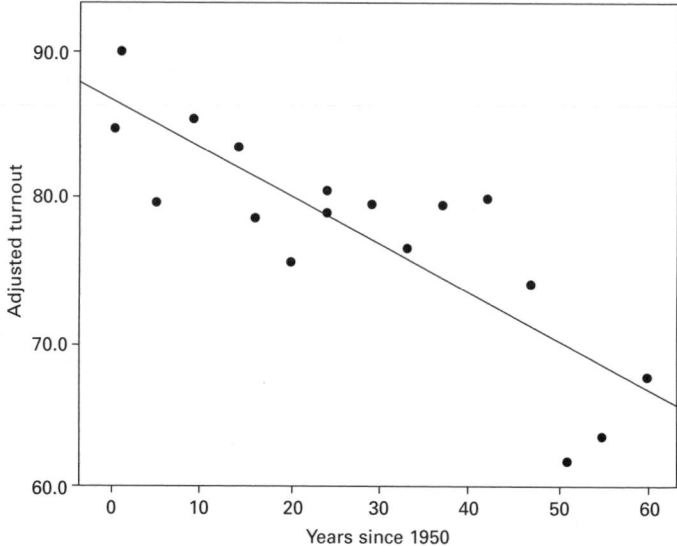

Figure 2.1 Turnout (adjusted) in Great Britain, 1950–2010

 The point of using years since 1950 on the *x*-axis (rather than just each election in turn) is that this measure is a **continuous variable** with scores on an interval scale. When we have two continuous variables (turnout is scored as a percentage) we can undertake some further interesting and informative analysis of the relationship between them. As a first step, a line has been drawn (by the relevant computer package) through the points. This is the 'best-fitting' line derived from **regression analysis**. Without going into the details of how the line is derived, it is apparent that it slopes down from left to right, indicating that turnouts have tended to fall over the period. The line can be described by a simple regression equation as follows: turnout = 86.7–0.33 (years). Thus, with a constant (starting point) of 86.7 per cent, turnout declined on average by about 0.3 per cent for every year that passed. Every regression equation has an associated **R-squared statistic (R^2)** which indicates the proportion of the **variation** in the **dependent variable** (in this case, turnout) that is explained or accounted for by variations in the **independent variable** (in this case, years since 1950). For this equation R^2 is 0.708, meaning that about 71 per cent of the variation in turnout in these 17 elections can be explained simply by the fact that there was a downward trend over time.

Research on turnout variations over time has suggested that they can be at least partly explained by the closeness (or expected closeness) of the election concerned, together with the extent to which the parties were perceived as offering significantly different choices (Heath and Taylor, 1999; Clarke *et al.*, 2004). This is in line with rational choice theory. There would appear to be more incentive for people to vote if they think that an election is likely to be close rather than a foregone conclusion, and if they believe that the winning party will bring in policies that are significantly different from those that the losing party would have pursued. These suggestions help to explain deviations from the trend shown in Figure 2.1. In three elections turnout was clearly higher than would be expected on the basis of the general trend: 1951, 1987 and 1992. The result in the first was very close, while polls also predicted a close-run thing in 1992. In 1987 an unusually large proportion of British Election Study (BES) respondents (84 per cent) perceived 'a good deal of difference' between the parties. Lower than expected turnouts occurred in 1970 (the first election after the lowering of the voting age) and 2001 (when both causes of low turnout were in operation: many voters believed that the result was a foregone conclusion and that there were no major policy or ideological differences between the parties). With many polls predicting a hung parliament, the result in 2010 was expected to be very close (at least in terms of votes) and this probably explains the slight recovery in turnout. (For a more detailed and complex analysis of turnout trends over time, see Clarke *et al.*, 2004: 261–74.)

Turnout variations across constituencies

In any general election, turnout varies markedly across constituencies. In 2005, Liverpool Riverside reported the lowest turnout for the third consecutive election (41.5 per cent) while Dorset West (76.4 per cent) had the highest figure. In 2010, Scotland's Renfrewshire East (77.3 per cent) took top honours whilst Manchester Central (44.3 per cent) stole the wooden spoon. Reflecting the almost 4 per cent overall rise from 2005, in which turnout was 70 per cent or greater in 34 British constituencies, it equalled or exceeded that percentage in 148 constituencies in 2010. At the other end of the scale, turnout was below 50 per cent in 6 constituencies in 2010, while in 2005 36 dropped below the 50 per cent mark. A more general indication of the extent of variations in constituency turnouts is given by the standard deviation, and the figures suggest that such variation had been increasing in recent elections, though 2010 has returned to the 1997 figure. The standard deviations of turnout in the last five elections have been as follows: 1987, 4.5; 1992, 5.2; 1997, 5.6; 2001, 6.4; 2005, 6.4; 2010, 5.6.

Clearly, variations such as this require explanation and investigations of the topic have drawn attention to four main sorts of explanatory factor: the practicalities of voting, the social composition of constituencies, the local electoral context and what, for want of a better term, might be called 'cultural norms'. The method of analysis most frequently used to investigate the problem is to try to account for variations in the dependent variable (constituency turnout) by reference to a series of independent variables, employing **correlation coefficients** and **multiple regression analysis** (see, for example, Denver and Hands, 1997b).

A particularly clear example of a simple practical matter affecting constituency turnouts occurred at the 1992 election. The election took place during a university vacation and, since most students had returned home, constituencies with large resident student populations recorded turnouts which were much lower than usual (see Curtice and Steed, 1992: 347). Practical considerations also relate to the accuracy of the electoral registers on which turnout calculations are based. If the registers in some constituencies are more inaccurate than in others – due to including more people who have moved away from the area or have died – then they will report lower turnouts; very low turnouts tend to be found in inner-city constituencies, for example. These tend to be areas in which there are large floating populations and it seems likely that the low reported turnout figures are in part a consequence of electoral register inaccuracy. Denver and Halfacree (1992b) tackled this problem more generally, arguing that in areas of high out-migration electoral registers will become more inaccurate more quickly than in areas of more stable population. They used regression analysis to demonstrate that the level of out-migration from a constituency does indeed have a significant negative effect on recorded turnout levels. People who move to a new area can apply to vote by post in their former constituency, of course, but these days it is easier for those who are keen to vote to get their names added to the register in their new constituency.

The fact that the social composition of constituencies is associated with varying levels of turnout is well established. In one of the first published analyses of British census and election data, Crewe and Payne (1971) showed that, as far back as the 1970 election, turnout in England was higher in seats with more professional and managerial workers, more owner-occupiers, a better standard of housing, more retired people and more people employed in agriculture. It was lower, on the other hand, where there were more households without a car, poorer housing and more immigrants from ethnic minority groups. This type of analysis is hampered by the fact that censuses (which provide details of the social composition of constituencies) are held only once every ten years. As a result, the social composition data can be somewhat out-of-date when applied to an election which is some distance in time from the census date. On the other hand, most constituencies do not change in character all that quickly and there is little dispute about the nature and strength of the relationships between turnout and the social characteristics of constituencies.

To say that constituencies do not change all that quickly does not mean that constituency social composition does not change, however. The Parliamentary Constituencies Act of 1986 requires that the Westminster constituency boundaries be re-examined and redrawn to account for shifts and changes in the relative size of constituency populations every eight to twelve years. Following the 2001 census, a major undertaking examined the boundary lines defining House of Commons constituencies, shifting constituency boundaries to reflect that more people are choosing to live outside some of Britain's major metropolitan areas. In the end most constituencies were changed in some way and in England, Wales and Northern Ireland these changed boundaries came into effect with the 2010 election (the Scottish boundaries had already been changed in the previous election). According to Curtice, Fisher and Ford (2010: 3), in the 2010 election the boundaries of only 73 constituencies in England and Wales were not changed.

Using the information for the 1983 and 2005 elections, Table 2.3 shows the simple correlation coefficients measuring the association between nine indicators of the social composition of constituencies and turnout. As explained in the Glossary, correlation coefficients indicate whether a relationship between two variables is positive or negative, and also how strong the association is. The closer the figure is to zero, the weaker the relationship; the closer to 1, the stronger the relationship.

All of these coefficients are **statistically significant** – they indicate relationships which are too strong to have occurred by chance – and two features of the data are immediately striking. First, despite being separated by more than 20 years, the pattern of relationships is identical in the two elections. Variables that correlated positively with turnout (as

Table 2.3   Correlates of constituency turnout, 1983 and 2005

	1983	2005
% Professional and managerial workers	0.33	0.54
% Manual workers	−0.23	−0.57
% Owner-occupiers	0.52	0.71
% Council tenants	−0.34	−0.66
% Private tenants	−0.37	−0.17
% Ethnic minority	−0.51	−0.40
% Households with no car	−0.63	−0.80
% Employed in agriculture	0.31	0.44
Persons per hectare	−0.66	−0.55
Previous marginality	0.27	0.72
(N)	(633)	(627)

Notes: For 1983, the scores on the social composition variables derive from the 1981 census, while for 2005 they are taken from the census of 2001. In 1983, what is described here as the percentage of the population belonging to ethnic minorities was actually the percentage born in the New Commonwealth and Pakistan. 'Previous marginality' is 100 minus the winning party's percentage majority in the preceding election.

the proportion with the given characteristic increases, so does turnout) in 1983 also did so in 2005; those that were negative in 1983 (as the proportion increases turnout declines) were also negative in 2005. In other words, although turnout was much lower in the 2005 election, the *pattern of variation across constituencies* was much as it had been 22 years before. Second, most of the coefficients were larger for 2005 than they were in 1983. This means that in the 2005 election there was a clearer and more consistent difference in turnout between the different sorts of constituencies. The country was more clearly divided into relatively low-turnout and relatively high-turnout constituencies, and the two were very different in social terms.

It is important to emphasize with respect to these figures that they tell us nothing about the behaviour of individuals, only about *constituencies*. Thus we cannot infer from the strong positive correlation between the proportion of owner-occupiers in a constituency and turnout that owner-occupiers as a group vote in greater proportions than others. Just because the proportion of households without a car is negatively related to constituency turnout does not of itself tell us that people without cars are less likely to vote. Both *may* be true but, from aggregate data, we can only draw conclusions about collectivities (constituencies in this case) and not about the individuals who comprise them. To do the latter is to commit what is known as the **ecological fallacy**. In addition, it is important to note that correlation coefficients tell us exactly what the word 'correlation' implies and no more. They tell us the extent to which two variables are co-related or associated (whether they increase and decrease in value together or whether, as one goes up, the other goes down). They cannot tell us whether variations in one *cause* the variations in the other; imputing causal relationships between variables is a matter for theory rather than statistical manipulation.

It is easy to hypothesize how different aspects of the electoral context might cause variations in constituency turnouts. It could be suggested, for example, that the more candidates there are the greater will be the turnout, since the choice before the voters will be more extensive and they are less likely to be able to use the excuse that there was no one that they wanted to vote for. Also, more candidates would presumably mean more local campaigning, and this could heighten awareness of (and interest in) the election. In fact this hypothesis, which is an aspect of the mobilization theory mentioned above, is not supported by the data. In 2005 there was a weak negative relationship between the number of candidates and turnout (a correlation coefficient of -0.13): the more candidates in a constituency, the lower was the turnout, on the whole.

Another aspect of the electoral context has been consistently found to have an important influence on constituency turnouts, however, and that is the marginality or 'safeness' of the seat. As with the closeness of the national contest, a simple application of rational choice theory would suggest that electors would be more inclined to go to the polls in places where the contest is likely to be close than in places that are rock-solid for one party or another. It is also the case that parties campaign harder in constituencies where the result may be in doubt than in those where they have no chance or expect to cruise to victory without much effort, so that there are elements of mobilization also involved. Previous analyses of this question have shown that the level of marginality has usually been strongly associated with constituency turnout, even when other variables are taken into account (Denver and Hands, 1974, 1985, 1997b; Pattie and Johnston, 1998; Denver, Hands and MacAllister, 2003). Table 2.3 shows the correlations between previous marginality and turnout in 1983 and 2005. In both cases the coefficients are positive: the more marginal the seat, the higher the turnout. Again, however, the relationship was much stronger in 2005 than it was in 1983. Figures for the intervening elections do not suggest a steady trend in the strength of this relationship but, for reasons that are not immediately apparent, the correlation between marginality and turnout became markedly more pronounced in 2001 (coefficient 0.70) and then reached a record level in 2005 (0.72). This may be because voters are now much more aware of the distinction between marginal and safe (or hopeless) seats. Alternatively (and perhaps more likely), it could be a consequence of the increased tendency of parties to concentrate campaigning resources and effort in more marginal seats while running much less intense campaigns elsewhere.

We can take the analysis of turnout variation across constituencies a step further by using **multivariate analysis**. The data in Table 2.3 are important and interesting, but they show the strength of the association between a series of variables and turnout separately (this is called **bivariate analysis** as it involves looking at only two variables at a time). The problem is that the various measures of social composition are themselves highly inter-correlated. Thus, constituencies in which a large proportion of households have no car tend also to have larger proportions of ethnic minority voters, local authority tenants and manual workers, as well as a higher population density (persons per hectare). By using multiple regression (regression analysis with more than one independent variable), we can sort out which variables are the most important influences on turnout, see whether a particular variable remains significant when all others are held constant and evaluate how successfully combinations of variables explain turnout variations. On the basis of all the variables shown in Table 2.3, the 'best' multiple regression equation (that is, the one that includes all significant independent variables) predicting turnout across all British constituencies in 2005 is as follows:

$$\% \text{ turnout} = 61.0 + 0.13 \ (M) - 0.05 \ (PPH) + 0.77 \ (AG) + 0.10 \ (OO) - 0.18 \ (PR) - 0.29(MW)$$

$$R^2 = 0.780$$

(M = previous marginality; PPH = persons per hectare; AG = % employed in agriculture; OO = % owner-occupiers; PR = % private tenants; MW = % manual workers)

'Predicting', as used in this context, has nothing to do with the future; it simply means calculating what a constituency's turnout should have been on the basis of its scores on the variables concerned, given the overall relationships identified by the analysis. As with simple regression, the R-squared statistic tells us how much of the variation in turnout is explained by this combination of variables (78 per cent in this case). So, turnout across constituencies varied a good deal in 2005 but we can account for over three-quarters of that variation – three-quarters of the variation is explained – by variations in marginality and five indicators of the social characteristics of constituencies.

This means, of course, that some variation remains unexplained. When all of the above factors are taken into account there remain a number of constituencies in which turnout is clearly higher or lower than expected. It is at this point that 'cultural norms' often come into play as a sort of residual explanation. In the 1950s and 1960s, for example, it was plain that coal-mining areas had much higher turnouts than would be expected on the basis of the social and political characteristics of the constituencies concerned. That is no longer the case (not surprisingly, given that we now have only ex-coal-mining areas). Indeed, examination of the most 'deviant' constituencies in 2005 suggests no real patterns. Factors peculiar to the constituencies concerned would be required to explain why, for example, Blaenau Gwent and Leicester East top the list of seats with higher than expected turnout.

The same sort of unexpected deviations are found at ward level in local elections. A study of turnout patterns in English county council and metropolitan borough elections during the 1980s (Rallings and Thrasher, 1990) produced results closely resembling those found for general elections. Turnout was lower in wards of low socio-economic status and was positively related to the marginality of the ward. As with constituency studies, however, Rallings and Thrasher found that even the 'best' combination of political and socio-economic variables left some turnout variation unexplained, with some individual wards regularly returning much higher or lower turnouts than expected. They conclude that: 'one is reluctantly driven almost to a cultural explanation of why turnout in Todmorden should be consistently 15 per cent above the average for Calderdale' (p. 89). Similar results have been reported from a more recent analysis of ward turnouts in Scotland (Denver and Hands, 2004).

Survey studies of non-voting

When we focus attention on the varying propensity of individuals to vote or not, rational choice theory suggests an arresting conclusion: it is irrational to vote. As has already been seen, the starting point of this approach is to assume that the individual weighs up the costs and benefits before deciding on a course of action and the argument then proceeds by logical deduction. It is clear that voting involves the individual in some costs (the time taken getting to the polls, for example, or the effort required to find out about the candidates). On the other hand, any benefit is not immediately apparent. The chances of an individual's vote making any difference to a constituency result, let alone the result of the election as a whole, are infinitesimally small. The chances that one vote will result in the voter's preferred party becoming the government and eventually benefiting the voter are so remote that they are hardly worth considering. Voting, therefore, is irrational and the question that should be posed is not why some people don't vote, but why anyone does! As we have seen, however, most electors do vote in general elections. This implies either that the costs involved are so small that they do not deter on the scale that rational choice theory would suggest, or that voters have reasons for voting that are not purely instrumental (see McLean, 1982, ch. 4). We return to this question at the end of the discussion.

As explained in Chapter 1, in order to study variations in turnout at the level of individual voters – to find out who votes and who doesn't, and why – we need to turn to survey data. This is not as straightforward as it may appear. In the first place (at least up until 2001) large majorities of electors do vote in general elections, so that sample surveys tend to have relatively few non-voting respondents and this inhibits analysis. Second, the problem is compounded by the fact that post-election surveys regularly find that more people claim to have voted than actually did so. In part this is because people who are willing to answer survey questions about politics are also more likely to have voted because they are more interested in politics. Partly, also, it is because (as explained above) official turnout figures take no account of the fact that some people on the electoral register will have died or moved away and these, of course, will not be contacted by a survey. In addition, voting is a culturally valued activity – the good citizen goes to the polls – and it appears that some people are unwilling, or perhaps ashamed, to admit that they failed to vote. By comparing official records with survey responses in a pioneering piece of research, Swaddle and Heath (1989) established that among respondents to the 1987 BES survey who had not in fact voted according to official records, about a quarter claimed to have done so.

In order to overcome the problem of small numbers, the first substantial individual-level study of non-voting in Britain used the combined results of BES surveys at the four general elections between 1966 and October 1974 (Crewe, Fox and Alt, 1977). Crewe and colleagues found, first of all, that in this period very few people were consistent non-voters. Only 1 per cent of their respondents who were eligible abstained in all four elections. Someone who did not vote in one election was quite likely to vote in the one after, or the one after that. This phenomenon was linked to the reasons people give for failing to vote, which were over-whelmingly 'accidental' or 'apathetic'. People said that they were away on polling day, or ill, or simply forgot. Very few were deliberate abstainers in the sense of refusing to vote on principle. In both respects, however, things have changed a bit. As seen in Chapter 1 (Table 1.3), a majority of non-voters in 2005 also did not vote in 2010 (amounting to 10 per cent of those eligible on both occasions). A larger core of persistent non-voters seems to be developing. In addition, when asked why they failed to vote, only a minority (47 per cent) indicated that they were prevented by circumstances. Others were simply not interested (21 per cent), thought that the outcome was not in doubt (9 per cent) or were hostile to the parties and politicians (16 per cent). Persistent non-voting is, then, much more common than it used to be and non-voters appear less likely to feel rather ashamed of it.

The second major conclusion of the study by Crewe, Fox and Alt was something of a surprise. They investigated the effects of a series of social variables on propensity to vote and found that, contrary to common assumptions, most seemed to have little effect. Working-class people were as likely to vote as the middle classes, women as likely as men, the poorly educated as likely as the highly educated, and so on. Only four inter-connected social factors were associated with poor turnout: being young (the most important), being unmarried, living in privately rented accommodation and being residentially mobile. Crewe, Fox and Alt explain higher levels of non-voting by these groups in terms of isolation from personal and community networks, which are charac-teristic of stable communities and which encourage conformity with the norm of voting.

In a later analysis, Swaddle and Heath (1989) sought to overcome the problem of respondents over-reporting voting by getting access to the official electoral registers used by polling officials to mark off the names of people as they actually voted in the 1987 election. They were, there-fore, able to tell which of their respondents had really voted, irrespective of what they told interviewers. This procedure has been followed in all subsequent BES surveys and has enabled analysis of 'genuine', as opposed to 'admitted', non-voters. Nonetheless, studies relating non-voting on this basis to social characteristics have generally confirmed the results originally reported by Crewe and his colleagues, although in some cases class and income have also been found to affect voting levels, with manual workers and poorer people having lower turnouts.

Table 2.4 shows the turnout of various social groups in the 2010 election. Apart from the simple 'flow-of-the-vote' table (Table 1.3) shown in Chapter 1, this is the first example in this book of a table based on cross-tabulations and it is worth making a few explanatory comments about this very common method of analysing and presenting data. Continuous variables enable each case to be given a specific score. Where cases can only be assigned to a category (male/female, say, or Conservative/Labour/Liberal Democrat) and not given a score, the variables concerned are known as **categorical variables**. The most common method of analysing categorical variables is cross-tabulation. Having assigned cases (usually survey respondents) to the categories of one variable (in this case, voted or didn't vote), they are then categorized on the basis of another (for example, occupational class). This would produce, in this example, six categories and these would constitute the cells of a table. Normally the independent variable (class) is shown along the top and constitutes the columns of the table, while the dependent variable (voted or not) is arranged down the side, constituting the rows, and the numbers in each column are converted to percentages totalling 100 for each column. Theoretically, additional variables can be added, but one of the problems of cross-tabulation is that as extra variables are incorporated the number of table cells multiplies very quickly. If the respondents classified by class and vote were further divided into six age groups, for example, the resulting table would contain 36 cells. Not only would such a table be difficult to read but at least some of the cells would inevitably contain a rather small number of cases, making the figures unreliable.

Another problem when analysing survey data in this way is that the figures derived are, of course, estimates based on a sample of the electorate. If we find differences in behaviour or in attitudes between different categories of respondents, it is important to know whether these differences are significant. We can do this by carrying out a test of statistical significance. Easily the most common test used for cross-tabulations is the **chi-squared test**. This calculates the probability that a difference found among survey respondents reflects a real difference among the population that was sampled. Nowadays, the necessary calculations are produced by suitable computer packages and all that we need to understand is what the results mean. Authors frequently simply report that what they have found is 'significant at the 95 per cent level', or '$p < 0.05$'. This means that there is only a 5 per cent chance, or a prob-

Table 2.4 Turnout of social groups in 2010 General Election

	%		%
Sex		*Housing*	
Men	64	Owner-occupiers	74
Women	63	Tenants	44
Marital Status		*Highest education qualification*	
Married	74	None	54
Live with partner	47	Occupational qualification	61
Separated/divorced	59	GCSE (or equivalent)	59
Widowed	75	A level (or equivalent)	64
Single/never married	51	Professional qualification	70
Degree	73		
Occupation		*Income*	
Professional and managerial	78	Lowest third	56
Other non-manual	64	Middle third	66
Manual	52	Top third	79
Age			
18–24	45		
25–34	52		
35–44	62		
45–54	67		
55–64	71		
65+	79		

Source: Data from BES 2010 cross-section survey. The original data have been weighted to reflect the actual turnout in the election.

ability of less than 0.05 (a very small probability), that the difference found in the sample does *not* reflect a difference in the population as a whole. In other words, the difference found is statistically significant; it is not due to chance. In subsequent tables details about statistical significance will not normally be given, but will be referred to in the text where appropriate.

Table 2.4 summarizes a series of separate cross-tabulations relating to whether or not respondents voted in the 2010 election. Marital status, occupational class, age, housing tenure and income level are clearly associated with variations in turnout (and the differences found are all statistically significant) but, confirming recent experience, there were no significant differences between men and women. As in previous elections, married people were more likely to vote than those who lived with a partner without being married, were separated or divorced, or were single. This may be because married people are more likely to conform to society's norms or – more tendentiously – because they are more likely to take their responsibilities seriously, but there could be other reasons. In terms of marital status, widowed people had the best turnout of all. This is related to age since older voters are also more likely to have been widowed. Middle-class groups voted more heavily than the working class, the better-off more than the worse-off, owner-occupiers more than renters and those with a university degree or professional qualification more than those without. Paralleling the results of the constituency analysis, the survey data reveal that, contrary to what was found in the 1960s, there is now a clear division in levels of turnout between relatively well-off, well-educated professional middle classes on the one hand and the less well-educated manual working class on the other.

Perhaps the most striking figures in the table, however, are those for age. The turnout of the youngest voters was only 45 per cent but this increased steadily with age and reached 79 per cent among those aged 65 and above. A simple, practical explanation for the heavy turnout of the oldest group is that it might just be a consequence of the fact that, being retired, they have more time to go to the polling station. At a more general level, however, it is widely suggested that as people get older they become more involved in the political process, acquire a greater sense of responsibility and are more likely to view voting as a civic duty. In the course of a full analysis of trends in turnout to 2001, Clarke *et al.* (2004, ch. 8) show that younger people have a much weaker sense of civic duty than their elders and are much less likely to think that non-voting is a serious neglect of a citizen's responsibilities. Moreover, this is not something that they seem to be 'growing out of', as it were, and for that reason we are unlikely to see a return to pre-2001 turnout levels for the foreseeable future.

In their original article, Crewe and his colleagues also investigated the impact of political interest and motivation on non-voting. Much of this sort of analysis comes close to tautology. To discover that people who are more interested in and knowledgeable about politics and who discuss politics more than average tend to vote in greater numbers is hardly surprising. However, one individual-level 'political' variable has been consistently found to have a strong effect on turnout levels, and

Table 2.5 Turnout by strength of party identification (%)

	Very strong	Fairly strong	Not very strong	No party identification
Regular voters (1966–74)	84	74	54	–
Voted 1992	92	90	80	58
Voted 1997	89	87	73	51
Voted 2001	81	72	50	28
Voted 2005	82	73	59	36
Voted 2010	85	78	60	39

Notes: The first row shows the percentages who voted in all four general elections from 1966 to October 1974; – = data not provided.

Sources: Data from Crewe, Fox and Alt (1977); BES 1992, 1997, 2001, 2005, 2010 cross-section surveys.

that is strength of party identification. This is linked to the approach which sees turnout as being related to the extent to which citizens are mobilized by parties. Butler and Stokes (1974: 40) reported that in the early 1960s some 64 per cent of very strong identifiers voted in local elections, compared with 54 per cent of fairly strong identifiers and only 39 per cent of not very strong identifiers. Figures from the analysis by Crewe, Fox and Alt (1977), together with data from the last five BES surveys, are given in Table 2.5 and the pattern is very clear. The stronger a person's party identification, the more likely he or she is to vote. This is not difficult to understand; people who are strong party supporters clearly have more incentive to go out and vote for their party than those who have only a mild preference for one party or another, or are indifferent. The figures also show that the turnout of people with no party identification has been very much poorer than that of even 'not very strong' identifiers. Moreover, the decline in turnout over the period is steepest among non-identifiers and slightest among 'very strong' identifiers. The problem is, as we shall see in later chapters, that there are now fewer strong identifiers than there used to be.

The data in Tables 2.4 and 2.5 show associations between voting and a variety of social and political characteristics separately. As already mentioned, however, some of the characteristics are themselves interrelated. Age relates to marital status and to strength of party identification, for example; class, housing tenure and income are also likely to overlap. What we really want to know, therefore, is whether differences in marital status, for example, would continue to be important if we also took account of age, and so on. Producing more detailed cross-tabulations to do this would not be very helpful, since a table combining voting versus non-voting, marital status and age group would contain some 60 cells, and adding a simplified three-category income variable would increase that to 180 cells. A table of this size would be difficult to present, never mind interpret.

Statistical techniques have found their way into mainstream electoral analysis which enable us to assess the impact of categorical variables in a way that is analogous to using multiple regression analysis with interval-scale variables. The best-known of these is **binary logistic regression**. This enables us to assess the impact of individual independent variables on a dependent variable while holding all the other independent variables in the analysis constant, and also provides measures of the combined effect of the included variables. The mathematics involved are as terrifying as the name of the technique suggests, but students of voting behaviour only need some (approximate) understanding of what it does and what the results tell us.

The dependent variable can only have two values or categories (such as 'voted' and 'did not vote'), and a category of each independent variable has to be used as a reference for that variable. The results tell us whether, and by how much, respondents in each category of each independent variable differ from the reference category in terms of the dependent variable (in this case, whether they voted or not) while holding all of the other independent variables constant. That sounds very complicated, but an example will help to clarify what is meant.

Table 2.6 presents the results of two logistic regressions with voting versus non-voting as the dependent variable. The first (column *A*) analyses the effects of all the social variables already discussed. The figures shown for each category are **odds ratios,** which indicate how more or less likely someone in the category was to vote in the election than someone in the reference category, while controlling for the other included variables. A ratio of less than 1 indicates that people in that category were less likely to vote, while a ratio greater than 1 shows that they were more likely to do so. Thus, those aged 65 and over were more than nine times (9.49) more likely to turn out than those aged 18 to 24. The analysis shows that sex, occupation and some categories of marital status (being widowed or single) made no significant difference to turnout levels when all characteristics are considered together: as suggested above, these categories overlap to a great extent with age so that, when we take account of the latter, widowed or single people show

Table 2.6 Logistic regression analyses of voting versus non-voting in 2005

	A	B
Sex (Reference = male)		
Female	1.07	1.09
Marital status (Reference = married)		
Living with partner	**0.72**	**0.66**
Separated/divorced	**0.69**	**0.67**
Widowed	1.37	1.24
Single/never married	0.96	0.96
Occupation (Reference = professional & managerial)		
Other non-manual	1.01	1.05
Manual	0.88	0.85
Age (Reference = 18–24)		
Aged 25–34	**1.52**	**1.62**
Aged 35–44	**3.41**	**3.43**
Aged 45–54	**4.00**	**3.78**
Aged 55–64	**7.61**	**6.85**
Aged 65+	**9.49**	**7.72**
Housing tenure (Reference = owner-occupier)		
Tenants	**0.57**	**0.56**
Education qualification (Reference = none)		
Occupational qualification	**1.83**	**1.95**
GCSE equivalent	**1.66**	**1.77**
A level equivalent	**2.71**	**2.72**
Professional qualification	**2.37**	**2.35**
Degree	**3.17**	**3.34**
Income (Reference = lowest third)		
Middle third	**1.28**	**1.27**
Top third	**1.31**	1.27
Strength of party identification (Reference = none)		
Very strong	–	**6.61**
Fairly strong	–	**3.96**
Not very strong	–	**2.06**
Nagelkerke R^2	0.198	0.270
% Correctly classified (original)	62.8	62.8
% Correctly classified (equation)	70.1	72.1
% Correctly classified (change)	+7.3	+9.3
(*N*)	(3,036)	(3,029)

Notes: Significant odds ratios ($p < 0.05$) are shown in **bold**.

no distinct pattern. On the other hand, the older voters were, the more they differed from the youngest age group, taking everything else into account. Electors with any educational qualification were more likely to vote than those without, but people with a degree showed the biggest difference, while those renting their homes were less likely to turn out than owner-occupiers even when other characteristics are taken into account.

The output from the relevant SPSS (Statistical Package for the Social Sciences) programme also provides a number of statistics to enable evaluation of each analysis. Some of these are incomprehensible to all but statisticians (and, perhaps, the odd psephologist) but some are easy to interpret and are shown in the table. The **Nagelkerke R^2** (named after the person who devised it and sometimes called a 'pseudo' R^2) gives an estimate of the proportion of variation in the dependent variable (voting versus non-voting) that is explained or accounted for by the variables in the analysis (in this case, 19.8 per cent). Second, the proportion of respondents correctly predicted to be, or classified as, voters or non-voters on the basis of the characteristics included can be calculated. Of course, we would get a good many of these predictions right by simply assigning everyone to the largest category (voters), and this is shown as the 'original' classification (62.8 per cent). The influence of the variables analysed can be gauged by the extent to which knowing how respondents are categorized on each of them improves our ability to classify them correctly. Here the improvement is 7.3 per cent.

In column *B* strength of party identification is added to the analysis. Very strong identifiers were more than six times as likely to vote as those with no identification. Even fairly strong and not very strong identifiers were significantly more likely to go to the polls than non-identifiers. There are only minor changes in respect of the other variables once strength of identification is taken into account. It can be seen that only one of the income categories is now significantly different from the reference group. On the other hand, age, housing tenure and level of education continue to have a significant independent effect. Adding party identification increases the variation explained to 27.0 per cent (R^2) and also improves the ability of the model to classify people correctly as voters or non-voters.

There is no doubt that logistic regression analysis looks and sounds daunting, and it is certainly not as easy to undertake or understand as simple cross-tabulations. Nonetheless, it has major advantages over the latter in that it enables electoral analysts to examine the combined impact of a large number of categorical variables on voting, and to assess the effect of specific variables while controlling for a large number of others. It seems likely that the use of the technique will become more common in electoral analysis and it is important, therefore, that those interested in the subject are able to understand the meaning of the results that it produces.

The significance of party identification in the preceding analysis helps to answer the question raised by rational choice theory: why do people vote when the costs outweigh the benefits? Back in the 1960s, Butler and Stokes (1969: 36–7) suggested that while rational choice theory assumes that people vote for *instrumental* reasons only (to achieve some end such as helping to elect a particular candidate), many actually vote for *expressive* reasons. Strong party identifiers vote to express their support for their party. Butler and Stokes go on to show that others have *normative* reasons for voting: they see it as a civic obligation, a duty for citizens. BES respondents in 2010 clearly exemplified the latter since 56 per cent agreed that they would feel very guilty if they didn't vote, 66 per cent thought that not voting was a serious neglect of their duty and 75 per cent agreed that it was a citizen's duty to vote (N close to 2,000 in all cases). Not surprisingly, people agreeing with these sentiments were much more likely to vote than those who did not. For example, turnout was 77 per cent ($N = 1,112$) among those who agreed that it is a citizen's duty to vote and 36 per cent among those who did not agree ($N = 348$).

Finally, it is worth looking briefly at the consequences of variations in individual turnout. Does one party consistently suffer as a result of the patterns that have been described? Aggregate turnout figures can be interpreted as suggesting that Labour suffers if turnout is poor and benefits if the turnout is high. As we have seen, turnout tends to be lower in poorer, more working-class constituencies, and these would be expected to be strongly Labour areas. Indeed, in 2010, mean turnout in seats won by Labour was 61.2 per cent ($N = 258$) compared with 68.2 per cent in those won by the Conservatives ($N = 305$) and 67.2 per cent in Liberal Democrat seats ($N = 57$). Survey data cast doubt on this interpretation, however. Although recent BES surveys have not asked non-voters which party they *would have* supported if they had voted, we can use party identification as an indicator of how they would have voted and Table 2.7 shows the relevant data for the last five elections. The Liberal Democrats consistently do worse among non-voters than among people who actually voted. Between 1997 and 2005, as Labour's share of the vote in elections fell, so did its support among non-voters. Unlike in the previous four elections where the party that won the election also 'won'

Table 2.7 Party identification of non-voters (%)

	1992	1997	2001	2005	2010
None	15	18	31	34	38
Conservative	41	21	16	19	18
Labour	30	46	40	33	29
Liberal Democrat	10	10	7	8	9
Other	4	5	5	6	6
(A)	(398)	(495)	(876)	(1,003)	(609)

Sources: Data from BES cross-section surveys 1992–2010.

among non-voters, in 2010 the non-voters continued to support Labour more than the Conservatives, though obviously this was not the case amongst the voting electorate.

Conclusion: what is to be done about low turnout?

All three of the theoretical approaches to participation in elections have found some supportive evidence in the preceding discussion. Some social characteristics (especially age) affect the propensity to vote and, if strong party identification is understood as an aspect of the mobilization of the electorate, then that too is clearly important. There is also evidence that the level of voting is affected by instrumental considerations relating to the costs and benefits of turning out. Participation is greater in more marginal seats and lower in second-order elections, for example. In addition, however, voting can also be an expression of support for a party or can simply be a matter of fulfilling one's duty as a citizen.

In this list we have not mentioned the actual process of voting: the fact that most people have to go to a polling station on a Thursday between 7 a.m. and 10 p.m. and mark a ballot paper. Nonetheless, that is the area on which the authorities have concentrated when considering what might be done to improve turnout. In other words, the focus has been on the costs rather than the benefits of voting. In the first place, opportunities for postal voting have been greatly increased in recent elections. Previously, anyone wanting a postal vote had to have a reason, such as being ill or absent on business. Now, however, anyone can have a postal vote simply by applying for it. Indeed the government has gone further by making postal voting compulsory in some regions at the 2004

European elections (and in the North East referendum on a regional assembly), while various local authorities have done the same in local elections. In general, easier (or compulsory) postal voting appears to boost turnout a little, although there is evidence from local elections that the effect fades as voters become accustomed to it in successive elections. On the other hand, fears have been expressed that extended postal voting gives greater opportunities for fraud and corruption in elections. These fears appeared vindicated just before the 2005 general election when a highly-publicized court case found evidence of serious corruption in Birmingham local elections with the presiding judge declaring that there had been activities that would 'disgrace a banana republic' (*Daily Telegraph,* 5 April 2005). In the light of this and other cases, there has been something of a reaction against compulsory voting by post but claiming a postal ballot is likely to remain much easier than it used to be.

There has been a variety of other experiments with the process of voting in local elections which have involved, among other things, locating polling stations in places such as supermarkets, keeping polling stations open for a few days and allowing voting via the Internet, telephone, or text messages. These have been largely a waste of time. As previously suggested, the costs of voting for most people are trivial and so we must look elsewhere for explanations of decreased turnout in recent elections. In addition to a decline in the sense of civic duty among younger voters, two further causes are structural and political (see Bartle, 2002).

As will be seen in Chapter 7, the first-past-the-post electoral system makes voting rather pointless in seats that are safe for one of the parties, and also leads parties to focus their local campaigns on a small number of 'target' seats. In addition, public opinion polls report a decline in the intensity of party identification and an increase in the proportions of voters who don't see great ideological differences between the main parties. Both of these are, at least in part, consequences of deliberate strategies pursued by the parties (see Crewe, 2002). After 1997, for example, New Labour clearly moved to the political centre by adopting what were, in many people's eyes, Conservative policies and doing little to enthuse their core vote. After the election of David Cameron as Conservative leader in late 2005, he too seemed concerned to reposition the party towards the centre rather than emphasizing differences between the two main parties. It is clearly in parties' interests to try to occupy the centre ground, since that is where most voters are positioned, so that distinguishing them on ideological grounds is likely to continue to be difficult. For that reason, the decline in the strength of party identification is unlikely to be reversed and this may result in future turnouts continuing to be relatively low. On the other hand, if future elections are thought likely to be close, as was the contest in 2010, and/or a greater ideological gap opens up between the parties, then the upturn in participation experienced in 2005 and 2010 could be repeated.

3

Alignment and Dealignment

This chapter is about two phases in Britain's post-war electoral history. The 1950s and 1960s are conventionally viewed as an 'era of alignment' in which most voters saw themselves as belonging to a particular social class and, in turn, identified with and voted for the party thought to do most for people of that class. Then, from around the beginning of the 1970s, a process of 'dealignment' – a weakening of voters' identifications both with social classes and with parties – quickly gathered pace. Of course, any attempt to divide history into distinct eras – or, for that matter, to divide the electorate into distinct groups – is bound to be an over-simplification. Voters did not wake up on New Year's Day in 1970 and decide to start dealigning themselves. Change within the electorate is a more gradual and piecemeal process and, as noted in the previous chapter on turnout, is often driven more by generational shifts in the make-up of the electorate than by individual voters changing their attitudes or identities. Indeed, plenty of voters did not change across the two 'eras'. Significant minorities of voters in the 1950s and 1960s felt no strong class or partisan attachment, while significant minorities today identify strongly with a party. Nonetheless, even if to talk of a change from alignment to dealignment is something of an over-simplification, electoral analysts generally agree that in broad terms it captures the major change in voting behaviour during the period since 1945.

There is much less agreement about the extent and (especially) the causes of dealignment. Disputes about the reasons for weakening class and party loyalties have been some of the most acrimonious in the usually fairly cordial field of British electoral studies. As we will see, some of these arguments pivot on what seem like quite technical details about how the basic concepts are measured but they also reflect the different theoretical perspectives on voting behaviour outlined in Chapter 1. The era of alignment is closely associated with the sociological approach and the Michigan model, while the key elements in rational models of party choice become more important once those old loyalties are eroded. In part, of course, theories of voting behaviour were updated in response to changes in the way that voters made their choices. However, we highlight another possibility: that voters changed less than has commonly been assumed and, instead, they just looked different as electoral researchers shifted their theoretical vantage-point.

Class and party

The investigation and understanding of British electoral behaviour in the 1950s and 1960s was strongly influenced by the first of the two broad theories introduced in Chapter 1. The first survey studies focused mainly on the social underpinnings of party choice. In doing so, they were not only following the lead given by early American voting studies but also treading the same path as an emerging comparative literature on party systems, best exemplified by the work of Lipset and Rokkan (1967), which argued that the various party systems in Europe were the products of the major social cleavages within the country concerned. In the first British studies based on national surveys, Butler and Stokes (1969, 1974) introduced the Michigan model (see Figure 1.2 for a reminder), which combined both the social influences on party choice and the effects of socialization in producing a psychological attachment to a party among voters: a party identification.

'Socialization' refers to the process of largely informal learning that almost everyone experiences throughout their lives as a consequence of interactions within families and with friends, neighbours, colleagues and so on. It is particularly important, however, in childhood when people are socialized by their families: they learn what is right and wrong, for example, and pick up what their parents' attitudes are on a whole variety of subjects, including politics. According to Butler and Stokes, most people learned to associate the different parties with classes (Labour was for the working class, the Conservatives for the middle class) and most also adopted their parents' party. We can speak, then, of the electorate being 'aligned' in two main ways. First, there was a class alignment: people in different classes aligned themselves with different parties. Second, there was a 'partisan alignment' in that individuals aligned themselves with a party by thinking of themselves as supporters of it. The inter-connected phenomena of class and partisan alignment were the twin pillars, as it were, that supported a strong and stable two-party system in the 1950s and 1960s. They divided the electorate into two large blocs which provided reliable and consistent voting support for the

Conservatives and Labour (see Table 1.2 and Figure 1.1), giving those parties about nine out of every ten votes and almost all of the seats in the House of Commons.

There are, broadly speaking, two types of class voting: that is, two reasons why voters might choose a party in line with their social class. The first is *subjective* class voting. In this case, voters identify themselves as belonging to a given social class and vote for the party that they see as best serving that class (see Butler and Stokes, 1974: 81–94). They may view the party struggle as reflecting opposing class interests: a case of 'us versus them'. Or they may simply see a party as representing their class interests without any implication that these are in conflict with those of another class. In any case, the key link is between voters' perceptions of their own class position and of what the parties are offering that social group. Put another way, the voters are thinking about party politics in terms of social class. Butler and Stokes found that this subjective approach was much better at explaining Labour than Conservative support. In 1966, for example, more than twice as many British Election Study (BES) respondents described themselves as working-class than described themselves as middle-class. Moreover, 91 per cent of working-class Labour supporters reported thinking about the parties in class terms, compared to just 35 per cent of middle-class Conservative supporters. The differences between the two groups reflected the different ways in which the parties portrayed themselves. Labour campaigned as the party for the working class while the Conservatives generally eschewed class rhetoric, claiming to be the party of the nation as a whole, at least partly because they could not win elections without a good proportion of working-class votes.

Nonetheless, the Conservatives still won very large proportions of the middle-class vote. This is where the second type of class voting, *objective* class voting, comes in. Voters in different social locations have different preferences and priorities. For example, those in middle-class occupations, who typically have higher incomes and greater job security than working-class people, tend to be less supportive of redistributive taxation and less concerned by unemployment. In short, the different classes have different interests. This is reflected in the British party system: the Labour Party was formed to serve the interests of the working class and, as Labour grew in strength, the Conservatives became the chief defenders of middle-class interests. Purely on the basis of the parties' policy offerings, then, we would expect working-class voters to gravitate towards Labour and middle-class voters to prefer the Conservatives. This does not require voters to be thinking about the parties in terms of class, or even to have a clear sense of their own class position. It is just a matter of choosing the party that shares their opinions and priorities. This is, in effect, class voting as rational choice, to use the term introduced in Chapter 1.

Measuring class and class voting

Despite its central position in voting behaviour theory, the concept of class is slippery and difficult to define precisely. It is even more difficult to measure or 'operationalize' in empirical research. When we say that a person is 'middle class' or 'working class' (to the extent that people still use these terms) we often have a variety of things in mind: wealth, income, occupation, education, accent, 'style of life', and so on. So how is a person's class to be determined? One way of doing this, of course, is to ask that person whether they think of themselves as belonging to a class (and, if so, which class). In line with the discussion above, this is measuring *subjective* social class. In measuring *objective* social class, voting researchers – like opinion pollsters and market researchers – have generally opted for occupation as a short-hand indicator. This can be justified on the grounds that most people have traditionally described different classes in terms of different occupations (see Butler and Stokes, 1974: 70) but it also gives rise to other problems. How many classes are there? Which occupations belong to which classes? The classes of bank managers and farm labourers may be fairly obvious, but what about personal assistants, police officers, or foremen on building sites? Another set of problems relates to the categorization of those not in work: should they be classified according to their previous job, or according to their spouse's or partner's occupation?

Clearly, the definition and measurement of this most basic social variable is fraught with difficulty. Indeed, as noted later in this chapter, the very definition of class came to be an important element in the debate over class dealignment. Various classification systems have been used in electoral research (see Evans, 2000, for an overview). Probably the best known is the six-category market research scheme. Because this is the system used by opinion pollsters, it has become familiar to election-watchers – indeed, Conservative electoral success in the 1980s was widely attributed in the media to its success among the 'C2s', that is, skilled manual workers. Whatever the original classification system, voting researchers also quite often collapse categories into just two groups, non-manual and manual workers. This is partly done to simplify matters. Partly, also, the reality is that most people used to think of – and talk about – the British class structure in terms of a basic division between a middle and a working class. Nevertheless, the manual/non-manual distinction is a very rough and ready approximation of what we mean when we talk about social class, and so in some cases finer distinctions are used. One of these, the five-class Goldthorpe scheme, is discussed later in the chapter.

The results in Table 3.1 make it clear that, whether class is considered in objective or subjective terms, it was strongly associated with party choice in 1964. Similar patterns can be seen in other elections during the 1950s and 1960s. In general, about two-thirds of manual workers and working-class identifiers were found to support the Labour Party and similar proportions of non-manual workers – rising to around three-quarters of those in clearly middle-class occupations – voted Conservative. Not everyone supported their 'natural' class party and there were, in fact, special studies of 'working-class Tories' in the 1960s (Nordlinger, 1967; McKenzie and Silver, 1968). Nonetheless, in comparison with other countries, Britain was considered to be the archetypal class-based party system (Alford, 1964). And it is easy to see how Peter Pulzer, writing in 1967, reached the much-quoted conclusion that 'Class is the basis of British party politics; all else is embellishment and detail' (1967: 98).

Table 3.1   Vote in 1964 by objective and subjective class (row percentages)

	Conservative	Labour	Liberal	(N)
Objective class				
Higher managerial/professional/ administrative	73	16	11	(91)
Lower managerial/professional/ administrative	68	18	14	(139)
Skilled/supervisory non-manual	59	24	17	(231)
Lower non-manual	54	28	18	(131)
Skilled manual	29	62	9	(564)
Other manual	25	69	6	(350)
Subjective class				
Middle class	66	19	16	(242)
Working class	25	67	8	(621)

Note: The objective class data are based on the occupation of the 'head of household'.

Source: Data from BES 1964 cross-section survey.

Other social influences on voting

Although class was the dominant source of party alignment in Britain in the 1950s and 1960s, other social and demographic characteristics were also consistently found to be associated with party choice. Two preliminary points about these relationships should be noted. First, while the job of establishing the existence of relationships between social attributes and party choice, whether at any single election or over a period of time, is relatively straightforward, explaining them is not. Voting researchers might agree about which groups tended to vote for which parties but that does not mean that they are in agreement about why they did so. Second, the importance of class as a determinant of voting was such that, for any other variable to be shown to affect party choice, it had to continue to have an effect when class was 'controlled'. That is, the variable in question would need to make a difference to party choice *within* at least one of the different classes. There would be little point in getting excited over a finding that most Roman Catholics voted Labour, for example, if it were also the case that most Catholics were working-class. The acid test would be whether, say, middle-class Catholics were more likely to vote Labour than middle-class people from other denominations. Many of the social characteristics associated with party choice in the era of aligned voting – notably union membership and housing tenure – were clearly class-related. We concentrate here on the three most interesting characteristics which were not obviously a function of class position: religion, age and sex. At this stage, we focus on the 'era of alignment' – that is, the 1950s and 1960s. For that reason, ethnicity is not covered here. At the time, ethnic minorities constituted a tiny fraction of the electorate and so there was limited scope for studying their voting behaviour. We deal with ethnicity when, in Chapter 8, we return to social factors and investigate whether they still have an influence on party choice.

Religion

As used in this context, 'religion' is a shorthand. In the context of British voting, what is usually being referred to is adherence (or not) to a Christian denomination, such as the Church of England, the Methodists and so on. Members of non-Christian religions constituted only a very small percentage of the electorate in the period to which this chapter refers. Religious or denominational divisions, stretching back to the Reformation, were identified by Lipset and Rokkan (1967) as one of the key sources of social cleavage giving rise to party divisions. In many Western European states, including Germany and the Netherlands, the Protestant–Catholic divide remains an important influence on party choice, while in predominantly Catholic countries (such as France) there is a tradition of party division over the role of the Church.

In Britain in the late nineteenth and early twentieth centuries, religion played a major role in party politics and in determining party support. In those days, the Church of England could fairly be described as 'the Tory Party at prayer' while the Liberal Party was strongly supported by Nonconformists. Issues such as support for Church of England schools from the rates (local taxes) excited much political passion, and the divide spilled over into other less directly clerical matters such as licensing laws, with the temperance/Nonconformist/Liberal forces opposing the brewers/Anglican/Tory nexus. In this period, too, the Conservatives (then widely known as the Conservative and Unionist Party) vigorously opposed Irish Home Rule and supported Ulster Protestants in attempting to preserve the union and, eventually, in forcing the partition of Ireland in 1922.

Although these events were in the distant past, even in the 1960s Butler and Stokes (1969: 124–34) found that religion had a 'political legacy'. According to the 1964 BES, support for the Conservatives in the 1964 election was stronger among Anglicans (46 per cent) and Scottish Protestants (mostly Church of Scotland) (45 per cent) than among Nonconformists (35 per cent) or, especially, Roman Catholics (26 per cent). The Conservatives were also relatively weak among voters with no religious attachment. As the size of these differences suggest, they are not simply a by-product of social class voting: there are similar denominational differences within each of the classes. By the 1950s and 1960s, therefore, although the influence of religious affiliation on political party choice had declined as compared with the early years of the century, it was still in evidence (and was, of course, of paramount importance in Northern Ireland).

Explanations of the continuing influence of religion have tended to focus on the fact that the Church of England, as the established church, is identified with the social and political establishment, while religious dissent goes hand in hand with political dissent. In addition, religious attachments at this time did not change a great deal from generation to generation, and the parents or grandparents of many voters in the 1960s would have been voting in the early part of the century when the connections between religion and politics were more direct. For example, many Catholics in Britain are descendants of Irish immigrants and, for them, the role of the Conservatives in the struggles over Irish home rule continued to play a large part in their political thinking. As this discussion illustrates, the influence of religion on party choice in the 1950s and 1960s was very much a legacy of past struggles, and Butler and Stokes were convinced that it was a legacy that was steadily disappearing.

Age

There is a well-known aphorism, the origins of which are obscure, which goes something like this: 'He who is not a radical at twenty has no heart, but he who is still a radical at forty has no head'. The precise ages referred to vary somewhat but the general sentiment of this piece of folk wisdom is clear enough and it found empirical support from voting studies in the 1950s and 1960s. Academic surveys and opinion polls regularly found that younger people, especially the youngest age group in the electorate, were more inclined to vote Labour, while older voters favoured the Conservatives. For example, according to the British Election Survey in 1970 (the first election after the voting age was lowered to 18), 37 per cent of 18 to 24 year olds voted Conservative, compared to 55 per cent of those aged 65 or over. This same pattern – the youngest age group being clearly the least Conservative and a sharp increase in Conservative support among the over-55s – could be observed among both manual and non-manual workers (and cannot therefore be attributed to social class). What is less obvious is why there should be this clear association between age and party choice.

As in the case of age differences in turnout (see Chapter 2), there are two main explanations. The life-cycle account is essentially the explanation implicit in the adage quoted above. Young people tend to be idealistic and to favour social and political change. As they grow older, however, people acquire more responsibilities (such as children of their own), more of a stake in society (such as property), more commitments (a mortgage) and become more aware of the difficulties associated with rapid social change. They thus become more cautious and conservative in outlook. The alternative explanation is generational, centring on the influential political phases or events at the time of political socialization. Voters brought up at the time of the Depression in the 1930s, for example, are likely to differ considerably in outlook from those who entered the electorate at the time of the Vietnam War in the 1960s. The idea of political generations could be used to explain the strength of Conservative support among older people in Britain in the 1950s and

1960s, since anyone aged over 65 in 1970 would have come of voting age in the 1920s or before, when Labour was a relatively new party. Their earliest influences, therefore, were unlikely to have been in a pro-Labour direction. When looking at just one time period, it is impossible to tell whether age differences reflect a life-cycle or a generational effect. More recent data, as presented in Chapter 8, help us to decide between the two.

Sex

Another pervasive feature of voting in the 1950s and 1960s was a sex difference in party choice: men were less likely to vote Conservative and more likely to vote Labour than women. The gap was not wide – five percentage points in the 1966 British Election Survey, for example – but it was consistent and it held within classes and within age categories (and so it was not simply a result of women, who tend to live longer than men, predominating in the more Conservative age groups). As with the association between age and vote, the reasons for this tendency are not wholly clear, although various hypotheses could be put forward. Probably the most convincing concerned women's role in the labour market: while men went out to work, women stayed at home to look after children and attend to other domestic duties. This insulated them from industrial conflicts and wider community pressures. If this is correct then we should expect to find the 'gender gap' narrowing as more and more women entered the workforce from the 1970s onwards. As we see in Chapter 8, this turns out to be the case.

Partisan alignment

As previously indicated, the alignment between classes and parties was only one of the main features of voting in Britain in the 1950s and 1960s. There was also a 'partisan alignment' in the sense that electors identified themselves with a party. The standard BES survey question designed to elicit the kind of generalized psychological commitment implied by party identification is: 'Generally speaking, do you think of yourself as Conservative, Labour, Liberal Democrat or what?' Surveys at the three elections between 1964 and 1970 found that the over-whelming majority of voters – around 90 per cent – were willing to nominate a party that they supported and, of those, most nominated the Labour or Conservative parties (see Table 3.2).

Table 3.2   Party identification, 1964–70 (per cent of electorate)

	1964	1966	1970
With party identification	92	90	89
With Conservative or Labour identification	81	80	81
'Very strong' identifiers	43	43	41
'Very strong' Conservative or Labour identifiers	40	39	40

Sources: Data from BES 1964–70 cross-section surveys.

It is possible that this survey question does not in fact tap the kind of enduring, deep-rooted commitment which is implied by the concept of party identification but that voters respond by simply naming the party which they currently favour. This possibility was considered by, among others, Butler and Stokes (1974: 39–47) and Crewe, Sarlvik and Alt (1977: 139–42). Both investigations found that voters were much more likely to change their vote without changing identification than to change their identification without changing their vote. Both suggested, on this basis, that the question 'works' and that party identification really did exist amongst voters. Butler and Stokes concluded (1974: 47) that in the 1960s 'millions of British electors remain anchored to one of the parties for very long periods of time. Indeed many electors have had the same party loyalties from the dawn of their political consciousness'.

As a standard follow-up to the party identification question in election surveys, respondents are usually asked: 'How strongly (chosen party) do you generally feel – very strongly, fairly strongly, or not very strongly?' In the three surveys reported in Table 3.2, more than two-fifths of the electorate were prepared to describe themselves as 'very strong' party supporters, and almost all of these were Conservative or Labour identifiers. Strength of party identification has important effects upon electoral behaviour. As seen in Chapter 2, stronger identifiers are more likely to turn out to vote and, in addition, they are more likely than weaker identifiers to vote for the party that they identify with and to be stable in their party choice over time. It could almost be said that these voters do not 'decide' whether and how to vote in an election; they have a 'standing decision' or commitment to a party, and voting for it is nearly automatic. In contrast, weaker identifiers are more likely to make their minds up about which party to vote for closer to election day itself, rather than well in advance of it, and they are more 'wobbly', in the sense of seriously considering voting for a party other than their eventual choice. We return to these important differences later in the chapter.

Table 3.3 Party identification in 1964 by parents' party preference (per cent)

	Both parents Conservative	Both parents Labour	Both parents Liberal	One parent Conservative; other none	One parent Labour; other none
Conservative	74	12	37	50	19
Labour	13	79	31	30	65
Liberal	6	6	28	12	11
Other/none	6	4	3	8	5
(N)	(320)	(309)	(102)	(76)	(107)

Source: Data from BES 1964 cross-section survey.

What was the source of the party identification adopted by voters? As Figure 1.2 illustrated, Butler and Stokes argued that it was largely inherited through the family, and they supported this contention with evidence similar to that shown in Table 3.3. As can be seen, where both parents had supported a major party, three-quarters or more of Butler and Stokes's respondents identified with the same party; even if only one parent had supported a party, there was still a clear effect on the subsequent party identification of their children. Studies like these show that the effects of parental socialization do tend to weaken over the life cycle. However, this is offset by another important feature of the Michigan model, which is that once people have acquired a partisan attachment (whether from their parents or elsewhere), the bond tends to strengthen over time. This is partly the result of habit, voters becoming accustomed to supporting their party and to justifying that behaviour. It is also the result of the 'perceptual screen' effect described in Chapter 1, whereby voters select and interpret political information in a way that reinforces a positive view of their own party (and a negative view of its opponents).

An alternative view of party identification

The Butler and Stokes view of party identification as an emotional loyalty to a party, learned early and changing little, has since come under strong challenge. Morris Fiorina (1981) puts forward a radically different interpretation, in which party identification is a kind of summary, or 'running tally', of positive and negative evaluations of a party. These running tallies are frequently updated as voters receive information about parties' records, leaders and policies. Such information can there-fore either strengthen or weaken party identification, even to the point at which voters may transfer not just their vote but also their loyalties to another party. So, whereas the Michigan model emphasizes stability, the 'running tally' model – as the phrase suggests – is a much more dynamic view of party identification. Another important distinction between the two models is that the notion of a running tally sits more easily with the rational choice approach. Rather than being an 'irrational' emotional attachment, unthinkingly inherited, party identification as described by Fiorina is responsive to political events and circumstances. This is not to say that voters need to remember details about these circumstances – it is also rational (given limited time and motivation for thinking about politics) to update the running tally and then to discard the specific information that fed into it.

Like the Michigan model, Fiorina's account of party identification was developed for the American voter but then imported by those study-ing British elections. In this case, the equivalents of Butler and Stokes were the BES team of Clarke, Sanders, Stewart and Whiteley (2004). Their re-analysis of the Butler and Stokes panel data showed consider-able instability in party identification. Over four interviews (1963, 1964, 1966 and 1970), only 61 per cent of respondents reported identifying with the same party on each occasion. Moreover, when a voter did trans-fer allegiance, the shift was usually predictable given that voter's assess-ment of the parties' performances – especially on the economy – and their leaders. In short, party identification seemed to be updated in response to political circumstances in exactly the way that the running tally model would suggest.

Rather than maintaining that one of these rival models of party iden-tification is right and the other is simply wrong, it is more sensible to acknowledge that party identifiers differ. This is clear in everyday life: we have all met dyed-in-the-wool partisans as described by the Michigan model (and may even recognize ourselves in that description), yet we also know plenty of people whose partisan sympathies are more fleeting or non-existent. A pure running tally model struggles to explain why parties seem to have a 'core vote', with both the Conservatives and Labour able to win support from over a quarter of the electorate even at their lowest point in terms of wider popular appeal. Equally, a pure Michigan model cannot easily account for electoral change of any kind, let alone the kinds of instability in party identification observed by Clarke *et al.* (2004).

It is hard to provide more than a rough estimate of the relative incidence of these two kinds of party identification during the 'era of alignment'. However, both the basic 1963–70 panel data and a more sophisticated statistical analysis of them (Clarke *et al.,* 2004: 193–4) suggest that between six and seven out of ten self-reported party identifiers (and thus over half of the electorate) were stable in their partisanship as suggested by the Michigan model. For different reasons, it is hard to judge whether this is a particularly high or low proportion. As suggested at the outset of this chapter, these things depend partly on theoretical perspective. At the time of these surveys, Butler and Stokes were investigating whether the Michigan model was also applicable in Britain. Understandably, then, they emphasized the extent and stability of partisanship (and, as we see in the next chapter, party identification was far more stable than reported opinions on the big policy questions of the day). Equally understandably, when scrutinizing what had become widely known as an 'era of alignment', Clarke and colleagues were struck by the fact that more than a third of reported identifiers looked to be anything but aligned.

The challenge to the Michigan model of party identification also raises questions about what lay beneath the apparent stability of electoral behaviour in the 'era of alignment'. The conventional wisdom had been that class and partisan alignment produced two blocs of voters which could be relied upon to turn out in election after election to support their party, thus buttressing the two-party system. We now know that these blocs of committed partisans were rather smaller than had been thought. In addition, later in the chapter, we show that with voting behaviour, as with party identification, aggregate stability during the 1950s and 1960s concealed a good deal of switching at the individual level. Some might conclude from this that the period cannot reasonably be termed an 'era of alignment'. This is a moot point. What is clear is that, even in ostensibly quite a tranquil period, there was at least the potential for volatility in electoral behaviour and thus in the party system. In the decades that followed, that potential was realized.

Dealignment

While electoral researchers might disagree about quite how to interpret the apparent calm of the 1950s and 1960s, even the most casual observer must have noticed that from the 1970s onwards things were different. The party system has been far from stable and electoral change has been swift and extensive. In general elections the two-party duopoly in

England has been eroded, at first by the Liberals, then by the Liberals in alliance with the SDP and finally by the Liberal Democrats. At the same time, in Scotland and Wales the nationalist parties have become important and established features of the political landscape. During these years electoral volatility rather than stability has been emphasized by election commentators. There was even a period in the late 1970s when single-party government could not be sustained and a 'Lib–Lab' pact was required to keep the Labour government in office. Clearly something had gone wrong with the (admittedly rather simplified) model of a stable, aligned electorate.

The key to explaining the relative electoral turmoil following the 1960s is *dealignment*: that is, a weakening of previously existing alignments. Just as there were two main forms of voter alignment, so there have been two distinct – though closely related – processes of dealignment, with voters becoming disconnected from social classes and from parties. By the second edition of their book, Butler and Stokes (1974: 193–207) had already detected an 'ageing of the class alignment'. Changes in the nature, policies and propaganda of the parties, the emergence of a more affluent working class and a revolution in lifestyles during the 1960s all contributed to a weakening of class–party links and an apparent increase in electoral volatility, especially among younger voters. However, the term 'dealignment' was first used in the British context in a seminal article published in 1977 by Ivor Crewe and colleagues (Crewe, Sarlvik and Alt, 1977). They regarded the election of February 1974 as marking a new departure and an appropriate point from which to date a marked change in British electoral behaviour. Since then, dealignment has become recognized by numerous writers (if not by their word-processing spell-checkers) as the major force for change in electoral behaviour over the last thirty or forty years.

Class dealignment

Presenting data showing the basic relationship between occupational class and party choice in all of the elections from 1964 to 2010 would be rather cumbersome. For illustrative purposes, then, Table 3.4 shows that relationship for the first two and last two of those thirteen elections. The proportion of non-manual workers who voted Conservative slumped from over 60 per cent in the 1960s to only around 40 per cent in 2005 and 2010, while the proportion voting Labour has increased (even though the party's overall vote share was a good deal lower in the more recent elections). Among manual workers, the proportion voting

Labour has fallen from around two-thirds to less than half, while the Conservative vote has fluctuated but remains in the region of one in four. In both classes, then, the proportion of voters supporting their 'natural' class party has declined markedly. The main beneficiaries, however, appear to be the Liberal Democrats (and, to a lesser extent, the minor parties). Most voters remain unwilling to cross over to the party that, on a traditional reading of class voting, would have been considered the natural enemy.

In order to make comparisons over time easier, voting researchers have devised a variety of summary measures of the relationship between class and party choice. Probably the most commonly used has been the Alford Index (devised by a political scientist called Robert Alford: see Alford, 1964). This is calculated by simply subtracting Labour's percentage share of the vote among non-manual workers from its share among manual workers. Thus for 2010 (Table 3.4) the score is (44–27) = 17. A little thought will show that the index can vary between 0 (equal percentages vote Labour in each class and there is, therefore, no class voting) and 100 (all manual workers vote Labour, but no non-manual workers do). By convention, it is Labour voting that is used as the basis for calculating the Alford Index but Conservative voting could just as easily be used (in which case we would subtract the percentage Conservative among manual workers from the percentage Conservative among non-manuals). The index is, then, a measure of the relative strength of a party in two classes. The Labour index scores for each election since 1964 are

Table 3.4 Occupation and party choice, 1964–66 and 2005–10 (per cent)

	1964	1966	2005	2010
Non-manual				
Conservative	63	62	38	41
Labour	22	25	31	27
Liberal (Democrat)	14	12	24	27
Manual				
Conservative	29	26	21	29
Labour	64	68	49	44
Liberal (Democrat)	7	5	20	18

Note: The columns do not total 100 because votes for 'others' are not shown.

Sources: Data from relevant BES surveys.

plotted in Figure 3.1. There was a sharp downturn in 1970 and a fairly steady fall thereafter with the Labour index reaching a new low in 2010. Even in that most recent election, however, the index is greater than zero, signifying that there still remains some class basis to party choice. Nevertheless, on this measure there has been a clear decline in class voting since the 1960s, confirming the pattern indicated by the results in Table 3.4. Clarke *et al.* (2004, ch. 3; 2009: 146) reach the same conclusion in their reports of recent BES surveys. Referring to a variety of measures, they record a sharp decline in the influence of class since the 1960s and conclude firmly that 'over time, British voters have become less "tribal" – less class-driven – in their electoral choices' (2004: 43).

Almost everyone now agrees that class voting has declined in Britain. However, the dealignment thesis was for some time the subject of considerable controversy. The challenge to the prevailing orthodoxy was first launched by Anthony Heath, Roger Jowell and John Curtice – co-directors of the British Election Study from 1983 to 1997 – in their report on the 1983 election, *How Britain Votes* (Heath, Jowell and

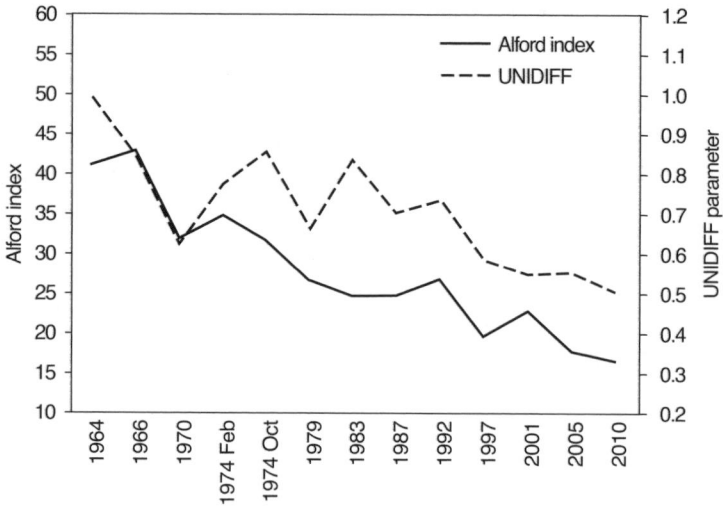

Figure 3.1   Two measures of class voting, 1964–2010

Notes: UNIDIFF scores (see p. 70 for definition) from 2001 onwards based on British Social Attitudes Survey data; otherwise, all scores calculated from the relevant BES data. In line with the practice of the original investigators, the figures for 1964–70 are based on the occupation of the 'head of the household'. From 1974 to 1979 married women are coded according to the husband's occupation. From 1983 the occupation of the respondent is used in all cases.

Curtice, 1985). They argued that there had been 'trendless fluctuation' rather than steady decline in the extent of class voting. More recently, the argument has been taken up by Geoffrey Evans who, in a book entitled *The End of Class Politics?* (1999), stated clearly his view that the answer to that question was 'no'. While these authors have now conceded that class voting has indeed declined, their arguments are worth outlining because they have important implications for the question – addressed later in the chapter – of the causes of this decline.

There are two key stages to the argument concerning class dealignment put forward by Heath, Evans and their various co-authors. The first is a rejection of the Alford Index. The problem with that measure of class voting, it was argued, is that it was too sensitive to changes in the overall popularity of a party. For example, suppose that Labour loses half of its support – that is, both its manual and its non-manual vote share are cut in half – between one election and the next. As a quick calculation based on any of the elections in Table 3.4 will show, the Alford Index of Labour voting will also be halved, suggesting considerable class dealignment in voting. Yet, since Labour lost support at the same rate in both groups, it is not clear that class voting has declined at all. Put another way, Labour is no less a class party; it is just a less successful class party. Given that this was a period in which both major parties lost significant support to the Liberals and others, it is easy to see how the Alford Index might exaggerate dealignment. In place of that index, Heath, Jowell and Curtice recommended an alternative measure of class voting called the 'odds ratio'. We will not dwell here on the calculation of this measure or on the rancorous controversy surrounding its use (odds ratios being described by Dunleavy (1987) as, among other things, 'quite inappropriate', 'distorting', 'peculiar', eccentric' and 'virtually meaningless'). A detailed treatment is available in Denver and Hands (1992, ch. 3). For present purposes, the key point is that a shift to odds ratios was not on its own sufficient to deny the downward trend in class voting. A second stage of the argument was required.

This second stage was a new way of allocating respondents to classes. Heath, Jowell and Curtice rejected the traditional manual/non-manual dichotomy as 'wholly inadequate for studying the social bases of politics' (1985: 13) and proposed a new five-class scheme consisting of the salariat, routine non-manual workers, the petty bourgeoisie, foremen and technicians, and the working class. This more refined grading attempts to take account of differences within the manual and non-manual categories which might be expected to lead to different voting patterns. In order to measure class voting, Heath *et al.* argued, it was necessary to consider the relative strengths of the parties (as measured by odds ratios) in all five class groups. Evans, Heath and Payne (1999) came up with a statistic to summarize all these odds ratios which they called the 'UNIDIFF' score. This can be calculated using BES data for all of the elections in our series, and so we plot it alongside the Alford Index in Figure 3.1. The overall downward trajectory of the graph is unmistakable, especially once the most recent elections are taken into account. Nonetheless, it is clear why authors using this measure tended to emphasize fluctuations rather than any trend in class voting. The different shapes of the two graphs in Figure 3.1 also carry rather different implications about the causes of this decline. Before addressing that point, however, we consider the other face of dealignment: a weakening of partisan attachments.

Partisan dealignment

In Table 3.2 we saw that in the 1960s most electors aligned themselves with parties in the sense of identifying – often quite strongly – with them. Table 3.5 compares levels of party identification in the two 1960s elections and the two most recent elections. The first row of the table shows the percentage of people volunteering a party identification and, while there has been a perceptible decline, it seems that the great majority of voters still do identify with a party. There has been a rather more pronounced drop in the percentage identifying with the two major parties, unsurprisingly given that the Liberal Democrats and other parties have many more supporters as compared with the 1960s. But the steepest fall is in the proportion of the electorate whose commitment to their party is 'very strong'. The trends in overall identification and the strength of such attachments in all elections since 1964 are shown in Figure 3.2. It is clear that the strength of the average party identification

Table 3.5 Party identification, 1964–66 and 2005–10 (per cent of electorate)

	1964	1966	2005	2010
Identify with a party	92	90	81	82
Identify with Conservative or Labour	81	80	63	62
Very strong identifiers	43	43	10	13
Very strongly Conservative or Labour	40	39	9	11

Sources: Data from BES surveys.

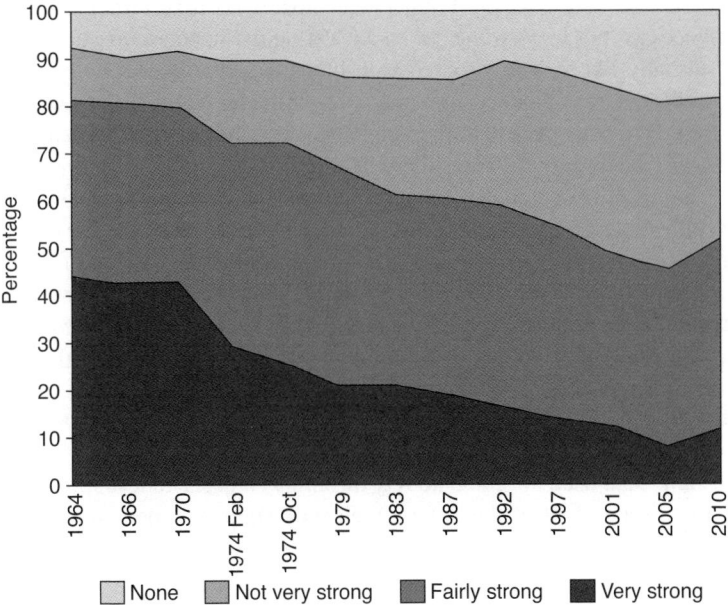

Figure 3.2 Party identification, 1964–2010

has been on a relentless downward trend since the 1960s. Despite a small upturn in 2010 – perhaps because the close race got people's partisan juices flowing – the proportion of very strong identifiers is barely a quarter of what it was at the start of the series. Similarly, 'very strong' Conservative or Labour identifiers, having comprised 40 per cent of the electorate before 1970, totalled only 11 per cent in 2010. They are now something of an endangered species.

It has been argued by Bartle (2001) that the standard survey question causes the percentage of party identifiers to be overestimated since it does not clearly indicate to respondents that it is acceptable to say that they have no identification. Evidence from different question wordings provides strong support for this contention. Since 2001, the BES has included an alternative question in which respondents are first asked whether they consider themselves supporters of a particular party, and only those answering 'yes' are then asked to name that party (see Sanders, Burton and Kneeshaw, 2002). According to this less presumptuous question, only around 50 per cent of the electorate are party identifiers, much smaller than the proportions recorded by the standard question over the years. Predictably, those who described their allegiances as 'not very strong' when answering the standard question were especially likely, if confronted with this alternative question, to report that they were not in fact supporters of a particular party. These 'not very strong' attachments might then be better described as partisan leanings rather than as genuine party identification.

Issues of measurement notwithstanding, the evidence is clear: most people do feel some sort of affinity with a political party, but they do so much less strongly than before (for a more detailed discussion of trends in party identification see Crewe and Thomson, 1999). When it is remembered that stronger partisanship is associated with more stable voting and with an increased propensity to vote, the wide-ranging implications of this weakening of partisan alignment are clear. In addition, the predominance of the two major parties in this respect has been substantially reduced. This means that whereas the Conservatives and Labour each used to be able to rely on solid and consistent support from about 40 per cent of the voters, their core support is now very much smaller.

The causes of dealignment

It is fairly obvious that class dealignment and partisan dealignment are closely related. As Crewe (1984: 193) put it some time ago, 'it is easier to vote against one's class once party loyalties weaken, easier to abandon one's party once class loyalties wither'. Although the two can be distinguished conceptually and some explanations are focused more clearly on one or other of them, there is such an overlap in practice that it seems sensible to outline the suggested causes of dealignment in general. It would be naive, of course, to expect that a phenomenon as complex as dealignment would have one simple cause; instead, it is a product of a series of interlocking developments. It is useful, however, to distinguish what might be described as 'bottom up' explanations and 'top down' explanations.

'Bottom up' explanations

By 'bottom up' we mean explanations which suggest that dealignment was produced by changes occurring, for a variety of reasons, among the voters themselves. Five explanations of this kind can be distinguished:

Changes in the occupational and industrial structures. Over the last 40 years the occupational and industrial structures of Britain have changed almost beyond recognition. Two related features are particularly noteworthy in the context of dealignment. First, there has been a shift from manual to non-manual work. Census statistics show that in 1961 manual workers comprised 58 per cent of the workforce; by 1981 this had fallen to 45 per cent (the first time since records began that manual workers had become a minority of the workforce). Although a reclassification of occupations for the 2001 census makes it difficult to give a figure, there has doubtless been further decline since then (and only around 30 per cent of respondents to the 2010 BES survey had manual occupations). One consequence is that many people from working-class backgrounds now have professional and other non-manual occupations, weakening the previously solid Conservative allegiance of the middle class. Second, there has been a shift from employment in manufacturing to the service sector. In 1961, roughly 38 per cent of employees worked in manufacturing and 47 per cent in services. By 2001 manufacturing was down to about 15 per cent and services (depending on the definition) to about 65 per cent. Put simply, there are fewer factory workers around today and more social workers, hairdressers and 'consultants' of various kinds. Moreover, even within manufacturing there has been an especially sharp contraction in heavy industries such as coal-mining, steel and shipbuilding. These were traditionally male-dominated, highly unionized industries with large plants, which tended to create distinctive and homogeneous working-class communities. In contrast, the emerging 'sunrise' industries are less heavily unionized and rarely located at the centre of established working-class communities. Taken together, it seems likely that these sorts of change have undermined the general level of class consciousness and class solidarity which underpinned the class–party relationship.

'Embourgeoisement'. In the early 1960s there was much agonizing in Labour circles over the fact that the party had lost three successive elections. Support seemed to be draining away and a popular explanation came to be known as the 'embourgeoisement thesis'. This suggested that the working class were becoming more affluent and hence more 'bourgeois' in their attitudes and behaviour, which extended to deserting their traditional Labour loyalties. The thesis was tested and largely rejected by Goldthorpe *et al.* (1968), but these authors detected a significant difference in the nature of the support given to Labour by affluent workers as compared with the traditional working class. In the terms introduced earlier in the chapter, affluent workers were objective or rational class

voters: they voted Labour because they expected a Labour government to bring them direct benefits. Support was thus conditional rather than 'solidaristic'. If Labour did not deliver the goods then their support would be withdrawn. The kinds of development that led people to speculate about the possibility of embourgeoisement at that time have continued apace ever since. Despite the persistence of pockets of poverty and the growth of a poor 'underclass' during the 1980s, manual workers on the whole have become even more affluent. More and more own their own homes and cars, go on foreign holidays, and so on. If, as Goldthorpe *et al.* argued, support for the Labour Party among more affluent workers is more conditional and less 'solidaristic' than it was among traditional workers, then the spread of affluence among the working class has created at least the potential for reduced working-class Labour voting.

Sectoral cleavages. According to Patrick Dunleavy (1980), party choice after 1970 was still basically a product of social location. What happened, however, was that the old cleavage based on occupational class was replaced by two new cleavages, each dividing the public from the private sector. The first relates to employment – whether a voter is employed by the state or in the private sector – and its importance is a consequence of the sharp growth in public-sector employment in Britain (at least up to the 1980s). The second cleavage relates to sector of consumption. People who live in council houses, rely on public transport and depend on the National Health Service (NHS) for medical treatment need these services to be collectively provided. They are consumers in the public sector. In contrast, people who own their own homes, use cars rather than buses or trains and have their own medical insurance arrangements are consumers in the private sector. The groups divided by these cleavages have conflicting interests which are translated, according to Dunleavy, into differential voting behaviour. Those in the private sector favour the Conservatives; those in the public sector do not. Dunleavy's theory is not without its critics (see, especially, Franklin, 1985, ch. 2) and supporting evidence is stronger on the consumption than on the production side. Nonetheless, the sectoral cleavage approach helps to account for the growth in non-Conservative support among white-collar employees in the public sector (such as teachers and social workers), and it provides a solid theoretical basis for the differences in party choice found among different housing groups.

Cross-class locations. An important consequence of these developments is that more and more people are in 'cross-class' locations: that is, they individually have characteristics that traditionally would be ascribed to different classes. Thus, buying one's house used to be thought a middle-class attribute and, according to BES figures, in 1964 only 35 per cent of manual workers were owner-occupiers. By 2010, however, the figure (for the sharply reduced number of manual workers) was 60 per cent. On the other hand, trade union membership, traditionally a characteristic of manual occupations, is now more common among non-manual workers (17 per cent) than among manual workers (13 per cent), according to 2010 BES data. Meanwhile, the growth of female employment (especially in non-manual jobs) has contributed greatly to an increase in the number of 'mixed-class' families. Even by the 1970s, over one-third of the growing number of households in which both husband and wife had jobs were 'mixed-class' in the sense that one partner had a non-manual job while the other was a manual worker. When the effects of inter-generational mobility are added to this, the result is that more than half of all extended families – grandparents, parents and children – are mixed in their class composition. Again, this reduces the potential for class solidarity in electoral behaviour.

At least on the surface, then, the differences between skilled manual workers and lower non-manual groups – or even traditionally middle-class groups such as school teachers – are not all that obvious. It is a moot point whether this is best described as a blurring or as a redrawing of class boundaries. An example of the latter interpretation is Crewe's (1984) distinction between the 'traditional' working class (manual workers who live in Scotland and the North, are council tenants, union members and public-sector employees) and a 'new' working class (manual workers who live in the South, are owner-occupiers, not union members and private-sector employees). The crucial points are that the traditional working class is dwindling in size and that it is being replaced by social groups whose support for Labour is a good deal weaker. Another conclusion worth noting is that, given the more complicated relationship between social class and political interests, continued reliance on the manual/non-manual distinction is inadequate for the study of the class voting.

'Cognitive mobilization'. The final 'bottom-up' explanation is more directly about partisan than about class dealignment. As noted in Chapter 1, one function of party identification was that it simplified the complex political world, giving voters 'cues' about how to evaluate policies, personalities and the actions of governments. Thus a very strong Conservative would believe, almost without thinking, that Conservative

policies on taxation or health or anything else were 'good', that Conservative leaders were 'best' by definition, and that the Labour Party and all its works 'bad'. In a landmark article, Russell Dalton (1984) argued that a process of 'cognitive mobilization' had left voters better able to deal with the complexity of politics, less reliant on this kind of simplifying device and thus less likely to be party identifiers. Dalton identified two main drivers of cognitive mobilization: higher levels of educational attainment, which enhanced citizens' capacity to process political information; and the expansion of the mass media, which lowered the costs of accessing such information.

It is certainly the case that, over the past 30 years, the amount (if not necessarily the quality) of education that the British electorate receives has steadily increased. The school-leaving age has been raised to 16; more and more pupils stay on at school beyond the minimum age (and more take 'A' level Politics); and a much greater proportion of 18 year olds now enter higher education than ever before. However, the fact that this trend has coincided with a decline in the intensity of party attach-ments does not mean that it caused it. And more recent studies have discredited Dalton's thesis by showing that, at the individual level, those who are 'cognitively mobilized' – the more educated and the more engaged with politics – are actually *more* likely to report strong identi-fications (Albright, 2009). A plausible theory thus falters in the face of the evidence. We mention cognitive mobilization here because of its prominence in the literature on partisan dealignment, not because it can do much to explain that trend.

'Top down' explanations

By 'top down' explanations we mean explanations which focus on events (in particular, political events) at national level, and see these as the main causes of dealignment. Four explanations of this kind can be identified:

Government performance. A fairly direct source of weakening party identification is the less than impressive record that both major parties have had in office. Governing a modern industrial society is a difficult and complex task and, no doubt, voters are over-optimistic about what the government can achieve and too quick to blame it when things go wrong (see King, 1975). Nevertheless, the series of disappointments, policy failures and U-turns that have marked government performances since the 1960s, together with the persistence of major problems facing the country, must surely have shaken any conviction voters might have had that 'their' party had all the answers. The link between government performance and party identification is highlighted by Miller, Tagg and Britto (1986) who suggest that dealignment began to affect Labour supporters in the late 1960s and Conservative supporters between 1970 and 1974. Further evidence in support of this interpretation is given in Table 3.6 which shows, first, the average net satisfaction ratings for governments since 1951. Up to the mid-1960s all governments – despite periods in the electorate's bad books – received positive ratings overall. The Labour government of 1966–70 plumbed new depths of unpopularity and thereafter, with the exception of Labour's first term under Tony Blair from 1997 to 2001 which just scraped into positive figures, the electorate was clearly dissatisfied with all governments. Moreover, while there are obvious peaks and troughs (notably the spectacularly low esteem in which the 1992–97 Conservative government was held), there is a perceptible downward trend in satisfaction.

Table 3.6   Average net satisfaction ratings for governments and Prime Ministers

Governments		Prime Ministers		
1951–55	9.9	Churchill 1951–55	12.6	(7)
1955–59	8.0	Eden 1955–57	28.1	(12)
1959–64	1.7	Macmillan 1957–63	18.7	(61)
1964–66	7.7	Douglas-Home 1963–64	7.8	(9)
1966–70	–23.2	Wilson 1964–70	1.4	(64)
1970–74	–14.9	Heath 1970–74	–13.2	(41)
1974–79	–17.6	Wilson 1974–76	1.8	(23)
1979–83	–28.1	Callaghan 1976–79	7.5	(38)
1983–87	–26.6	Thatcher 1979–90	–14.6	(124)
1987–92	–27.5	Major 1990–97	–26.0	(74)
1992–97	–62.9	Blair 1997–2007	–1.7	(111)
1997–2001	0.4	Brown 2007–10	–26.2	(33)
2001–05	–25.4			
2005–10	–38.4			

Notes: The figures to 1979 are based on Gallup data and thereafter on monthly polls by MORI. Gallup asked for approval/disapproval of the government record while the relevant MORI question concerns satisfaction with the way the government is running the country. The figures show the mean net score (positive minus negative responses) over the period in question. For Prime Ministers the number of separate observations is shown in brackets.

Sources: Data from King and Wybrow (2001); Ipsos MORI website.

As the table also shows, satisfaction with the performance of Prime Ministers has declined as well. Overall, people were significantly more satisfied than not with Winston Churchill, Anthony Eden and Harold Macmillan in the 1950s and early 1960s. Even Alec Douglas-Home in his short spell in office was positively rated. Every Prime Minister since has done worse. There were, of course, times when the electorate was very happy with each of them: for example, over his first term (1997–2001), Tony Blair had strongly positive ratings (+22.0). Taking their periods in office as a whole, however, it has clearly become more difficult for Prime Ministers to keep the electorate content. This may not only reflect performance while in government. Some suggest that there has been a decline in deference among the electorate: people have become less trustful of, and willing to accept the authority of, government and political leaders (Beer, 1982). This also relates to the argument about declining party identification, however, since identification itself implies a kind of deference to the authority of a political party.

Ideological disjuncture. Ivor Crewe (1985a: 138–41) argues that a significant source of weakening identification with the Labour Party during the 1970s was the fact that a gap opened up between the opinions of Labour supporters and the policies and principles espoused by the party. Between 1964 and 1979, among the declining number of Labour identifiers, the proportions favouring each aspect of Labour's 'collectivist trinity' of public ownership, trade union power and increased spending on social welfare fell by more than 20 percentage points. By 1979, according to Crewe, there was an 'ideological chasm' between the Labour Party and its supporters. This problem became even more critical in the early 1980s as Labour lurched to the left, adopting a series of left-wing policies. This move was noticed by the electorate (half of the 1983 BES sample believed that Labour had moved to the left since 1979) and was unpopular. Almost half (47 per cent) of 1979 Labour supporters who thought that the party had moved left defected to other parties in 1983 (see Heath, Jowell and Curtice, 1985: 146–50).

Clearly, if there is an increasing disjuncture between the basic tenets of a party and the opinions of its supporters (let alone its potential supporters) we would expect commitment to the party on the part of its supporters to become more and more strained. Labour, of course, recognized this problem and in the late 1980s embarked on a series of policy reviews designed to bring the party more in line with the attitudes of voters (see Shaw, 1994). The process culminated in the election of Tony Blair as Labour leader and the subsequent transformation of Labour into

'New Labour', with a whole set of new policies designed to make the party more attractive to the electorate. While this certainly worked wonders for Labour's popularity among voters in general, the new approach may have been less than rapturously received by at least some committed members and supporters, who had been attracted by the old ideology in the first place.

A similar argument can be applied to the Conservatives. Under Margaret Thatcher, the Conservatives clearly moved to the right during the 1980s. This undoubtedly pleased Conservative activists and the party was very successful in electoral terms, but the evidence suggests that the broader electorate was far from persuaded of the virtues of Thatcherism. Crewe (1988) highlights widespread opposition to a raft of Thatcherite principles and policies and Milazzo, Adams and Green (forthcoming) show that, in every election between 1987 and 2001, Conservative party identifiers were more moderate on economic matters than their party. On being elected party leader, David Cameron made clear his intention to move the party back to the centre ground in order to reconnect with these supporters and in 2010 he appeared to reap at least some electoral benefit. Yet there remains the danger, as with Labour under Blair, that the party becomes so moderate that it alienates traditional identifiers. Supporters want neither an extreme party nor one that is barely distinguishable in ideology or policy from its opponents.

Changing rhetoric. There is a problem with the argument about ideological disjuncture. It implies that ideological convergence – the meeting of political parties on the centre ground – encourages dealignment by weakening the commitments of traditional supporters who want to see their party standing by its principles and policies, not retreating from them. This sounds plausible enough but runs headlong into the fact that the 1950s and 1960s were not only the heyday of aligned voting but also, as discussed in the next chapter, a period of centrist consensus. How, then, were the major parties able to maintain such solid and socially distinctive support bases when their policy offerings were far from distinctive? One possible answer lies in the way that they talked to voters and especially in the role of class in Labour's rhetoric. While the language of class conflict had been toned down since the inter-war period, it was nonetheless common during the 1950s for leading Labour figures to talk of the party as representing the interests of 'the workers' rather than 'the owners'. The distinction between objective and subjective class voting is useful here. Ideological convergence can explain a decline in objective class voting because it becomes less easy to identify the party that is serving the interests of a particular social class (see Evans and Tilley, forthcoming). However, since the subjective version hinges on voters linking their class identity to one of the parties, we can expect that kind of class voting to be stronger when parties make class-based appeals – that is, when the parties draw those links themselves.

Today, it is almost unthinkable that Labour, or indeed any of the mainstream parties, would refer explicitly to serving the interests of a particular social class. The rhetorical aim is now to find a label – such as the recently popular 'hard-working families' – in which everyone across the class spectrum would recognize themselves. Labour and the Conservatives have long sought to become what Kirchheimer (1966) termed 'catch-all' parties: that is, they aim to downplay social boundaries and to appeal instead to the electorate as a whole. On this account, the crucial class dealignment has been among parties rather than voters. This is consistent with the evidence – accepted on both sides of the class voting debate (Evans, 1993; Clarke *et al.*, 2004: 44) – that the proportion of voters who regard themselves as belonging to a particular social class has altered little since the 1960s. The point is that those class identifications have largely ceased to translate into party identifications.

The impact of television. It was not until the 1960s that ownership of television sets became well-nigh universal in Britain, so that partisan dealignment has been closely paralleled by the rapid growth of televised political coverage. Before the advent of television, radio coverage of elections had always been minimal. For example, during the 1950 campaign, as Nicholas (1951: 126) notes, 'the BBC kept as aloof from the election as if it had been occurring on another planet'. The broadcasting authorities feared that if they covered the election they would be in breach of the laws regulating the conduct of elections. It was only in the 1960s that campaign reports of the kind we are now familiar with began to develop. At the same time, the style of political coverage has undergone a revolution. Even outside campaign periods, television coverage of politics was initially circumspect in the extreme. When leading politicians deigned to be interviewed, they determined the questions to be asked and were treated in a highly deferential manner by interviewers. News broadcaster Leslie Mitchell began a 1951 interview with then Foreign Secretary Anthony Eden thus: 'With your very considerable experience of foreign affairs, it's quite obvious that I should start by asking you something about the international situation today. Or perhaps you would prefer to talk about home – which shall it be?'

The contrast with today could hardly be greater. Intense and detailed coverage of politics is available for those who want to watch it and, during election campaigns, there is more or less round-the-clock coverage on rolling news channels. Two particular features of this coverage are liable to weaken partisan attachments. The first is the collapse of deference. (Imagine Leslie Mitchell's words in the mouth of Jeremy Paxman.) Politicians of all parties are questioned aggressively and, indeed, if a party leader appears to have been given an 'easy ride' by an interviewer, complaints are loud and long. Meanwhile, away from the news, impressionists such as Rory Bremner and programmes such as *Have I Got News for You* hold politicians of all parties up to ridicule. The second feature is the balance of televised politics. Broadcasters are tightly regulated with a view to ensuring impartiality in their coverage. As a result, news reports on political issues typically involve contributions from both major parties and often from the Liberal Democrats too (as well as from smaller parties such as UKIP or the Greens when the issue is especially pertinent to them). This contrasts with political coverage in the press which is not regulated in this way and is often stridently partisan. By choosing newspapers that share their political allegiance, party identifiers can largely avoid messages and arguments which challenge their party's position (see Chapter 6). But they would need to be very quick with the remote control (and to have a very tolerant family) in order to mute all such dissenting views on television. It is very difficult, if not impossible, to measure the impact of this pluralistic coverage; by their nature, the effects of television are diffuse and subtle. It would be surprising, however, if the decline in the strength of partisan commitment since the 1960s was unrelated to the ways in which politics and politicians have been projected by television.

* * *

As suggested above, none of these explanations by themselves account for class and partisan dealignment. There is, of course, no single explanation; instead, a variety of social changes at the 'bottom' has interacted with other (mainly political) developments at the 'top' to produce a weakening of the old alignment between class and party and to weaken voters' commitment to the major parties especially. This interaction could take a cyclical form: the decline of traditional and highly unionised industries contributes to a weakening of working-class identification with the Labour Party, which in turn discourages Labour from mounting a class-based appeal, which in turn further weakens manual workers' sense of Labour as the party for them. In any case, whatever the precise causal process, the key point is that the largely aligned electorate of the 1950s and 1960s has given way to a largely dealigned modern electorate that behaves in a very different way.

The consequence of dealignment: electoral volatility

A priori, one would expect the decline in the average strength of party identification among voters in Britain to have had important consequences. Strong party identification acted as a sort of psychological anchor in the sea of electoral politics. It provided an element of stability, and for very strong identifiers party choice at elections was almost automatic. When the anchor is removed, or becomes more weakly attached, voters are likely to be more open to persuasion, more indecisive about which party to vote for, and more likely to switch parties. The core of support upon which each party can rely is much diminished in size. The party system, rather than being set in stone, as it were, is more unstable; its foundations are less solid and secure. In short, partisan dealignment is likely to produce an electorate that is very different from that described by voting studies in the 1950s and 1960s. Fewer people base their vote on tradition or a 'standing decision', enhancing the importance of short-term factors such as their perceptions of the competence of the parties or the quality of the party leaders. Rather than being stable and predictable so far as party choice is concerned, many voters are likely to be volatile and unpredictable in their behaviour.

Defining and measuring electoral volatility is not straightforward, however. First of all, we have to distinguish between *net* and *overall* or *individual* volatility. The distinction is similar to that between swing and the 'flow of the vote' between elections (see Chapter 1). Net volatility usually refers to changes in the parties' shares of the votes at two successive elections (although it could also apply to the share of voting intentions received in successive opinion polls), while overall volatility refers to change on the part of individual voters and the total amount of changing that takes place in order to produce the net outcome. Thus, self-cancelling changes – some people switch from Conservative to Labour while others switch from Labour to the Conservatives – are part of overall volatility but would not affect net volatility if similar proportions went in each direction. Indeed, it is perfectly possible to imagine a situation in which there is no net volatility at all, while overall volatility is high.

Second, we can distinguish three different contexts giving rise to three types of volatility which can be labelled 'inter-election volatility', 'mid-term movements' and 'campaign swithering' (to use a descriptive Scots word, which means being indecisive or leaning one way and then another). Inter-election volatility relates to voter behaviour in successive elections. Those who switch parties are clearly behaving in a volatile way, but it is less clear whether those who move between voting and non-voting should also be classed as volatile. They may support the same party in both elections but simply have been prevented from voting for one reason or another. There are also opportunities to display volatility in the period between general elections. All electors can vote in European Parliament elections and local elections; Londoners have mayoral and assembly elections; the Scots, Welsh and Northern Irish elect devolved institutions; and there are occasional parliamentary by-elections. In addition, monthly opinion polls give estimates of how the electorate would vote if there were a general election 'tomorrow'. In these contexts we can register mid-term movements on the part of the electorate. Finally, during general election campaigns there are almost daily opinion polls and some panel surveys. These show that while some voters have their minds made up about which party to support when the campaign begins and never waver from that position, others are slow to decide, hesitant, or actually switch between parties. This sort of campaign 'swithering' represents another form of electoral volatility.

Inter-election volatility

We have already briefly discussed net inter-election volatility, as measured by the Pedersen Index, in Chapter 1 (see Table 1.2). Although there is no consistent upward trend, it is significant that the three most volatile elections (February 1974, 1983 and 1997) all took place after the onset of dealignment. Nonetheless, the dealignment thesis does not necessarily imply that all elections will display high levels of net volatility. The net figure may conceal self-cancelling changes, or short-term factors may favour the same party in successive elections.

In order to measure overall or individual volatility in its different dimensions, survey data are required. It is well established, however, that when asked to recall their vote in an election held a few years previously, a significant proportion of survey respondents do not recall their behaviour accurately. They tend to remember voting even if they did not turn out, and they also tend to make their past vote consistent with their current preference (Heath and Johns, 2010). Both biases mean that surveys are liable to understate change in behaviour between elections. Nonetheless, most of the major BES surveys have had to rely on recall of past vote in order to estimate the extent of inter-election volatility. Table 3.7 presents two measures of volatility for pairs of elections since 1959, as indicated by the BES surveys. The first column shows the percentages of those who voted in both elections who switched parties in successive elections. The trend in the proportion of switchers is not perhaps as clear or as strong as might be expected on the basis of the party identification figures but it is, nonetheless, certainly on an upward track. Moreover, the timing of the upturn is consistent with the notion that the impact of dealignment really began to be felt after 1970. The mean figure for party switchers in the first three elections in the series is just under 15 per cent; in the last three the average is just under 25 per cent (almost a quarter of those who voted in each pair of elections), and 2010 saw an unprecedented level of switching.

The percentages in the second column are based on everyone eligible to vote at each pair of elections and, this time, switchers include those moving from voting to non-voting and vice versa. Not unexpectedly, this increases the estimates of volatility. (Indeed, as we noted in Chapter 1, moving between voting and non-voting is usually the most common

Table 3.7   Trends in inter-election volatility (per cent)

	Switched parties	Switched (incl. non-voters)
1959–64	18	35
1964–66	10	22
1966–70	16	34
1970–74 (Feb)	24	42
1974 (Feb)–1974 (Oct)	16	28
1974 (Oct)–1979	22	37
1979–83	23	40
1983–87	19	37
1987–92	19	34
1992–97	25	35
1997–2001	22	34
2001–05	24	37
2005–10	28	38

Sources: Data from Heath, Jowell, Curtice with Taylor (1994: 281) and relevant BES surveys.

form of individual change between elections. Switching between the Conservative and Labour parties is the least common form.) When abstention is included in the measure of volatility there is only a slight upward trend. However, the story might be different if we could calculate both measures for elections in the 1950s, and the trend is also likely to be constrained by the fact that reported turnout has declined much less quickly than actual turnout (and so these days there are probably more switchers in and out of non-voting than the surveys suggest). In any case, the extent of volatility is clear. Between all pairs of elections since October 1974, more than a third of the electorate have changed their behaviour in one way or another.

Mid-term movements

A cursory glance at the results of recent mid-term elections and of monthly opinion polls shows that they fluctuate wildly as compared with the preceding general election. The evidence from polls and parliamentary by-elections suggests that, in net terms, mid-term movements in party support became much more violent from the late 1960s onwards (see Crewe, 1985a: 104–5; Norris, 1990), and this form of volatility remains at a high level today. A striking recent example of a large midterm movement occurred in the European Parliament elections of 2009 when the UK Independence Party leapt from 2.3 per cent in the 2005 general election to 16.5 per cent (while the British National Party rose from 0.7 to 6.2 per cent) and the overall effect was a Pedersen Index score of 34.8. These rocketing vote shares were propelled partly by the proportional electoral system used in European Parliament elections, which means that votes for smaller parties are far less likely to be wasted (see Chapter 7). Yet dealignment is an important factor, too. Voters who remain strongly attached to one of the major parties are likely to vote for that party, regardless of the electoral system. The prospects for minor parties have improved as the proportion of such strong identifiers has declined.

For evidence of individual volatility in the mid-term we have to turn to panel surveys involving mid-term waves. The best recent evidence of mid-term volatility comes from a series of surveys known as the British Election Panel Survey (BEPS), which involved interviewing the same respondents every year from 1992 to 1997 and asking them how they would vote in a general election. Although the panel suffered from attrition (respondents dropping out over the years), this series provides much fascinating data, and Table 3.8 is an example. This shows the percentage

Table 3.8   Mid-term volatility (percentage of 1992 voters still supporting party in subsequent years)

	1993	1994	1995	1996	1997
Conservative	63	54	49	56	59
Labour	87	88	92	89	83
Liberal Democrat	73	63	49	49	50

Source: Data from British Election Panel Survey, 1992–97.

of 1992 voters for each of the three main parties who indicated at each subsequent interview that they would still support the same party. By 1995, just under half of 1992 Conservatives were intending to vote Conservative again. But there was also massive defection from the Liberal Democrats: in 1995 only around half of those who voted Liberal Democrat in 1992 said that they would do so again. Labour, on the other hand, largely held on to its 1992 supporters. (The difference between the two major parties reflects the unpopularity of the Conservative government at the time. A panel survey during the 2005–10 term would no doubt have shown Labour having particular difficulty in retaining its support.)

Even these data underestimate the extent of party switching in mid-term as they do not tell us about respondents who nominated different parties in the different interviews. Considering those who were interviewed on all six occasions, and confining the analysis to support for the three major parties, we find that only 43 per cent of respondents were consistently loyal – that is, they indicated each time that they would vote for the same party. Clearly, in the mid-1990s, party support was extremely fluid between general elections. Due to a lack of comparable data from the 1950s and 1960s, we cannot be sure that this represents an increase in mid-term volatility compared with the 'era of alignment'. However, there is strong circumstantial evidence from a breakdown of the 1992–97 loyalty rates by strength of party identification. Among strong party identifiers, 53 per cent were consistently loyal, compared to just 35 per cent among not very strong identifiers. We can reasonably infer that, since the strength of party identifications has declined sharply, the extent of volatility has increased.

Campaign swithering

This form of volatility takes two main forms: switching parties, or moving between indecision and a firm voting intention ('churning', as the pollsters describe it). Evidence of net campaign volatility between 1964 and 1992, based on the results of campaign polls, suggests that this too increased sharply after 1970 and, with the exception of 1987, remained at a higher level thereafter (see Farrell, McAllister and Broughton, 1995). Panel surveys enabling us to measure this form of individual volatility during campaigns are relatively recent and still rare (because they are expensive). However, the polling company Ipsos MORI has estimated 'churning' among the electorate at each election since 1979 and has found an unmistakeable upward trend (Fallon and Worcester, 1992; Worcester and Mortimore, 2001).

BES research on the 2010 election involved interviewing a panel of voters just before the official campaign began and again immediately after the election. In the pre-campaign survey, fully 50 per cent of respondents ($N = 767$) said that they had not decided how to vote. Of those who had decided and named their party preference ($N = 666$), 80 per cent eventually voted for the party, while 9 per cent didn't vote and 11 per cent voted for another party. Of those who were undecided but indicated which party they were leaning towards ($N = 459$), only 54 per cent eventually voted for it while 27 per cent opted for another party and 19 per cent didn't vote. It is worth noting that this volatility is not specific to the 2010 election, with its close race and fluctuating poll ratings (especially for the Liberal Democrats). The figures were similar in the 2005 BES, indicating a high level of campaign swithering even in an election which saw relatively stable opinion polls and in which the result was thought by many to be a foregone conclusion.

Although campaign panel surveys are relatively recent, the main BES surveys provide a valuable series of data going back to 1964 which measures what Heath *et al.* (1991) call 'hesitancy' during campaigns: the percentage of voters who decided which party to support during the election campaign itself, and the percentage who thought of voting for a party other than the one that they ended up voting for. The figures are shown in Table 3.9. There were clearly more late deciders from 1974 onwards, and the proportion reached a peak in the 2010 election when over a third of those who responded ($N = 888$) claimed that they made up their minds about which party to support during the campaign itself. The trend in the proportion of switherers is less clear, but the figures from 1979 onwards are generally larger than those for the previous five elections.

Analysis of the various dimensions of volatility is handicapped by the absence of suitable data from the 1950s. Nonetheless, there is plenty of

Table 3.9   'Late deciders' and 'switherers', 1964–2010 (per cent)

	Decided during campaign	Thought of voting for other party
1964	12	25
1966	11	23
1970	12	21
1974 (Feb)	23	25
1974 (Oct)	22	21
1979	28	31
1983	22	25
1987	21	28
1992	24	26
1997	27	31
2001	26	–
2005	33	–
2010	37	–

Note: The question asking whether respondents thought of voting for another party was not included in the three most recent surveys.

Source: Data from BES surveys.

evidence – from both surveys and election results – that individual voters and the electorate as a whole are more volatile and less predictable than at a time when strong party identification was widespread. Admittedly, the upward trend in volatility is less consistent than is the clear and steady decline in strength of party identification. Yet that is to be expected. The point about dealignment is that it creates the *potential* for short-term electoral change. Whether this potential is realized depends on the circumstances of the period in question. For example, this supposedly volatile electorate produced stable electoral outcomes in general elections from 1979 to 1992 (see Table 1.2). Yet it is a mistake to regard, say, the 40-odd per cent of the vote that the Conservatives consistently garnered from 1979 to 1992 as constituting a stable bloc of core supporters. Instead, the Conservatives were able to put together temporary coalitions of voters (which then dissolved in the inter-election periods). These coalitions were based on voters' short-term judgements about the parties: their competence in running the economy, their leaders, their general image, and so on. When – as between 1979 and 1992 – these judgements tend to favour the same party, the results of elections can be expected to remain fairly stable. The electorate remained potentially volatile, but the potential was not realized largely because of the relative unattractiveness of Labour. Once the short-term factors moved in Labour's favour, as they had by 1997, the result was a huge swing from the Conservatives, by far the biggest swing in post-war electoral history (see Denver, 1998a).

These arguments should not be taken as implying that voters' judgements – about party policies, the record of the government in office and the capabilities of the party leaders – were unimportant prior to dealignment. In fact, since the core support for the two major parties was roughly equal in size, elections in the 1950s and 1960s were also decided by short-term factors rather than long-term loyalties. The impact of dealignment has been to magnify the effects of these factors and thus to generate the potential for swings dwarfing those seen in the era of alignment. Judgements about the parties, their policies and their records, always crucial in determining aggregate election outcomes, have also become more and more important in determining individual voting decisions. The nature and basis for such judgements are discussed in the next three chapters.

4

Issues, Policies and Performance

If a political commentator or politician of the 1920s or 1930s were able to read the previous chapter then he or she would be amazed at the relative lack of attention given to party policies or to topical events and political issues. Before survey studies of voting behaviour began, elections and voting were conceived of largely in terms of choices between competing sets of policy proposals. The voter was pictured as weighing up the policies of the different parties, or the qualities and positions of candidates, and on that basis deciding whom to support. The party which won an election was thought to have a 'mandate' from the electorate for all of its policy proposals as detailed in its election manifesto. In the nineteenth century, the political philosopher John Stuart Mill (1963 edition: 302–4) said this about the voter:

> His vote is not a thing in which he has an option ... he is bound to give it according to his best and his most conscientious opinion of the public good ... the voter is under an absolute moral obligation to consider the interest of the public, not his private advantage, and give his vote to the best of his judgement exactly as he would be bound to do if he were the sole voter and the election depended upon him alone.

This idealized view of the voter informed much comment upon elections until well into the twentieth century. Even today, if we ask politics students how they think a voter *should* reach his or her decision, most refer to the scrutiny and comparison of party manifestos.

In the preceding two chapters, in contrast, we have considered voting behaviour as almost entirely a function of the voter's social location (class, religion, and so on), socialization experience or psychological attachments (party identification), hardly mentioning party policies or 'the interest of the public'. It would, of course, be going too far to claim that before 1970 not a single voter decided how to vote after carefully evaluating the parties' policies and considering the public interest, or that policy considerations played no part at all in the decision processes of most voters. Indeed, the Michigan model explicitly contains 'issue orientation' as a short-term factor affecting party choice. Most studies of British voters also found that voters did have generalized images of the parties that were not without policy content. Thus the Labour Party was widely perceived as the party which was 'for the working class' or in favour of nationalization and higher welfare spending. Nonetheless, when researchers in the 1950s and 1960s tried to be more precise about the effects of electors' political opinions and judgements on their voting choices, their results did not suggest that there was a very strong connection between the two.

There is a broad consensus, however, that as the impact of class and party identification declined, the importance of voters' assessments and judgements increased. There was no parallel consensus about what voting on the basis of issue or policy opinions should be called. The terms used include 'issue voting', 'policy voting', 'consumer voting' and 'instrumental voting'. A variant on the basic idea is 'retrospective voting'. Despite this diversity of terminology, all of these involve the voter making a more or less calculated decision about which party to support (or, as we have seen, about whether to vote at all) on the basis of his or her policy preferences and assessments of the parties' positions or performance. In terms of the theories outlined in Chapter 1, as the Michigan model became less relevant, so voting as a form of rational choice came to be seen as a more useful way of explaining voters' decisions.

Issue voting

In their discussion of issue voting, Butler and Stokes (1974: 292) made an important distinction between what they call 'position' issues and 'valence' issues. The former are issues on which people take positions: for or against fox hunting, compulsory identity cards, student tuition fees, or whatever. Of course, on some of these issues there are more than two possible positions. For example, a voter may want taxes and spending to be slashed, to be trimmed, to be substantially increased, or some intermediate position. The key point is that people's stances vary. On the other hand, there are many issues on which there is broad agreement among the electorate about the goals that government should pursue. What is at issue is the competence or performance of the parties in seeking to achieve these goals. Not many people, for example, are in favour of increased crime or economic recession; not many are against improving standards of health care. These are valence issues and the disagreement is about which party would be best at achieving what people want. It is worth pointing out that the position–valence distinction is not always clear-cut, with the status of an issue potentially varying across people and across time. For example, immigration could be seen as a position issue – since voters differ in their views on what is an appropriate amount of immigration – but also has a valence flavour, with a focus during recent election campaigns on the Labour government's handling of immigration and on which party is most likely to manage the issue competently. One reason why immigration might have become more of a valence issue is that, at least until the 2010 election, the major parties have tended not to adopt markedly different stances. This illustrates a key point – when the parties' positions on an issue converge, that issue inevitably takes on valence characteristics. Denied the choice between different policy positions, a voter can only decide among parties on the basis of their likely competence on the issue.

Which issues matter?

As far as position issues are concerned, Butler and Stokes (1974: 276–95) suggested that four conditions must be met if an issue is to influence voting and a voter is to qualify as an 'issue voter':

1   The voter must be aware of the issue concerned. Clearly if someone failed to notice that in 2004 the government introduced 'top-up' tuition fees for university students, then that policy could not affect his or her vote in a subsequent election.
2   The voter must have some attitude towards, or opinion about, the issue. Someone might be well aware that many people have strong views about university tuition fees but be completely indifferent themselves, or else unable to make up their mind on the question. In these cases the issue could not affect their vote.
3   The voter must perceive different parties as having different policies on the issue. If he or she believes that, whatever they might say, all the parties are basically in favour of tuition fees, then there is no scope for choosing between them on the basis of that issue.
4   Finally, and most obviously, the voter must vote for the party whose position on the issue is, or is perceived to be, closest to his or her own position.

These conditions refer to an individual voter but it is easy enough to derive from them the conditions necessary for a position issue to affect the overall election outcome. An issue needs to be fairly prominent, such that a lot of people are aware enough of it to have formed opinions, and it must also divide the electorate and the parties. In the 1960s, for example, many voters had strong opinions on the question of immigration but believed (correctly, as it happened) that there was no real difference between the parties on the issue. As a result, the immigration issue did not, on the whole, influence party choice (see Butler and Stokes, 1974: 303–8).

A parallel list of conditions can also be drawn up for valence issues. As with position issues, voters must be aware of and care about the issue in question in order to be influenced by it when voting. However, given the definition of valence issues, we would not expect them to divide the electorate or the parties in terms of the objectives or direction of policy. In this context, the crucial gap between the parties is in terms of likely performance. If a voter believes that the major parties are equally able (or, perhaps more likely, equally unable) to deliver lower crime rates, then that issue cannot be a basis for his or her choice between those parties. Moving from the individual to the aggregate level, a valence issue will only influence the election outcome if there is an imbalance in perceived competence – that is, if one of the parties is seen overall as better able to handle that issue. The 2010 election campaign – indeed, not only the campaign but also the two years or so leading up to the election – was dominated by the battle between Labour and the Conservatives to be seen as the party best able to handle Britain's economic troubles.

The first of Butler and Stokes's conditions concerns voters' awareness of an issue. It is hard to imagine anyone in 2010 being unaware of the economic issue; we can probably also assume that it weighed quite heavily in many voters' decision-making. In the jargon of electoral studies, the economy was a highly *salient* issue in 2010. The salience of different issues – that is, the extent to which they are in people's minds at the time of the election – is of obvious electoral relevance. As Sarlvik and Crewe put it, 'one would expect a stronger relationship between issue opinions and voting among those who consider a given issue important than among those who are less concerned' (1983: 222). Salience is usually gauged by questions such as this one from the most recent BES surveys: 'As far as you're concerned, what is the single most important issue facing the country at the present time?' (It is an 'open-ended' question, by which we mean that respondents could answer with any issue that came to mind rather than having to choose from a list of issues decided in advance by the survey designers.) Table 4.1 shows, for

Table 4.1   Issue salience rankings in 2001, 2005 and 2010 (% citing issue as 'most important')

	2001		2005		2010	
Rank	*Issue*	*%*	*Issue*	*%*	*Issue*	*%*
1	Health	24	Immigration	24	Economy	50
2	Economy	12	Health	14	Immigration	15
3	Education	12	Crime	13	Crime	6
4	Europe	8	Iraq	9	Unemployment	6
5	Crime	6	Economy	5	Debt	4

Sources: Data from relevant BES pre-election surveys.

the three most recent elections, the five issues mentioned most often in response to that question.

There is a mixture of continuity and change in salience across elections. Some issues, like the economy and crime, preoccupy at least some voters each time. Others emerge at a particular election – such as Iraq in 2005 – but then slip off most people's radars. (These are sometimes called 'flash issues'.) The really striking difference across elections, however, is in the percentages. In 2001 and 2005, the clear leader in terms of salience was most important for less than a quarter of the electorate and the top three issues accounted for only around half of responses. Clearly, voters' concerns varied widely. In 2010, by contrast, the economy was seen as most important by fully half of the electorate (and closely related issues, like unemployment and debt, push that proportion still higher). The first two can probably be seen as 'normal' elections in this regard, while 2010 shows what can happen when a major crisis causes one issue to dominate voters' thinking.

Given the prominence of the economy in the 2010 election, it might be thought surprising that well over one-third of voters chose non-economic concerns as their 'most important issue'. As this indicates, voters' priorities are not simply a reflection of the prominence of issues in the election campaign. Of course, the voters' agenda tends to be similar to those of the media and the parties – similar enough to trigger a number of studies examining the causal relations (that is, the question of who sets the agenda and who follows) between the three (see Chapter 6). Nevertheless, some voters have a particular and longstanding concern that will remain their top priority, even if the issue barely registers during the election campaign. (For one respondent in the 2010 BES, the most important issue was the need to 'tell the truth about alien contact [and] use their technology to save this planet'. It is easy to see how this might overshadow fleeting economic concerns.) So, while results like those in Table 4.1 are often used to give an impression of the overall campaign agenda, we should not lose sight of the fact that they are an aggregation of individuals' priorities. Moreover, if the aim is to explain an individual's choice of party, it makes more sense to ask what mattered most to him or her rather than what mattered to the average voter.

Methodological problems in analysing issue voting

It is generally agreed among voting researchers that the dealignment of the electorate has been accompanied by an increase in issue voting, in one form or another. This is not to say, however, that people – apart perhaps from a few very odd cases – are beginning to resemble that 'ideal voter', assessing parties across the range of issues in their manifestos and using this comparison to calculate the appropriate vote. Those seeking to estimate the extent of issue voting need to consider three important methodological points. The first of these is the matter of salience raised just above. It is rare that people's policy preferences or evaluations of government performance all point towards voting for the same party. The difficulty then is that we do not know how the issue voter decides which issues are the ones that will determine his or her vote. In practice, the commonest way out of this problem is simply to tot up the balance of voters' preferences over a number of issue areas. This is not satisfactory, however, because it ignores salience; that is, it presumes that all issues are weighted equally when, in reality, a voter's opinion on one issue may outweigh his or her preferences on all others. Voters' assessments of issue importance need to be incorporated into any analysis of issue voting.

The second methodological point concerns causation. If we find a clear relationship between voters' policy opinions and their choice of party, then at least two interpretations of this are possible. The issue voting interpretation is that voters make their decisions by comparing their policy preferences with the stances taken by the parties. The second interpretation puts party identification in the driving seat. In Chapter 1 we noted that partisanship acts as a 'perceptual screen' such that, for example, a strong Labour identifier is predisposed to believe that the Labour Party not only has the right policies (on position issues) but is also more likely to deliver (on valence issues). The problem, then, is that a strong correlation between issue positions and party choice is consistent with both interpretations. People could be voting according to their issue opinions, or bringing those issue opinions into line with their vote choice. There is no simple way of resolving the problem of causal direction empirically. We can demonstrate the extent to which voters fulfil the conditions for issue voting, but ultimately it cannot be proved that issue preferences cause or determine party choice.

The third problem was highlighted in an important essay by Philip Converse, one of the authors of *The American Voter*. Using a panel study of US voters, he observed a good deal of apparently random fluctuation in issue attitudes and famously concluded that 'many citizens do not have meaningful beliefs, even on issues that have formed the basis for intense political controversy among elites' (1964: 245). Butler and Stokes (1974: 281) then showed that this was not just an American phenomenon. In each wave of their 1963–70 panel study, British voters were asked a question about the extent to which they thought major industries should be nationalized (publicly owned). This issue had long been at the centre of political controversy in Britain and in the 1960s the parties took clearly different stances on the question. Yet, over four separate interviews, less than half (43 per cent) of BES respondents were consistent in either supporting or opposing further nationalization. This suggests that, for many people on many issues, the second condition for issue voting – that the voter must have a real attitude on that issue – is simply not met. This would matter less but for the considerable reluctance among survey respondents to admit it when they have no opinion on an issue. Instead, respondents are prone to pluck an answer more or less out of the air (either to try and keep the interviewer happy or just to save face). Converse coined the term 'nonattitudes' to describe these off-the-top-of-the-head responses. The problem for voting researchers is that it is difficult to tell whether a reported opinion is genuine or a nonattitude. If it is the latter, then any correlation between it and party choice has to be coincidence rather than evidence of issue voting.

Position issues, policies and ideology

When aligned voting was the norm in Britain, the evidence suggests that relatively few voters fulfilled the four conditions for issue voting. As in the Grand National, large numbers fell at every fence. First, on the question of awareness of issues, studies consistently found that large numbers of electors managed to get through life with only the haziest notion about the topics exercising the interest of MPs and political journalists. In 1964, around 40 per cent of respondents to the British Election Study survey were unable to name two important questions facing the country (quoted in Franklin, 1985: 128). Butler and Stokes concluded that '[u]nderstanding of policy issues falls away very sharply indeed as we move outwards from those at the heart of political decision-making to the public at large' (1974: 277). It is therefore unsurprising that many voters did not have genuine opinions about the issues concerned – they could report only 'nonattitudes' – and hence failed to meet the second condition for issue voting.

Perception of differences between the parties (the third condition for issue voting) varied considerably depending upon the nature of the issue. On 'big' or broad issues, such as welfare spending or nationalization, voters were mostly able to see a difference between the Conservatives and Labour, but on a whole series of more precise or detailed policy questions (and on immigration, as noted earlier) this was not the case. In addition, 1960s voters were seldom able to assign policy stances to the Liberals. Finally, even voters who successfully passed the first three issue-voting tests were prone to fall at the last fence. Despite having an opinion which they knew was contrary to a party's policy, some would nevertheless go ahead and vote for that party. This was particularly true of Labour supporters, a majority of whom were regularly found to oppose the party's central policy of nationalization. A survey of Bristol voters in 1955, for example, found that 39 per cent of Labour voters were pro-Conservative in their policy preferences with a further 27 per cent being neutral (Milne and Mackenzie, 1958: 119). The authors of the report on this survey also noted that 'the proportion of electors claiming that an issue had finally decided their vote is minute' (p. 160).

For those writing on voting during the era of alignment, the reason for the weakness of issue voting was obvious enough: the strength of party identification. Voters were much more likely to adopt policy preferences to suit their long-standing party attachments than to switch loyalties in line with their policy positions. Predictably, then, interest in issue voting was rekindled by dealignment. With fewer votes effectively predetermined by strong party identities, there was more scope for issue positions to influence choice. Fittingly, it was in their book entitled *Decade of Dealignment*, a report on the 1979 BES, that Sarlvik and Crewe (1983) provided the next detailed analysis of issue voting. They analysed opinions on eight position issues by asking respondents to choose between policy alternatives in each case. They found that most respondents (an average of 88 per cent) fulfilled the first two conditions for issue voting: being aware of the issue and taking a position on it. An average of 78 per cent fulfilled the third step in the model: perceiving the parties as having different positions. Sarlvik and Crewe then examined the influence of policy preferences and perceptions by calculating correlation coefficients measuring the extent to which respondents voted for the party that they thought was closest to their own position on each issue. In every case the coefficients were positive and significant, averaging 0.36 and ranging from 0.19 on how to improve race relations to 0.48 on whether there should be more or less nationalization. Sarlvik and Crewe also incorporated salience into their analysis by grouping respondents according to their rating of each issue as 'extremely important', 'fairly important' or 'not very important'. In each case the correlations between issue position and party choice were consistently strongest among respondents who considered the issue extremely important (averaging 0.49) and weakest among those who considered it not very important (0.30).

Looking to bolster their argument about issue voting being a consequence of dealignment, Sarlvik and Crewe also compared the impact of issue opinions with the impact of class and other social characteristics on party choice. (It should be noted that this comparison was based not only on the eight position issues but also on four assessments of party performance on valence issues.) They concluded that 'the voters' opinions on policies and on the parties' performances in office "explain" more than twice as much as all the social and economic characteristics taken together' (1983; 113). Numerous other studies have corroborated Crewe and Sarlvik's conclusion that issue voting became more evident from the late 1970s onwards. Franklin (1985), for example, used complicated statistical techniques to examine the relative extent to which class and issue positions contributed to explaining party choice between 1964 and 1979. He found that in 1964 class exerted a stronger influence but that by 1979 it was issue opinions that had the greater impact. In a later piece, Franklin and Hughes (1999) confirmed that in elections from 1987 to 1997 issue opinions remained significantly more important than class (even though 'class' was widely defined to include not only occupation but other factors such as education, parents' class and trade union membership).

Issues or ideology?

If 'aligned voting' was the orthodoxy of electoral analysis in the 1950s and 1960s, then 'issue voting' quickly became the orthodoxy of the

1970s and 1980s. However, as more attention was paid to voters' opinions, the model of issue voting and the ways in which it had been studied came to be criticized. As with the class voting controversy, the most trenchant criticism of Sarlvik and Crewe's findings came from Heath, Jowell and Curtice (1985) in their report on the 1983 BES, *How Britain Votes*. They showed that, if people had voted in the 1983 general election for the party which they saw as closest to them on the issue they considered most important, then the election would have resulted in a dead-heat between Labour and the Conservatives. Since Labour was in fact trounced, Heath and colleagues argued, the policy voting model can be rejected. A better model, they suggest, is what might be called 'ideological voting'. Ideology – a set of interlinked values relating to politics – rather than issue opinions was what was important in determining party choice. While voters may know little about specific issues or policy areas, they did have broader political values and preferences. Moreover, they could link these values to parties and thus derive an overall impression of what the parties stand for.

Heath, Jowell and Curtice (1985) used survey respondents' answers to questions about issues and policies to demonstrate the existence and role of more general enduring values. In 1983, the issues which were most important in differentiating between Conservative and Labour supporters were nationalization, trade union legislation, income redistribution, defence spending, private education and job creation (p. 109). Not all of these were campaign issues in the election, say Heath and his colleagues, but they were bound up with the overall images of the parties and 'constitute[d] the main ideological divisions between the parties' (p. 109). So, while they utilized responses to issue questions, and showed that opinions on these issues were clearly associated with party choice, Heath, Jowell and Curtice saw the questions as 'not so much tapping discrete issues as a general ideological dimension' (p. 111). Further support for this contention was presented in the BES study of the 1987 election which showed that opinions on a variety of issues were intercorrelated in ways that would be expected if voters did indeed subscribe to general political values (Heath *et al.*, 1991: 174).

A somewhat similar account of the role of issues and opinions in influencing party choice was put forward by Rose and McAllister (1986, 1990) after the same pair of 1980s elections. They too reject the view that issues – defined as 'topical issues of the moment, which are transitory by definition' (1986: 117) – are an important influence on voting behaviour. They add (p. 147) that 'how a person votes is a poor guide to what a person thinks about most issues today' (and, presumably, vice versa). What is important, however, are the 'political principles' or 'values' which voters hold: 'underlying judgements and preferences about the activities of government [which] are general enough to be durable... [and]...concern persisting problems of public policy' (p. 117). Rose and McAllister (1990) concluded that 'durable political values are more than ten times as important in explaining voting as is the government's handling of issues' (p. 141).

Despite using different data sources and methods of analysis, Heath, Jowell and Curtice and Rose and McAllister are agreed on two fundamental points about these general or core values: first, they matter more for voting than do specific issue opinions; second, during the 1980s at least, these values became more strongly associated with party choice while the influence of family background decreased. For example, Heath *et al.* (1991: 33) reported that: 'In 1983 and 1987 voters' attitudes towards the issues were more closely associated with the way they voted than had been the case in previous election studies. Attitudes have become better predictors of how people will vote.' The timing of this development is consistent with Sarlvik and Crewe's contention that it was dealignment that gave voters' issue attitudes an increasing influence over their choice of party. However, in another echo of the class voting debate, Heath *et al.* were sceptical about the role of dealignment and instead suggested that it was parties rather than voters that had changed. In particular, they argued that the strength of the correlation between (position) issue opinions and vote is related to the extent to which voters see a difference between the parties. If the major parties move further apart then the third condition for issue voting – that voters perceive the parties as offering distinctive policies – is more often fulfilled. This, claim Heath and his colleagues, is precisely what happened in 1983 and 1987. They present data showing that their respondents saw a much greater difference between the two main parties in these elections than was the case before. Since issue positions and ideology had become a more serviceable means of deciding between parties, it is not surprising that their influence over vote choice increased.

Ideology: a spatial view

The debate about whether it is opinions on issues or more general ideological values which influence party choice is, in the end, really much ado about not very much. For one thing, whatever the phenomenon is called, the evidence for the most part suggests that voters' opinions on matters of public policy have come to play a larger part in determining their choice of party as opposed to a reliance on family tradition and class location. For another, most of those who have sought to discover the broad principles or values that voters hold have done so on the basis of responses to questions on specific issues anyway. However, there is another way of thinking about ideological voting which more closely reflects the way the term is used in common political parlance. This is the *spatial* model of ideology, so called because both voters and parties can be seen as occupying a space on a continuum or ideological dimension. The principal such dimension, not only in British politics but throughout Europe and beyond, runs from left to right. (In the US, the terms 'liberal' and 'conservative' describe a similar continuum.) This spatial conception also underlies the frequently heard references to the 'centre ground' of British politics.

Spatial models of voting have generated a great deal of complicated and often heated argument. Sidestepping this debate, we concentrate on the simplest version, the proximity model, which was famously set out by Anthony Downs (in the same (1957) book in which he discussed the rationality of turning out to vote). This 'Downsian model' hinges on two assumptions: first, voters can locate themselves and the parties on an ideological dimension; second, voters then choose the party that is located closest to their position. Downs regarded ideology as a useful simplifying device for voters because it served as a summary of what parties stand for, thus saving the effort involved in comparing parties on their multiple policy stances. Another key feature of his work is that, based on the assumptions about voters, Downs drew inferences about the behaviour of parties. Specifically, he concluded that they would converge into the centre ground in order to maximize their vote share (in the same way that two rival retailers setting up shop on a street would maximize their market share by locating towards the middle – otherwise, their competitor would be the nearest option for more than half of the customers).

The proximity model is appealingly simple but its performance is mixed when it comes to explaining British post-war electoral history. For one thing, the major parties have not hugged the moderate voter in quite the way predicted by Downs. Measuring parties' ideological positions is fraught with difficulty but one sustained attempt has been made by the Manifestos Research Group (see Klingemann *et al.*, 2006), which analyses the priorities and preferences in a party's manifesto at each election and thus calculates a statistic summarising its left–right position. Figure 4.1 shows how the left–right scores for the Conservatives and Labour have fluctuated in the post-war period. There have been two

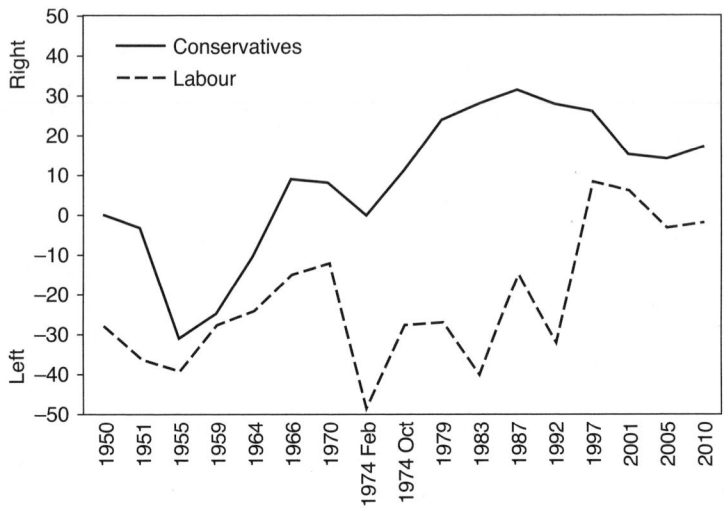

Figure 4.1 Conservative and Labour left–right positions, 1950–2010

Notes: Positions calculated by subtracting percentage of left-wing stances from percentage of right-wing stances, so negative scores denote more left-wing positions.

Source: Bara (2010).

periods of consensus in which the parties behaved as Downsian logic implies. The first of these, in the later 1950s and 1960s, saw the parties converging on what became known as 'Butskellism' (named after Conservative Chancellor of the Exchequer R. A. Butler and the former Labour chancellor Hugh Gaitskell). Labour accepted the basis of a market economy but the Conservatives, as their left-wing scores indicate, accepted the welfare state and other significant government interventions in that market. The second period of consensus followed New Labour's sudden shift to the centre ground during the 1990s under Tony Blair, and the ideological gap between the parties remained relatively narrow in 2010. In between those outbreaks of consensus, however, there was a protracted period during which the parties were sharply divided ideologically. Moreover, this was not just due to one party lurching to an extreme position. Both Labour's manifestos were more left-wing and the Conservatives' more right-wing than would have been the case had either party conformed to the Downsian model.

Turning from parties to voters, we find another mixed picture. Despite its supposed potential as a simplifying device, ideology seems to be too difficult or abstract a way of thinking about politics for many voters. Butler and Stokes (1974) report that, in the 1960s, electors did have views about what the main parties stood for but that these were expressed mainly in terms of class and rarely in terms of ideology. Fully 80 per cent had minimal or no recognition of the meaning of the terms 'left' and 'right' in a political context (p. 334). Butler and Stokes concluded that there was little evidence that the British electorate could be described as 'ideological' and few if any studies since have provided direct evidence that voters see electoral politics in these spatial terms. Of course, one reason for the electorate's apparent 'innocence of ideology' in the 1960s could be the consensus between the parties at the time. Ideological thinking was of little use to voters until the parties moved apart again in the 1970s. At the heart of the ensuing period of ideological divergence are the 1983 and 1987 elections, those in which Heath *et al.* (1991) recorded unusually high levels of ideological voting. Echoing their conclusion, we can say that voters' propensity to use ideology when voting depends on how useful a device it is at that election – that is, how much 'clear blue water' there is between the main contenders. (Ironically, then, Downs's assumptions about voters become more plausible as his predictions about parties go awry.)

There are other reasons for caution in applying the simple Downsian model to elections and voting in Britain. Some of these concern the assumption that there is only one relevant ideological dimension. Several studies (e.g. Palmer, 1995) have suggested that British voting is influenced not only by left–right attitudes but also by where voters and parties sit on a libertarian–authoritarian spectrum (which subsumes attitudes on various matters relating especially to law and order, such as the death penalty or identity cards). And there are other issues, such as climate change and European integration, which are often prominent but which do not fit neatly within the left–right framework. Finally, and perhaps most fundamentally, the limits of proximity voting are clear from the fact that the Liberals (latterly the Liberal Democrats) have typically finished a distant third in British elections despite on most occasions being closer to the median voter than either of the major parties. Plainly there is a good deal more to voting than simple ideological proximity.

Nevertheless, the Downsian model does capture an important feature of British electoral politics: the widely-held view among politicians and commentators that the major parties need to occupy the centre ground in order to attract enough voters to win a general election. Quite what the 'centre ground' means is open to dispute; also, it seems likely that voters in that moderate territory are non-ideological (rather than committed

centrists) and hence not choosing between parties on grounds of proximity. The key, therefore, is probably party image rather than position.
The electoral cost lies in being perceived as an ideologically extreme or
doctrinaire party (which, as we see in the next chapter, was a persistent
problem for Labour in the 1980s). Given the limited evidence that voters
interpret politics in the spatial framework of the Downsian model, an
account of ideological voting as a matter of broader party image seems
more plausible.

Valence issues and performance

One corollary of ideological convergence is that there are fewer position
issues on which Labour and the Conservatives take distinct stances. As
far as the voters are concerned, the parties appear to be pursuing broadly
the same objectives. The upshot is that valence issues become propor-
tionately more important, with parties judged by their ability to deliver
these agreed objectives. In the light of the trends in Figure 4.1, it is
therefore not surprising that the team reporting on the most recent BES
– the 2001, 2005 and 2010 studies – has emphasized valence over position issues (Clarke *et al.*, 2004, 2009). And the man who coined the
valence–position distinction, Donald Stokes, has also argued (1992) that
valence concerns have become increasingly important in elections (in
Britain and beyond). However, Clarke and his colleagues go further.
They argue, contrary to the received wisdom among analysts, that
valence issues have always (at least since 1964, when the first detailed
data become available) been uppermost in voters' minds. They acknowledge that proximity voting was more common in the 1980s than during
the preceding and subsequent periods of consensus, but suggest that,
even then, valence outweighed positional or ideological considerations
in voters' minds (Clarke *et al.*, 2004: 63).

There is good reason to suppose that, regardless of the parties' ideological manoeuvrings, voters are preoccupied by valence issues. As
already noted, the average elector has little detailed knowledge of politics, may well lack clear opinions even on some prominent issues and is
certainly unlikely to think about politics in ideological terms. He or she
is likely to be on the lookout for ways to simplify the voting decision,
perhaps quite drastically. One means of doing this is to focus on one or
two key issues and to judge whether the government has performed
competently on them – and, if not, whether the opposition looks likely
to do better. Fiorina encapsulates this reasoning: 'what policies politi-

cians follow is their business; what they accomplish is the voters' business' (1981: 13). For instance, while the issues of law and order and health subsume a huge range of policy questions (on which the parties may take differing positions), the average voter is likely to focus mainly on whether the government seems to be cutting crime and improving standards in the NHS. This underlines the point that few issues are valence by definition; rather, it is the voters' – and the parties' – approach that makes them function as valence issues.

The claim that valence issues predominate over position issues in voters' thinking receives support from the salience statistics for the past three elections. These are repeated in Table 4.2, this time accompanied by party preference scores which record the advantage on that issue enjoyed at the time by the leading major party over its main rival. These are calculated on the basis of a question asking respondents which party they regarded as best able to handle what they had just designated as their 'most important issue'. There remains a difficulty in classifying issues like crime or immigration as purely valence or purely position – some voters are simply looking for a governing party to reduce crime and effectively manage immigration, while others might prefer a particular party because it takes a particular stance on those issues. Nonetheless, valence issues clearly predominate in the table. Europe in 2001 and Iraq in 2005 are the only straightforwardly position issues, while the core valence issues of health and the economy are prominent.

The party preferred scores provide further – albeit still indirect – evidence that valence issues are more influential over voting behaviour.

Table 4.2 Parties preferred on salient issues in 2001, 2005 and 2010

2001		2005		2010	
Issue	*Party preferred*	*Issue*	*Party preferred*	*Issue*	*Party preferred*
Health	Lab +35	Immigration	Con +23	Economy	Con +7
Economy	Lab +38	Health	Lab +15	Immigration	Con +16
Education	Lab +37	Crime	Con +13	Crime	Con +9
Europe	Con +18	Iraq	Lab +4	Unemployment	Lab +6
Crime	Lab +12	Economy	Lab +28	Debt	Con +9

Notes: The party preference score is the percentage of those mentioning the issue who preferred the policies of the leading party on the issue minus the percentage preferring the other major party.

Sources: Data from relevant BES pre-election surveys.

In 2001, Labour enjoyed substantial leads on the three most salient issues, all of them valence issues, and won a landslide victory. By 2005, Labour's leads on health and the economy had narrowed and it had lost its advantage on crime; moreover, the Conservatives were clearly ahead on the emerging (and at least partly valence) issue of immigration. This could explain why that election was a much closer contest than the previous election. Five years later, Labour trailed on all but one of the key issues, and notably on the dominant valence issue of the economy. In sum, the outcomes of the three elections could be pretty accurately predicted on the basis of these (pre-election survey) evaluations of the leading parties' ability to handle valence issues.

These are aggregate-level results which cannot demonstrate directly that these valence issue evaluations drove voting behaviour at the three elections. However, there is some individual-level evidence bearing on exactly that point. At all three of the elections discussed just above, Clarke *et al.* (2004, 2009) find that BES respondents were markedly more likely to vote for the party that they deemed best able to handle their 'most important issue', even holding constant their social class, their party identification, their position issue attitudes and so on. Further evidence comes from Sarlvik and Crewe's analysis (mentioned earlier in the context of position issue voting) of 1979 election survey data. They classified four issues – strikes, unemployment, prices, and law and order – as valence issues, reasoning that few people would actually favour more strikes, heavier unemployment, higher prices or crime. Almost all respondents (an average of 96 per cent) were willing to offer assessments of the ability of the Conservative and Labour parties to handle the problems, and opinions correlated strongly with party preference (an average coefficient of 0.49, rising to 0.53 among respondents considering the issue extremely important). This supports the claim made by Clarke *et al.* that valence issues are not newly salient but have in fact long been a key influence over party choice.

However, this apparent evidence of valence issue voting has been dismissed by some researchers (e.g. Heath, Jowell and Curtice, 1985: 89–90). The basis for criticism is the second point raised in the earlier section on methodological problems, namely the biasing effect of partisan predispositions. Whenever analysts use voters' judgements about the performance or competence of parties to measure issue voting, they face the problem that these judgements are inextricably bound up with a pre-existing party preference. For instance, those who vote Conservative at a given election are likely to think that that party is best equipped to handle transport but that is because most of them are Conservative supporters in the first place. They may well have little idea about what the party's transport policies are or even care much about the issue in question. The judgement is a consequence of party preference, not a cause of it.

It is hard to deny that these sorts of valence issue judgements are influenced by partisan preferences. There are two reasons why this point should not be overstated, however. First, all three of the elections in Table 4.2 show considerable variation in responses to the party competence question across the different issues. The same is true of other valence measures, such as the series of BES questions about how well or badly the government has handled various issues. For instance, in 2005, 62 per cent of BES respondents thought that the government had managed the economy very or fairly well. Of these, however, 26 per cent thought that the government had handled the National Health Service badly and 34 per cent that it had handled crime badly. Only 23 per cent consistently said that the government had done either well or badly on all three issues. Clearly, at least some people must have been assessing the parties' particular strengths and weaknesses rather than simply delivering a blanket and biased verdict. Indeed, some familiar themes from British party politics – Labour traditionally regarded as stronger on public services like health and more concerned about unemployment, the Conservatives preferred on immigration and crime – can be picked out from Table 4.2. In the run-up to elections, the parties are concerned not only with boosting their general reputation for competence but also with trying to propel 'their' issues – that is, those on which a long-standing reputation gives them a head start – up the campaign agenda.

The second reason why valence judgements cannot simply be attributed to partisan preferences is the size of some of the differences in the table. In 2001, Labour identifiers clearly outnumbered Conservative identifiers and the same is true of voters. Yet the gaps in partisanship and vote share were on nothing like the scale of the nearly 40-point leads that Labour enjoyed over the Conservatives when it came to perceived ability to handle key valence issues. The extent of Labour's advantage means that there must have been some people who inclined towards other parties but were nonetheless willing to give Labour credit for economic competence and public service delivery. At the same time, the consistency of Labour's advantage suggests that many voters, rather than deliberating over the parties' likely performance issue by issue, were guided by an overall impression of which party appeared generally most competent. The gradual transfer of this advantage from Labour to the Conservatives over the next two elections – witness the sharp fall in

Labour's lead on health – indicates that the party was losing this general reputation for competence. More broadly, the pattern of results in Table 4.2 seems to confirm that valence issue judgements are influenced not only by the respondents' partisanship and by the parties' traditional strength or weakness on that issue, but also by a general impression of that party's capacity to deliver.

This idea of a party's general air of competence – or incompetence – is closely related to the notion of the *credibility* of party proposals, or the extent to which voters believe that parties will or will not be able to achieve its goals. The importance of this notion was underlined by the misfiring of the issue voting model during the 1980s. In the 1987 election, Labour led very clearly on three of the four most salient issues and in 1992 they also had clear leads on the top three issues: the NHS, unemployment and education. In both cases, if electors had voted purely on the basis of their issue judgements then Labour would have won the election, but the party lost both decisively. In attempting to resolve this paradox as far as 1987 is concerned, Crewe (1992b) argued that voters were mainly concerned with their own private prosperity and the Conservatives were seen as the party most likely to create or maintain prosperity. Similarly, in 1992 Labour's leads on specific issue areas were outweighed by more general perceptions that Labour could not be trusted to run the economy effectively, which called into question the party's wider credibility. This highlights the critical role played by the economy: by economic prosperity as a valence issue in itself, and by a party's economic reputation in shaping overall impressions of that party's likely performance across the board. The centrality of the economy in British elections is such that it deserves special attention.

The economy and voting

During the 1992 US presidential election the communications director of Bill Clinton's campaign hung a sign over his desk which said, 'It's the economy, stupid!' This was to remind him that, no matter what happened, the state of the economy was the issue that would win the election for Clinton (and he was proved right). That phrase has become a commonplace on both sides of the Atlantic and was endlessly repeated at the 2010 UK general election, somewhat redundantly since no one needed reminding of the significance of the economy in that campaign. The view that the economy is *the* issue that matters above all others is one that many other politicians and commentators have long shared.

Harold Wilson, Prime Minister in the 1960s and early 1970s, believed that 'all political history shows that the standing of a Government and its ability to hold the confidence of the electorate at a General Election depend on the success of its economic policy' (quoted in Norpoth, 1992: 2).

The state of the economy is a classic 'valence' issue. There are some economic position issues – for example, savers and borrowers are liable to take a different view of a policy of increasing interest rates to control inflation – but the valence aspects dominate. In broad terms everyone wants prosperity and few would be opposed to more specific economic goals such as full employment, stable prices and increasing real incomes. What is at issue, therefore, is how well different parties have performed, or might in future perform, in delivering these shared goals. In analysing the impact of the state of the economy on voting there has been a marked shift in approach. The 'traditional' approach, based on the aggregate or 'objective' economy, has been largely supplanted – or, at least, supplemented – by a focus on the 'subjective' economy as perceived by individual voters.

The 'traditional' or aggregate approach

It is almost a psephological law that governments get re-elected in good times but get punished when they have presided over bad times. As Norpoth (1992: 1) puts it, 'In the dictionary of political economy, prosperity spells r-e-e-l-e-c-t-i-o-n for governing parties at the polls, whereas recession spells d-e-f-e-a-t'. The traditional understanding of economic voting was based on this simple relationship between two aggregate-level variables: the state of the economy – as measured by standard macroeconomic indicators – and the popularity of the government. That relationship did a good job of accounting for the results of post-war British elections. A more statistically rigorous attempt to assess the economy-popularity link was made by two econometricians (Goodhart and Bhansali, 1970). Analysing polls and economic data covering the period 1947–68, they found that a good prediction of the level of government popularity could be obtained using just two economic indicators: the level of unemployment and the rate of inflation. This combination came to be known as 'the misery index'.

Convinced of the electoral potency of economic indicators, governments tried to manage the economy such that 'booms' were timed to coincide with an election (typically by raising taxes early in their term and then cutting them as the election approached). This appeared to work, so much so that a phenomenon known as the *electoral cycle* came to be recognized as a regular feature of inter-election periods. Just after an election, the winning party usually enjoys a 'honeymoon' with the voters and its support increases for a short while. Quite soon, however, the government begins to become more and more unpopular – it suffers from 'mid-term blues' – but as the next election approaches there is an upswing in support. This cycle is reflected in by-election results as well as in opinion polls (see Norris, 1990). It should be said that there are other reasons, political rather than economic, why we might observe this electoral cycle (Miller and Mackie, 1973). In mid-term, with no immediate prospect of power changing hands, the government is judged against an abstract standard: 'how well it *ought* to be doing'. Come the election, the government is judged against the concrete alternative of the major opposition party. It is not surprising that governments fare better when compared to the latter. Nonetheless, it seems likely that economics plays a part in explaining these trends in government popularity. Goodhart and Bhansali's evidence pointed clearly to a link between the macroeconomic cycle and the electoral cycle, and governments before and since have found a variety of macroeconomic justifications for expansionary policies in the run-up to elections.

The trend in the Labour government's popularity between 2005 and 2010 is plotted in Figure 4.2, along with quarterly GDP growth statistics. The basic 'U' shape predicted by the electoral cycle can just about be made out, with government popularity at first falling and then climbing steadily, if slowly, in the final year or so of the term. The trend is anything but smooth, illustrating another feature of cycles: they are subject to 'random shocks'. The first major shock in the 2005–2010 term was the replacement of Tony Blair with Gordon Brown, the latter making a favourable impression during his first few months in office. There was another spike in Labour popularity with the onset of the global economic crisis in late 2008. As is often the case, however, the effects of these shocks soon faded and the basic underlying pattern was reasserted. Moreover, for much of the term, a similar pattern can be discerned in the economic growth graph. It also shows considerable fluctuation but around a broad downward trend until mid-2008 and a definite recovery from mid-2009. The late upturn in both graphs could be attributed at least in part to the government's major economic stimulus (a big increase in public spending along with 'quantitative easing', that is, the injecting of new money directly into the economy). Amid division among economists over the wisdom of the stimulus and its scale, Labour could claim plenty of expert support in arguing that the

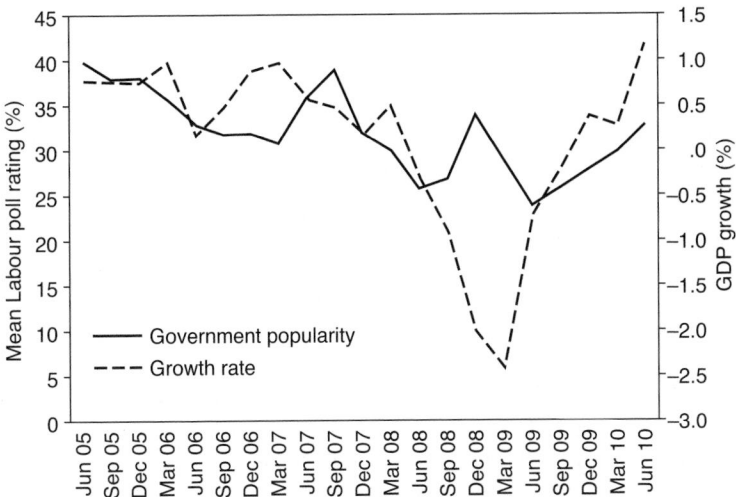

Figure 4.2   Government popularity and economic growth, 2005–2010

Note: Government popularity measured as the mean Labour percentage in that month's major regular polls; GDP growth measured as annual rate (adjusted for inflation) in quarter ending in that month.

policy was driven by macroeconomic rather than political considerations. Nonetheless, it is hard to deny that the timing of it was electorally convenient, and on the face of it appears to have brought the economic and electoral cycles back in step.

As this indicates, there was a period during the 2005–2010 term – specifically, between June 2008 and June 2009 – in which the economic and electoral cycles were far out of step. As the economy plunged into severe recession, the government's popularity actually rallied, whereas the economic upturn was greeted by new lows in Labour vote intention. This is by no means the first time that the relationship between aggregate economic and electoral indicators has been disrupted; it adds to a stockpile of evidence challenging the traditional view of the economy and voting. By examining that evidence, and the limitations of the traditional approach that it exposes, we can highlight the advantages offered by the alternative ('subjective' or individual-level) method of analysing economic voting.

An early casualty of the troubles for the traditional view of economic voting was the tight relationship between the 'misery index' and voting behaviour. If Goodhart and Bhansali's original equation is worked out using 1983 figures for inflation and unemployment, then it suggests that the Conservatives should have received *minus* 156 per cent of the vote in the 1983 election! (See Crewe, 1988: 28.) In the 1970s, both prices and joblessness had reached levels far above those seen during the 1947–68 period analysed by Goodhart and Bhansali. And the electoral implications of mass unemployment were less grave than their model would imply. Rising jobless figures were of limited relevance to those in secure employment, and the patterns of economic restructuring during the Thatcher years meant that unemployment was highest in those northern industrial areas dominated by Labour anyway.

One response to the eventual failure of the Goodhart and Bhansali model, then, could be to argue that the idea remained right but the economic indicators needed to be revised. In an important study of government popularity in the lead-up to the 1983 election, Sanders, Ward and Marsh (1987) introduced interest rates as a key economic variable. The interest rate was not only an important influence over investment and economic growth but also impinged on many people – more than were personally hit by unemployment – directly by affecting how much they had to pay for their mortgages. Sanders and his colleagues found that their combination of economic indicators – notably unemployment, the interest rate and the exchange rate – were able to account for much of the trend in Conservative support. At the time, this was most noticeable because the rally in Conservative support had been widely attributed to the Falklands War of 1982 and the beneficial effects that military success is thought to have on incumbents. It is significant here because it highlighted the continuing potential of economic variables to account for government support, and triggered a range of other (increasingly complex) models of the relationship between the two, using a variety of economic indicators (see Denver and Hands, 1992, part III).

However, in addition to varying the aggregate economic indicators used, Sanders introduced another important innovation into his model of economic voting (see also Sanders, 1993, 1995, 2005; Sanders *et al.*, 2001). As well as using objective economic indicators to predict election outcomes, he also introduced opinion poll results about personal economic expectations (often referred as 'the feel-good factor'). This takes a step in the direction of the individual-level or subjective approach to economic voting, since it acknowledges that macroeconomic conditions can only affect party support to the extent that they are noticed by voters. Yet it maintains key features of the traditional aggregate approach. In Sanders's analyses, individual respondents' expectations are not matched to their individual voting intention. Rather, the net aggregate level of expectations in each month (the percentage of respondents who think that the financial situation of their household will get worse subtracted from the percentage who think that it will get better) is related to monthly aggregate voting intentions. And economic indicators remain the driving forces in the basic model. While the statistics used by Sanders can become very complicated, that basic model is easy to grasp. A simple schematic representation is as follows:

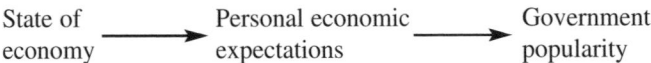

| State of economy | → | Personal economic expectations | → | Government popularity |

Economic indicators like interest rates influence how optimistic or pessimistic voters feel about their economic prospects and this in turn affects their reactions to the government.

The model could account easily enough for the revival in Conservative fortunes in the run-up to the 1983 election. While the three million unemployed probably took a different view, falling interest rates and a general economic upturn had left many voters broadly optimistic about their personal economic circumstances. On the basis of variations in interest rates and economic expectations Sanders (1993) was able to explain over 90 per cent of the variation in government popularity between 1987 and 1990. Further, he found that variations in expectations themselves could in turn be explained largely by changes in the levels of inflation and interest rates (and by the temporary effect – illustrating that random shocks remained important – of the introduction of the poll tax in 1990). Eighteen months before the 1992 election, when the Conservative government was very unpopular, Sanders (1991) suggested that if interest rates and inflation were steadily reduced, personal expectations would become more optimistic and government popularity would recover enough for the Conservatives to win the election. Moreover, he forecast what the Conservative share of the vote would be, given different levels of interest rates and inflation, and these forecasts turned out to be extremely accurate. Given that most people – including the opinion pollsters (see Chapter 6) – seriously underestimated Conservative support at the 1992 election, the accuracy of Sanders's economic forecasting was all the more striking. It also highlighted the dynamic aspect of the relationship between the economy and voting: since government support was driven by economic expectations, the level of unemployment or inflation might matter less than whether these indicators were moving in the right direction.

The success of Sanders's model notwithstanding, the 1992 election outcome was plainly at odds with the traditional view of the economy and voting. One reason why few people had forecast a Conservative victory was precisely that a severe recession was assumed to mean defeat for the incumbent. Instead, the Conservatives were re-elected comfortably. The 1997 election then further undermined the traditional model by showing that prosperity did not necessarily spell re-election. Most economic indicators had been steadily improving for some time when polling day arrived, and yet the government was thrashed. The 1997 outcome challenged not only the simple view but also Sanders's expanded version based on the personal economic expectations. The improvements in the objective economy had translated into a greater optimism among voters, but this produced only a very modest increase in government support (see Gavin and Sanders, 1997).

One possible conclusion is that, at least in 1992 and 1997, the economy must have been less important than everybody had thought. Most electoral analysts instead preferred to find ways of extending the traditional model in order to account for these election outcomes. They identified two political variables that needed to be considered alongside economic indicators and expectations. The first is the extent to which the government is held responsible for economic outcomes, whether good or bad. One reason why the 'misery index' ceased to predict government popularity was that high inflation was at least partly due to problems – such as the spiralling world price of oil – that were hard to blame on the government of the day. And Newton (1993) found that, while voters were well aware that the economy was not performing well in 1992, they were not inclined to blame the government because the former Prime Minister, Mrs Thatcher (whom they did blame), had been replaced by John Major just over a year before the election. Equally, however, the Conservative government gained little credit for the encouraging economic outlook towards the end of the 1992–1997 term. This was because the party had not recovered its longstanding reputation for competent economic management following 'Black Wednesday' (16 September 1992), when Britain was forced to withdraw sterling from the European Exchange Rate Mechanism (ERM) (see Denver, 1998b). While most voters probably had only a hazy idea of what that meant in economic terms, its political implications were clearer: a central plank of government policy had splintered in humiliating circumstances. From that point on, voters appeared to assume that any economic improvement had come about despite rather than because of the Conservative government's efforts.

The second key political variable is voters' assessments of the economic competence of the opposition – in short, would they do better? This depends partly on the first point about responsibility. To the extent that economic problems are blamed not on the government but thought to originate elsewhere – such as a hike in world oil prices – then they will not be remedied just by electing the opposition. However, even if voters are inclined to hold the government at least partly responsible, it would only make sense to replace them with a party thought likely to improve matters. Herein lies the crucial difference between 1992 and 1997. In the former election, Labour's economic competence was widely doubted and so the incumbent Conservatives, whether or not they were to blame for the recession, were thought better equipped to lead Britain out of it. By 1997, Labour's economic credentials were much strengthened due to a new leader and generally enhanced party image and so the party was deemed ready to take over from the Conservatives whose own economic reputation was still to be rebuilt following Black Wednesday.

The importance of these political considerations was reinforced by developments after 1997. During Labour's first two terms, the performance of the 'objective' economy – unemployment, interest rates, inflation and so on – had little effect on the trend in government popularity. Personal economic expectations did play a role in 2001 – a growing optimism in the last months before the 2001 election served to increase Labour's margin of victory – but, between 2001 and 2005, government support had become decoupled even from this subjective 'feel-good' factor (and was instead driven by other factors such as the popularity of the party leaders and the Iraq war). However, trends in government popularity throughout these two terms were very closely related to the fluctuating ratings of the parties' ability to manage the economy (Sanders *et al.,* 2001; Sanders, 2005).

The individual-level approach

The key independent variables used in studies of economic voting had thus shifted from objective aggregate indicators, like inflation or interest rates, to subjective individual-level variables. These might be collected under the heading 'economic perceptions'. A variety of perceptions had been shown to matter: of the economic situation; of the extent of government responsibility for this; and of the competing parties' capacity to improve it. There was a parallel shift to the individual level when it came to the dependent variable, so that the relationship of interest was between a voter's economic perceptions and his or her party choice. As with issues more generally, there are considerable difficulties in measuring both these perceptions and their impact on voting behaviour.

The phrase 'perceptions of the economic situation' is rather vague, and in the course of research two important distinctions relating to these perceptions have emerged. On the one hand, perceptions about the economy may involve *retrospective* or *prospective* judgements, and on the other they may be *sociotropic* or *egocentric*. 'Retrospective' judgements refer to the recent economic performance of the government and the economic well-being of individuals and their families, while 'prospective' judgements concern how well the parties might run the economy in future, if elected, and how individuals view their economic prospects. 'Sociotropic' (society-centred) is the term applied to assessments of national economic conditions, while assessments of how the individual concerned has fared, or might fare in future, are labelled 'egocentric' or 'egotropic' (self-centred). Another term for egocentric economic voting is 'pocketbook' voting, named after the American word for wallet and thus neatly illustrating what is on voters' minds according to that model.

It is not clear whether we would expect voters to be more influenced by retrospective or prospective considerations, or whether we would expect them to pay more attention to sociotropic or egocentric considerations. It might be thought irrational to vote according to retrospective judgements in the same way that there is no point crying over spilt milk – the choice of a future government should be driven by prospective judgements. On the other hand, economic expectations are by nature uncertain and so voters may be guided by their rather clearer view of the recent economic past. There is similar ambiguity surrounding the relative importance of egocentric and sociotropic evaluations. Although Butler and Stokes (1974: 370) noted that 'changes in personal economic conditions are overwhelmingly salient to the mass of electors and evoke in them strong and definite attitudes', they also cautioned that 'many will be responsive to the more generalized information about economic conditions that reaches them through the mass media'. Further complicating matters is the fact that the four types of economic judgement – retrospective egocentric, retrospective sociotropic, prospective egocentric and prospective sociotropic – are all causally intertwined. People are liable to judge the future based on the past, general economic performance based on their own experience, and perhaps their personal economic prospects based on recent national conditions. The result is that the different types of perception are strongly correlated with one another, which in turn makes it difficult to discern which have a stronger effect on voting behaviour.

Studies of economic voting have not led to a consensus in that last regard. We have seen that David Sanders used prospective egocentric judgements – that is, personal economic expectations – in his analyses of government popularity. In similar analyses for the period from 1979 to 1992, Clarke and Stewart (1995) found that the four different perception variables were strongly correlated with one another and that there was little to choose between them in terms of how well they predicted government popularity. However, in the immediate run-up to the 1992 election, and in predicting the election result, the national economic expectations variable performed better than personal expectations, which in turn was more successful than the two retrospective variables. The same pattern – mixed results but a slight edge for prospective and for sociotropic judgements – can be seen in studies with individual party choice (rather than aggregate government popularity) as the dependent variable. Heath *et al.* (1991) concluded from their analysis of 'pocketbook voting' in the 1987 election that, in the economic sphere, 'individual experiences do not seem to carry as much weight as collective ones' (p. 142). On the other hand, other studies have found that both sociotropic and egocentric considerations have a role to play, with party choice most strongly influenced by expectations of future national economic conditions (Miller *et al.*, 1990: 248–55; Clarke *et al.*, 2004, ch. 4).

Economic perceptions are worth particular attention in 2010 given the centrality of the economy in that election. The retrospective perceptions are predictably downbeat (see Table 4.3). Although Figure 4.2 suggests that the economy had been on the mend – at least in terms of growth – for a while by the time of the 2010 election, clearly this had yet to be felt in perceptions or bank balances. Having said that, the prospective evaluations indicate that most voters thought the worst was over and indicate a significant degree of optimism about the national economy in particular. On the egocentric side, there is less difference between retrospective and prospective evaluations because household budgets are influenced by a range of idiosyncratic factors of which macroeconomic conditions are only one. With sociotropic perceptions, by contrast, the object being evaluated is the same for everyone – the national economy – and so there is a discernible shift from an overwhelmingly dim view of the past year to a somewhat more positive outlook. Yet there are still substantial differences of opinion about national economic prospects and even the recent past. One reason for this is party identification. For many people, partisanship operates as a

Table 4.3   Economic perceptions in 2010 (%)

	Retrospective		Prospective	
	Egocentric	*Sociotropic*	*Egocentric*	*Sociotropic*
Worse	50	72	24	25
Same	36	11	47	25
Better	14	17	29	50
N	*1923*	*1911*	*1867*	*1826*

Note: The figures are based on answers to questions asking how the financial situation of the respondent's household (egocentric) and the general economic situation of the country (sociotropic) has changed over the past year (retrospective) and will change over the next year (prospective).

Source: BES 2010 pre-election survey.

lens through which their observation of the national economy is refracted. People who support the incumbent party are unlikely to believe (and even less likely to admit) that the government had made a mess of the economy or was about to do so, whereas those who oppose the government are prone to take a particularly jaundiced view of conditions. In the 2010 BES, 55 per cent of Conservative identifiers said that they felt Britain's economy had got 'much worse' over the past year, compared to only 32 per cent of Labour identifiers. These were evaluations of the same national economy. Nevertheless, as with valence judgements in general, reality tends to intrude on the economic perceptions of even the most partisan. Retrospective evaluations in 2010 were predominantly negative even among strong Labour identifiers.

Turning to the impact of economic perceptions on voting behaviour, we can see that all four perceptions have the expected relationship with party choice (Table 4.4). In each case, the Conservatives enjoyed a healthy lead over Labour among those with negative views of the economy, but little or no advantage among those reporting a more positive view. Interestingly, aside from the Conservatives, it was the minor parties rather than the Liberal Democrats which look to have benefited from economic dissatisfaction – the latter actually perform better among those with positive economic perceptions. Consistent with previous studies (Heath *et al.*, 1991; Clarke *et al.*, 2004), it is the prospective evaluations, and especially the expectations about national economic conditions, that have the strongest association with vote choice, Labour enjoying a slight lead among optimists but trailing badly among pessimists. However, it would be premature to conclude that these eval-

Table 4.4 Economic perceptions and party choice in 2010 (%)

| | Retrospective | | | | Prospective | | | |
| | Egocentric | | Sociotropic | | Egocentric | | Sociotropic | |
	Positive	*Negative*	*Positive*	*Negative*	*Positive*	*Negative*	*Positive*	*Negative*
Conservative	37	43	34	42	31	46	34	52
Labour	33	28	33	27	34	23	37	17
Liberal Democrat	27	22	30	25	29	22	25	22
Other	3	7	3	7	5	9	4	9
N	*171*	*625*	*167*	*904*	*312*	*292*	*551*	*327*

Note: Respondents thinking that things have stayed/will stay the same are not included in the table.

Source: BES 2010 post-election cross-section survey.

uations have a causal impact on party choice. There remains the problem – highlighted at several points in this chapter – that economic
perceptions, like other issue opinions, are coloured by partisanship.
Since Labour supporters are more likely to evaluate the economy positively *and* to vote for the government (and the converse is true of those
who support opposition parties), we would expect a correlation between
economic optimism and incumbent support even if there is no causal
connection between the two. A more satisfactory test of the impact of
economic perceptions would be to incorporate other variables – social
characteristics, opinions on other issues, perceptions of leaders, and
above all partisanship – into the analysis. Such analyses are reported in
Chapter 8 and they suggest that prospective sociotropic evaluations do
indeed have an independent influence on party choice.

In a previous edition of this book, Denver (2006: 110) presented data
corresponding to those in Table 4.4 but from the 2005 BES. They
showed a stronger relationship between economic perceptions and party
choice than in 2010. This is counter-intuitive given that, by any standard, the economy was a more important issue in 2010 than in 2005.
One possible explanation lies in the point raised earlier about the
perceived competence of the parties. Alongside the standard perception
questions, recent BES surveys have also included a question asking
respondents to choose which of the two major parties they regard as best
able to handle the situation if Britain was in economic difficulties.
Unlike at previous elections, this was not a hypothetical question in
2010, and Labour trailed the Conservatives by 42 per cent to 33 per cent.
The similarity between these pre-election survey responses and the
parties' eventual vote shares tends to reinforce the view that it was
indeed 'the economy, stupid' that explains the 2010 outcome. On the
other hand, the fact that only 42 per cent of the electorate saw the
Conservatives as clearly superior on this key yardstick can help to
explain why the party was unable to win the election outright.

Considering the unusually gloomy economic climate, that rather slim
advantage for the Conservatives is surprising. This only reinforces the
point that the relationship between the economy and electoral politics is
far from simple. The predictive failures of Goodhart and Bhansali's
'misery index' and Sanders's 'feel-good factor' model are a reminder
that there is no 'last word' in this area. The 'perceptions' model currently
in vogue may well suffer the same fate in future elections. Nonetheless,
few would dissent from the view that, in one form or another, economic
considerations significantly influence party choice. There are also two
established asymmetries in economic voting: it tends to be driven by

assessments of the governing party rather than the opposition; and it is more likely to involve punishing a bad performance rather than rewarding a good one. (During periods of relative and stable prosperity, economic considerations seem to fade in voters' minds and so governments receive less recognition. For obvious reasons, people are especially loth to give governments credit for improvements in their personal economic circumstances.) Both of these spelled trouble for the incumbent party in 2010. According to the Harold Wilson interpretation of 'political history' quoted above, Labour went into the 2010 election holding a losing hand.

Conclusion: 'performance politics'

Voters Begin to Choose was the title chosen by Richard Rose and Ian McAllister for their (1986) book on British electoral behaviour following dealignment. Their point is overstated: plenty of voters had been choosing all along, and even those with strong party loyalties may well have thought of themselves as deciding afresh at each election, even if they invariably reached the same decision. Nonetheless, loosening ties between social classes and the parties, together with the weakening of party identifications, have meant that an increasing proportion of voters can be accurately described as choosing a party at election time.

Plainly, voters need a basis for these choices. At times over the last forty years – most notably during the 1980s – the major parties have been clearly distinguishable in terms of policy and ideology. In such circumstances, the voters' own issue and ideological positions are a useful basis for party choice. But ideological divisions have narrowed sharply and, in any case, ideological thinking was always something of a minority pursuit. Indeed, even on the most prominent position issues, strong opinions may be the exception rather than the rule within the electorate. The salient concerns for voters are typically valence issues; in other words, most people agree about what the government is there to do – to improve standards in health and education, to reduce crime, to manage the economy effectively – and they vote for the party that they regard as likely to do it best. In short, party performance is the key to understanding electoral choice in Britain today.

This 'performance politics' model of electoral choice has been outlined and forcefully defended by the current BES team (Clarke *et al.,* 2004, 2009). They make a compelling case that the average voter is concerned primarily with competence and delivery rather than policy and ideology. What is striking, however, especially in the context of this chapter, is that individual issues are largely incidental to this case. (The sidelining of issues is all the more noteworthy given that they are at the heart of Stokes's (1963, 1992) discussions of valence politics, an approach which is often treated as synonymous with 'performance politics'.) The focus is much more on overall impressions of competence across the issues board; that is, on whether a party looks generally 'fit to govern'. This parallels the argument of Heath *et al.* (1985, 1991) that voters are guided not by parties' specific issue positions but by a broader sense of what the party stands for. And it is consistent with what we know are quite severe limitations on voters' knowledge of and interest in politics. Just as few voters would contemplate a thorough comparison of manifesto commitments, few have the capacity or inclination for detailed evaluations of party competence across a wide range of issues.

The vital role played by these broad evaluations of competence (or incompetence) raises the question of where they come from. This is easier to answer in the case of the incumbent party, since there is a recent record to go on. Yet few governments are uniformly successful or unmitigated disasters and so there is still a judgement to be reached. Moreover, as with the economy, past performance is an imperfect guide to the future performance that is the ultimate concern of voters. Assessing opposition parties is markedly harder. As with the Conservatives in 2010, the past record in government may be several years – even several leaders – back, and voters have to form impressions based largely on a party's performance in the rather different task of opposition. An even clearer case is that of the Liberal Democrats. Readers may have noticed – perhaps even lamented – the lack of attention given to that party in this chapter. This is because, until a few weeks before polling day in 2010, they were almost universally regarded as having no hope of governing. Their likely competence was, as in previous elections, widely thought to be irrelevant (and so, for example, BES respondents were asked to choose between Labour and the Conservatives as the best equipped to handle economic difficulties). However, when the Liberal Democrats briefly took the lead in the opinion polls during the 2010 campaign, at least some voters will have tried to estimate the party's likely performance in office. Given that the party had no post-war experience in government or even as principal opposition, there was little concrete evidence to go on. How voters might nevertheless form evaluations of competence, and impressions of likely performance, is the subject of the next chapter.

5

Party Image and Party Leaders

A judicious comparison of the parties' stances across the full range of issues might still be regarded as the way that voters *should* decide. However, it is obviously an extreme case: at most, a tiny minority of people really *do* choose in that way (and probably few people ever did). The key conclusion from the previous chapters is not the trivial point that British voters are unlikely to pore over party manifestos. The point is rather that issues and policies, long regarded as the main currency of electoral politics, actually carry much less influence over voting behaviour than has generally been supposed. One reason for this is that a substantial proportion of voters continue to identify quite strongly with one of the parties and, as a consequence, tend to approve of its policies and performance on an issue anyway. Yet, even if dealignment has meant that many 'voters begin to choose', there remain two key reasons why these choices are not driven by policy. One reason has to do with limits on voters' political awareness. Few have detailed knowledge about parties' policies, let alone over multiple issues, and there are easier ways of choosing between parties than by accumulating such information at election time. Second, for much of the post-war period in Britain, even if a diligent voter did undertake a comparison of policy positions then he or she would have found more similarities than differences. Issue stances are not a very useful basis for choice during such periods of consensus. Instead, parties compete – and voters choose between them – on the basis of general impressions of competence. With the parties broadly agreed on the objectives of governing, the decision concerns which party is most likely to achieve those objectives. In short, despite dealignment, electoral choice continues to be more about parties than about issues.

This still leaves the question of how voters judge a party and its likely performance. The assessments of party identifiers are obviously likely to be swayed by partisan sentiments; indeed, the judgements of strong identifiers might be said to be predetermined rather than formed afresh at each election. However, the result of dealignment is that many British voters lack such 'standing judgements' of the parties. Moreover, while parties are familiar objects on the political landscape, many voters may still lack detailed or up-to-date knowledge about parties' records or policies. Short of such information, voters can be guided by their broader images of the party – as moderate or extreme, as united or divided, as 'in touch' or 'out of touch', and so on. Since these images are often rather hazy, however, voters are also inclined to use a convenient short cut: their evaluations of party leaders. Judging leaders is a much simpler task since we can all react to people without necessarily knowing much about what parties have been doing or might do in future. Party leaders are also prominent figures, widely recognized by even the less politically attentive voters. Not only that but, in 2010 and probably subsequent elections, these leaders are placed squarely in the electoral shop window via televised debates. As we show in this chapter, these two aspects of parties – images and leaders – are not only core components of the 'performance politics' model but also crucial influences on voting behaviour in their own right.

Party image

Party images are the mental pictures that voters have of the political parties. As defined by Butler and Rose (1960: 17), 'a party image is nothing more than a party as it appears to the public, the picture left by its surface characteristics'. These definitions are as broad as they are simple. As we will see, there are numerous sources of party images and so the contents of these mental pictures could vary considerably across parties, across the electorate and across time. Even an individual voter may well have a vague or inconsistent picture of a given party. Nonetheless, and in line with our arguments in previous chapters, voters' inclination to simplify their political thinking means that their images of parties will tend to be dominated by one or two key mental associations. And these associations are often persistent over time and shared by large proportions of the electorate. These prominent associations are the core of a party's image.

Considering that politics in Britain (and elsewhere) are often characterized – usually pejoratively – as having become image-dominated, it is surprising that the term 'party image' is largely absent from recent studies of British elections. It is not as if the notion is new to electoral analysis. Party images were first discussed by Graham Wallas, in a (1910) book entitled *Human Nature in Politics*, in which he pointed out that a political party was no different from any other object in people's lives – when they heard its name mentioned, they would automatically call up whatever mental image they had formed of that party. Party image was also a prominent concept in early election survey work, notably Milne and Mackenzie's (1954, 1958) studies of voters in Bristol North East at the elections of 1951 and 1955. Academic attention probably peaked in 1959 at an election which also saw a wider preoccupation with these images, not least because it was widely regarded as the first 'television election' (or, at least, the first at which a large majority of British households had a TV set). Trenaman and McQuail (1961: 36), in a study of the role and impact of television in 1959, noted that 'the term "party image" has been on the lips of the party leaders, the newspaper columnists, and of the many political commentators who have been discovering the reasons why Labour lost'. Interest in the concept persisted during the 1960s and questions measuring party image were included in the first BES surveys, Butler and Stokes (1974: 338) concluding that such images did much to shape voters' behaviour.

Since then, however, the notion of 'party image' has been shelved by most electoral researchers. This is partly just a matter of changing terminology. Many features of parties identified in later work as important influences over electoral choice could reasonably be described as aspects of image. It is also the result of class dealignment. In the 1950s, many voters referred to social class when asked to describe the parties and what they stood for. Interest in this facet of party images predictably waned as class moved from a central to a peripheral role in British elections. These points can be illustrated by looking in more detail at the diverse content of party images.

The content of party images

Not surprisingly, given that many political parties arose out of social divisions, voters' overriding image of a party is often its association with a particular social group. The relevant group will obviously depend not only the party but also on those social divisions that have been most prominent in a country's politics. Thus, for example, American voters' images of their parties include associations with race and (increasingly) religion, in addition to the traditional differences in socioeconomic status between Democrats and Republicans (Brewer, 2009). In Britain, where all else was 'embellishment and detail' compared with the dominant class cleavage (see Chapter 3), early studies of party image assessed how closely voters associated the Conservatives and Labour with their traditional class bases (e.g. Benney, Gray and Pear, 1956). A party's image and its class image were treated as more or less synonymous. These studies confirmed that social class featured prominently in voters' images of both major parties. They also revealed two persistent tendencies. First, class images were shaped by partisan sentiment. Party identifiers were prone to see their party as serving the country as a whole while denouncing its opponent as narrowly focused on the interests of a particular class. Second, voters associated Labour with the working class more closely than they associated the Conservatives with the middle class. This difference was often invoked as one reason for the Conservatives' electoral success in the 1950s. While Labour was seen – including by its own supporters – as a party battling for the working class against the middle class, the Conservatives were more likely to be seen as a 'one nation' party, concerned with improving prosperity across the board rather than fighting the corner of one class against the other. This helps to explain why, as we saw in Chapter 3, the party was able routinely to win substantial chunks of the working-class vote.

As the power of social class to predict party choice has declined, so has interest in the class images of parties. One consequence is that we do not have up-to-date survey data bearing on this issue. However, there is some evidence from a question asked in most BES surveys during the 1970s, 1980s and 1990s. Respondents were asked, for both Labour and the Conservatives, to say whether they would describe that party as 'good for one class' or 'good for all classes'. The responses are shown in Table 5.1. Typically, more than half of the electorate chose the 'one class' option, suggesting that each party retains a class image in many voters' minds. The glaring exception is New Labour in 1997, when many voters responded to the party's explicit aim of reaching out to middle- as well as working-class voters. This may be due partly to a popularity effect: Table 5.1 suggests that parties which are out of favour anyway tend also to be condemned as good for only one class. Nonetheless, the scale of the difference between Labour's 1992 and 1997 results also signals a considerable blurring of the party's class image. There were corresponding large shifts on other questions, asking about how closely the parties look after the interests of class-related social groups. Labour in 1997 was seen as somewhat less concerned than in 1992 with the unemployed and the trade unions, and more concerned than previously with the interests of big business (Heath, Jowell and Curtice, 2001, ch. 7). Yet, while these shifts brought

Table 5.1   Class images of Labour and the Conservatives, 1974–1997
(%)

		1974 (Feb.)	1974 (Oct.)	1983	1987	1992	1997
Labour	Good for one class	45	50	61	64	57	22
	Good for all classes	55	50	39	36	43	78
Conservatives	Good for one class	65	65	62	62	56	75
	Good for all classes	35	35	38	38	44	25

Note: Respondents answering 'neither', 'both' or 'don't know' have been excluded. The question was not asked prior to 1974, in 1979 or since 1997.

Sources: BES 1974, 1983, 1987, 1992, 1997.

Labour's image rather closer to that of the Conservatives, there remained pronounced differences with the Conservatives clearly seen as pro-business, anti-union, and oriented towards middle-class rather than working-class interests. Even after decades of dealignment and a studious avoidance of class rhetoric by the parties, voters have not wholly abandoned their sociological images of the parties.

Even in the era of alignment, however, there was a good deal more to party images than social class. Survey questions asking what voters liked or disliked about a party, or what they thought that party stood for, elicited a wide variety of responses about that party's issue positions and priorities, its leadership, its trustworthiness, its competence, and so on (Milne and Mackenzie, 1958, ch. 9; Trenaman and McQuail, 1961, ch. 3; Butler and Stokes, 1974, ch. 16). We noted in the previous chapter that ideological thinking is the preserve of a minority and, consistent with this, few voters spontaneously used ideological terms or spatial reasoning when describing the parties. Instead, in identifying a party's basic orientation or values, voters tended to cite its position on one or two core issues. A prominent stance on an important issue, such as being hostile to the European Union, can become central to a party's image. As Milne and Mackenzie (1958: 130) argue, enduring relevance is more significant than current salience: 'Party images, then, are symbols; the party is often supported because it is believed to stand for something dear to the elector. It matters little that the 'something' may be an issue no longer of topical importance; the attachment to the symbol, and to the party, persists'. We should add that the durability of these issue images is not necessarily beneficial to a party. In the 1950s and 1960s, Labour profited from its association with the quest for full employment but lost out because it was also widely associated with the increasingly unpopular policy of nationalization. More recently, the Conservatives' long-standing image as a party of lower taxes and spending proved an electoral advantage in 1992 but, then and since, has cost them support among those fearing the impact of cuts on public services like health and education.

As these examples illustrate, a party is on safer ground if its image involves associations with valence rather than position issues. According to Butler and Stokes (1974: 23), 'the parties have achieved their prominence as political actors in the public's mind by linking themselves to goals that matter to the electorate whose support they seek'. While some voters may have doubts about the state intervention required to achieve full employment and investment in schools and hospitals, these are broadly agreed objectives and so it was advantageous for Labour to be clearly associated with them. Most of all, parties seek to connect themselves in voters' minds with the purest valence issue, economic prosperity. One reason for the preoccupation with party image at the 1959 election was a widespread perception – borne out by voter surveys – that the Conservative Party had become associated with economic success and improved standards of living. This image had been cultivated by then Prime Minister Harold Macmillan in a famous 1957 speech reminding voters that most of them had 'never had it so good', and was hammered home by the campaign slogan 'Life's Better with the Conservatives. Don't Let Labour Ruin It.' Trenaman and McQuail's (1961) analysis suggests that the Conservative image as a party of prosperity was the key to their late surge in support. Electoral history before and since indicates that parties are indeed virtually unbeatable if associated with economic prosperity – and more or less doomed to defeat if associated with economic failure. Moreover, as underlined in the previous chapter, the parties' economic images and reputations are at least as important as objective economic indicators in determining voting behaviour.

These arguments demonstrate the central role played by party image in the 'performance politics' approach to voting behaviour set out by Harold Clarke and his BES colleagues (Clarke *et al.*, 2009). While they do not use the term 'party image', they place heavy emphasis on a party's reputation for competence and delivery on core valence issues, especially the economy. When such a reputation – whether good or bad – is clearly established in electors' minds, it becomes a central element of that party's image. It is also likely to become a general reputation rather than one tied to any single issue. This point was noted by Butler and Stokes (1974: 339) in their assessment of party images:

[s]ome qualities of party image, such as strength or modernity or reliability, are so broad that they could be linked to almost any set of government outputs. A party may be seen as trustworthy or as bound to make a mess of things without any necessary reference to the area in which it can be trusted or in which it is bound to make a mess. Indeed, some image qualities have much more to do with 'intrinsic' values of party, which are not related to outputs of government at all.

Butler and Stokes refer to these qualities as 'valence' aspects of party image because, just as no voter wants economic decline and rising crime, no voter wants a governing party that is weak or incompetent.

Beyond attributes such as strength and competence, there are other elements of party image that are also related – if more indirectly – to performance politics and might well influence voters' willingness to support that party. For example, Labour's electoral success in the 1960s was often credited to their image as a more progressive and modern party. Against a Conservative Party perceived as ageing and backward-looking, Labour was better placed to capture the mood of youthful excitement and reaction against tradition (Butler and Stokes, 1974, ch. 16). During the 1980s, Labour and the Conservatives shared an image problem in that both were widely seen as extreme. When asked to describe each party as 'extreme' or 'moderate', more than half of BES respondents in 1983 and 1987 chose the former option. In these polarized conditions, it is not surprising that the SDP/Liberal Alliance achieved the highest post-war vote shares for the centrist option. Perceived moderation is clearly not a necessary condition for electoral success given that Thatcher's Conservatives won both 1980s elections. Nevertheless, it is hard not to suspect that New Labour's advance was owed partly to a dramatic fall in the proportion of voters perceiving the party as extreme.

Perhaps concluding that ideological convergence had rendered the extreme/moderate question redundant, BES researchers have dropped it from recent surveys. However, they have included questions about four valence aspects of party image. Respondents were asked whether they see parties as 'united' or 'divided'; as 'in touch' or 'out of touch with ordinary people'; as a party that 'keeps' or that 'breaks its promises'; and as a party 'capable' or 'not capable of being a strong government'. In Table 5.2, we show responses to these questions for the three main parties at each of the past three elections.

There is the same popularity effect as in Table 5.1. The Conservative results show that an improvement in a party's overall standing tends to boost its image across the board. Conversely, as Labour lost electoral

Table 5.2   Four valence aspects of party image, 2001–2010 (%)

		2001	2005	2010
United	Conservatives	9	24	61
	Labour	70	33	25
	Liberal Democrats	88	85	49
In touch with ordinary people	Conservatives	17	28	36
	Labour	54	48	43
	Liberal Democrats	68	65	54
Keeps its promises	Conservatives	30	28	34
	Labour	43	25	24
	Liberal Democrats	70	56	29
Capable of being a strong government	Conservatives	35	46	71
	Labour	84	67	42
	Liberal Democrats	47	32	30

Note: To save space, we report only the proportions giving the positive response in each case. Respondents answering 'neither', 'both' or 'don't know' have been excluded from the analysis.

Sources: BES 2001 (post-election survey), 2005, 2010 (self-completion surveys).

ground, all aspects of its image suffered at least somewhat. Nonetheless, party images are obviously more than simply a reflection of a party's general popularity. Labour retained most of its credit – and its lead over the Conservatives – in terms of being in touch with ordinary people. And the Conservatives' advance was evidently not achieved by persuading voters that it would keep its promises. The big swings between the two major parties were on the (probably related) matters of party unity and capacity for strong government. On the surface, at least, these look the more electorally potent aspects of party image.

The results for the Liberal Democrats illustrate two final points about the content of party images. First, these impressions can be rather vague. The Liberal Democrats projected a strikingly favourable image in 2001 and 2005 but, with the party having neither held nor seriously contended for power for decades, it is difficult to imagine voters having a clear picture of its capacity to govern or even the value of its promises. Second, if impressions of a party are rather superficial, they can change quickly. The positive image of the Liberal Democrats had largely worn off by 2010 – especially when it came to trustworthiness and unity (in a survey conducted following the party's decision to join the

Conservatives in a coalition government) – and their ratings look much more like those of the other two parties. As the example of 'Black Wednesday' (see Chapter 4) illustrates, it is not only the Liberal Democrats whose reputation is precarious. Compared to the durability of social class associations, parties' valence images are much more transient.

Party images and party choice

In order to measure the impact of party image on voting behaviour, it is necessary first to find out what these images are. Political parties often use focus groups to explore how they are perceived by voters – or, in marketing terms, to investigate their 'brand image'. (Participants might be asked 'if the Labour Party were a breakfast cereal, what kind of cereal would it be?' and, if the group settled on All Bran, Labour strategists would have to decide whether the implied wholesomeness and dependability compensated for a lack of youthful excitement.) Meanwhile, most academic research into party images has been conducted via large-scale surveys and using one of two methods. In the *open*-ended approach, survey respondents are asked to describe in their own words what they like and dislike about the parties (or perhaps – again in their own words – what they see the parties as standing for). This has been the standard approach in the American National Election Surveys and was also used in early studies of party image in Britain. As Trenaman and McQuail (1961: 23) put it, if there are common elements in people's open-ended responses about a party, 'one might reasonably describe this commonality as the party image'. The alternative *closed* approach is illustrated by the results in Tables 5.1 and 5.2. Respondents rate the parties on various aspects of party image that have been decided in advance by the survey researcher. In effect, open questions ask voters for their images of a party as it actually is, while closed questions specify what that party should be and ask voters about how closely it conforms to that ideal.

Both approaches have pros and cons. Open questions reveal great diversity in the content and clarity of party images. Some attribute might dominate one voter's thinking but go apparently unnoticed by others. Different parties call different kinds of attributes to voters' minds. And the contents of party images can vary considerably across elections. This variety is suppressed by simply asking for ratings of each party on the same standard list of attributes at each election. On the other hand, open questions also show that some themes – like competence, unity and trustworthiness – recur at more or less every election. If the aim is to assess the overall images of the parties at election time and to relate these assessments to voting behaviour, closed question ratings are much easier to use than a mass of open-ended material.

However party image has been measured, its impact on voting behaviour cannot be determined without also taking account of partisan bias. The argument, familiar from previous chapters, was stated clearly in this context by Butler and Stokes (1974). Having noted the strong tendency for those who evaluated a party's image positively to report voting for that party, they observe: 'We do not from this suppose that these aspects of party images are pre-eminent in determining party choice; the extent of agreement between the two is largely due to electors' making their images of the parties fit their pre-existing preferences' (p. 347). The extent of bias should not be overstated, however. For one thing, as we have seen, around half of the electorate is either non-partisan or only weakly aligned with one of the parties. These voters have more clear-eyed images of the parties and, since they are also more likely to be undecided in the run-up to an election, there is more scope for party image to influence their choices. The results in Table 5.2 confirm that image ratings are not simply reflections of partisanship. Labour in 2001 and the Conservatives in 2010 enjoyed much bigger leads in terms of unity and strong government than they enjoyed in terms of partisanship or electoral support at those elections. The pattern can only be explained if, in the reasonably objective view of a substantial proportion of the electorate, Labour's image deteriorated while that of the Conservatives improved. It does not stretch credulity to suggest that this contributed to the considerable Labour to Conservative swing between those elections.

The point about partisan bias does have an important methodological implication. In order to estimate the impact of images on voting decisions, it is necessary to hold constant those factors – notably party identification – that predispose some people both to vote for a party and to have a particularly flattering view of it. Researchers doing so have demonstrated that party images still do have an independent effect on party choice. Butler and Stokes (1974: 416) found that popular images of the parties were an important reason for vote-switching between the elections of 1964, 1966 and 1970. More recently, Andersen and Evans (2003) showed that an overall image variable – consisting of the 'united/divided', 'keeps/breaks promises' and 'capable/not capable of strong government' questions from Table 5.2 – was a powerful predictor of party choice in 2001, even with an array of other variables held constant. Trilling's (1976) analysis of US elections showed that party images were not only independent of partisanship but could even override it, especially in cases of relatively weak party identification. Finally, perhaps the most direct evidence of image effects comes from Milne and Mackenzie's (1958) early study. When they asked voters in Bristol 'What made you finally decide to vote the way you did?', party image was mentioned more often than any other kind of reason. They concluded simply: 'it seems that images are much more important in determining voting behaviour than are issues' (p. 159).

The sources of party image

Given the potential electoral importance of party images, it is worth considering where they come from. Figure 5.1 sketches a model of how voters form and update these mental pictures of the parties. Like any such model, it is a highly simplified account but captures the essential features of the process.

The model begins with what we have called political 'reality'. This umbrella term takes in both 'internal' features of a party – its policies, decisions, leadership, and so on – and external circumstances such as the performance of the economy or any of the huge range of events that can befall a party. (When asked about what determined a government's fortunes, former Prime Minister Harold Macmillan is said to have replied 'events, dear boy, events'.) While it would be hopelessly naïve to see party images as nothing but simple reflections of political circumstances, it is just as unrealistic to suggest that there is no link between the two. The steep fall during the 1990s in the percentage of voters describing Labour as 'extreme' reflects a genuine shift in the party's outlook and policy agenda, while the decline between 2001 and 2005 in its reputation for unity resulted from real divisions over the Iraq war. Economic indicators provide an unusually objective means of judging a

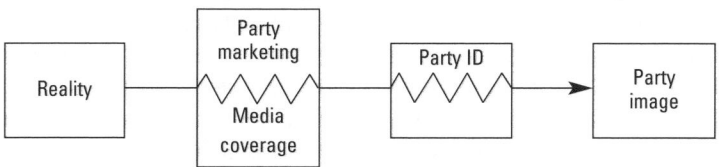

Figure 5.1   A model of party image formation

governing party and, although Labour won credit in some quarters for its response to the global financial crisis, it is hard to imagine that adverse trends in growth, unemployment and public debt did not tarnish its image as a competent manager. Judging opposition parties is less straightforward, images being formed on the basis of behaviour in opposition as well as – if applicable – past record in office. Some events cast such long shadows that even the distant past is reflected in party images. More than a decade after 'Black Wednesday' (see Chapter 4), Conservative politicians were still struggling to restore their reputation for economic competence. And the parties' enduring class images may well have little to do with what they say or do today. As Milne and Mackenzie (1958: 130) vividly put it, 'some party images resemble images of distant, disintegrating stars; the image is still clearly perceived by means of light-waves at a moment when the star no longer exists'. Nonetheless, even if party images are reshaped only slowly as circumstances change, the key point – that these images originate in what parties actually do and what actually happens to them – holds true.

Of course, voters do not typically experience political events at first hand, and the parties do not report impartially on their own records and policies with a view to educating and informing the citizenry. Voters encounter political reality as it has been shaped and interpreted – or 'spun', to use the familiar derogatory term – by parties and the media. Parties not only provide a running commentary on political events in terms designed to protect and boost their reputations; they also make proactive attempts to build their own images and to associate themselves in voters' minds with popular symbols and objectives. This process, termed 'brand-building' by those in the marketing field, had been anticipated by Graham Wallas (1910: 84) in his introduction to the concept of party image: 'It is the business of the party managers to secure that these automatic associations shall be as clear as possible, shall be shared by as large a number as possible, and shall call up as many and as strong emotions as possible'. The Conservatives' brand image in the 1959 election, thought by many to have been the key to their victory, had been carefully developed by public relations professionals. This was a pioneering example of an approach that is now ubiquitous. To the extent that their resources allow, all British parties draw on professional expertise and use an array of marketing techniques (such as the focus groups mentioned earlier) in order to identify and develop the desired image. Some of the most famous examples are ostensibly the most superficial, such as the changes of logo by Labour in the 1980s (from a red flag to a red rose) and the Conservatives in 2006 (from a torch to an oak tree).

Such manoeuvres are unlikely to change a party's image unless coupled with more substantive shifts of policy or rhetoric, echoing the earlier point that reality will intrude. However, the simplest marketing device can make a huge contribution to a process of branding or rebranding. Through its informal rechristening as 'New Labour', the party's strategists were able to sell the desired image to the electorate every time this name was mentioned.

Parties also make considerable efforts to shape the images of their opponents, aiming in particular to reinforce negative associations in voters' minds. For example, in the 2010 election campaign, Labour likened the Conservatives' planned spending cuts to a similar retrenchment programme in the 1980s, repeating notorious phrases from Conservative Ministers at that time such as 'if it isn't hurting, it isn't working' and unemployment being 'a price worth paying'. As with parties' attempts to build their own brands, their attempts to tarnish those of their opponents vary widely in their effectiveness. Some posters or slogans strike a chord with the public while others go unnoticed or even backfire. Moreover, the way that a party deals with its opponents can give a signal to voters about its own image. Evidence from the 2007 Scottish Parliament election (Pattie *et al.*, 2011) suggests that voters were turned off by parties perceived as conducting negative campaigns (that is, criticizing other parties rather than promoting themselves and their policies). The negative messages may hit home but the messengers also bear a cost.

Chapter 6 includes a detailed discussion of the role and impact of the media in British elections. For the moment, we need to note the crucial interdependence between the parties and the media when it comes to shaping voters' party images. On the one hand, the media are the principal channel through which parties promote their own brand images (and undermine their opponents'). On the other hand, the media do not simply convey the parties' chosen messages to the public. They edit, interpret and comment on parties' images and messages, as indeed on all political issues and events. As a result, much political marketing consists of attempts to put the appropriate 'spin' on the media's coverage of a party. It hardly needs saying that a party's image can be damaged by stridently negative coverage by its opponents in the partisan press. The image of Labour as an extreme party in the 1980s was enthusiastically propagated by *The Sun* and the *Daily Mail* in stories about extremes of political correctness in Labour-run local councils. However, even the ostensibly neutral coverage of the broadcasters has the potential to shape party images, again usually in a negative direction. The unavoidable fact that mistakes are more newsworthy than their absence, along with the media's determination to seize on even the slightest sign of internal dissent, means that TV and radio coverage is likely to undermine parties' reputations for competence and unity.

As shown in Figure 5.1, and as noted earlier, the images of parties depicted by the parties and the media are then seen by voters through their own partisan lenses. The strongest identifiers cast virtually any political information in a light favourable to their own party and unflattering to the images of their opponents. Yet, as we have seen, the proportion of such strongly attached voters has sharply declined. The effect of dealignment should not be overstated: even a non-partisan voter will still have attitudes and preconceptions towards the parties that will shape his or her reading of new information. Ultimately, however, the weakening of party loyalties will make party images more responsive both to changing political reality and to the biases in the way that these circumstances are communicated to voters by parties and the media.

Party leaders

At the beginning of the previous chapter, we noted that a reader from the 1920s or 1930s would be startled by the lack of emphasis given to issues and policies in this book. Such a reader would be equally bewildered at the attention about to be devoted to party leaders. The first survey study of voting in Britain (Benney, Gray and Pear, 1956) mentions each party leader only once (and then only to report the number of radio broadcasts they made during the election campaign). However, the advent of television put party leaders into the spotlight and, very quickly, the general view among many political observers shifted from one extreme, that leadership was basically unimportant for voting behaviour, to the other, that leadership was the key to explaining election outcomes. At the time of reporting on the 1959 election, Butler and Rose (1960: 72) perceived a popular impression that leaders mattered above all:

> It has been suggested that, in so far as a campaign is designed to help voters to choose a government, it does not much matter what issues predominate; the ordinary elector is better as a judge of men than of measures, and any argument will bring out the personal qualities of the contending leaders. It has become fashionable to say that an election is a choice between rival political teams more than between rival programmes: voters choose leaders, and leaders choose policies. This view can be pushed too far.

As their final remark shows, Butler and Rose were inclined to correct or at least to modify that common view and, for decades, academic analysts of elections downplayed the impact of leadership. Anthony King (2002a) outlines the reasons for this scepticism, drawing on Butler and Stokes's (1974) reasoning about the conditions under which issues have an electoral impact (see Chapter 4). Leadership meets the requirements of awareness and 'opinionation', Butler and Stokes (1974, ch. 17) finding that the Prime Minister and the Leader of the Opposition were highly visible figures about whom most voters had opinions. However, King argues, there will seldom be a large gap between the major parties on the 'leadership issue': that is, the leading contenders for Prime Minister are likely to be quite closely matched in terms of popularity. One reason is that leaders, having the usual human blend of positive and negative qualities, will receive correspondingly balanced assessments from voters. For example, while Gordon Brown scored few points for likeability and charisma, he was credited by the public with commitment and intelligence. The second and more important reason to expect a narrow popularity gap between leaders is the effect of partisan bias. Those who support a particular party are strongly inclined to see the best in its leader – and to see rival party leaders in a less flattering light. As a result, the balance of preferences among leaders tends to mirror the balance of support among the parties.

Such partisan bias obviously reduces the scope for party leadership to have an independent effect on voting behaviour. The other consequence of party loyalties is that, even in those rare cases where party and leader preferences conflict (that is, where voters prefer the 'wrong' leader), it is their party attachment that is likely to win out. The point is stated clearly by Crewe (1981b: 274–5):

> The purpose of general elections is not primarily to choose a party leader to become prime minister but to choose a party to form a government. More importantly, the British electorate tends to vote according to what a party represents rather than who represents the party ... British voters, if forced to choose between leader and party, tend to abandon the leader.

These arguments – that leader evaluations are strongly influenced by partisan sympathies and that, even when the two conflict, party preferences trump leader preferences – underpinned the old 'limited effects' orthodoxy about the impact of leaders on party choice. This view enjoyed a fair bit of support from early studies of voting behaviour. However, most electoral analysts regard it as outdated and believe that the personal appeal of the party leaders has become more important in swaying votes. The weight of evidence now clearly supports the argument that evaluations of leaders have come to play an important role in electors' calculations. An analysis of the changing impact of party leaders (relative to party policies and performance) in elections from 1964 to 1992, using Gallup data, concluded that evaluations of leaders began to increase in importance during the mid-1970s and their effects became significantly more pronounced in 1987 and 1992 (Mughan, 1993). Before examining the evidence of leadership effects in more detail, we outline four key reasons why these effects have strengthened over time.

Why leadership matters (more)

Since the old orthodoxy was based on the premise that party loyalties stifled leadership effects, it is not surprising that *dealignment* is a primary reason why these effects have strengthened. The original Michigan model did allow for 'candidate orientation' as a short-term influence on party choice but that model was, of course, developed with presidential rather than parliamentary elections in mind. In Britain, the long-term forces of social class and family socialization would be presumed to have overridden the purely temporary consideration of who happened to be the leader of each party. Indeed, as noted above, we would expect voters' assessments of the party leaders to have been themselves products of basic party loyalty. With the erosion of the importance of long-term factors, however, we might expect an increase in the electoral impact of party leaders. The competence, personality and image of individual leaders might be regarded as akin to issues which could swing votes in the short term.

There are also *institutional* reasons to expect party leadership to have a growing influence over voting behaviour. In recent decades, Prime Ministers have become stronger within their governments (especially with respect to the Cabinet) and leaders have become stronger within their parties. These developments, at their most rapid during the premierships of Margaret Thatcher and Tony Blair, have created what Michael Foley (2000) calls the 'British Presidency'. The trend does not apply only to parties in government; leaders of the opposition (and of parties in general) have also enjoyed an accumulation of powers, both formal and informal, around their office. Now that leaders have become more influential relative to their parties, we would expect a rational voter to pay more attention to the characteristics of those leaders – and less to the characteristics of parties – when deciding how to vote.

A third reason to expect a strengthening of leadership effects is the nature of political coverage in the *mass media*. We address the role of the mass media in campaigning in Chapter 6. For the moment, it seems safe to assume that, in the days before extensive television coverage of politics, the influence of party leaders on voting was minimal. For the great mass of voters, their only knowledge of political leaders was through photographs, newspaper reports of speeches and the occasional radio broadcast. By the 1960s, however, political television was well established and the faces, voices and personalities of party leaders became very familiar to voters. Moreover, the media encourage voters to focus on leaders by reporting and portraying politics in highly personalized terms. This tendency is even stronger during election campaigns, during which leaders are subject to intense scrutiny in the broadcast media and character assassination in the partisan press. And, of course, as we describe in the next chapter, leaders were even more prominent in the 2010 campaign because of the introduction of televised debates. It is hard to say whether personalized media coverage is a cause or a consequence of the institutional changes described above – probably a bit of both, and certainly the parties tend to place leaders at the heart of their national campaigns (Foley, 2000). What is plain is that the trend of presidentialization extends to the mass media.

The final reason to anticipate leadership effects has to do with the way voters think about politics. Given that the average person neither thinks nor knows all that much about politics, he or she is prone to seek ways of simplifying political choices, including the voting decision. Party leaders serve as one such simplification. We are used to judging people and will (automatically) make a number of politically relevant judgements – about a leader's intelligence, honesty, competence, and so on – based not only on what they say and do but also on their faces, voices and body language. In contrast, it is much harder – especially for the less politically aware – to judge complex abstractions like issues and parties. Some voters may, therefore, simply choose between party leaders – in effect voting for a Prime Minister rather than a government. Others may use leaders as a simpler means of evaluating parties. This is a particularly useful device when a party has been out of power for a while. For example, the widespread perception that Labour had by 1997 become a plausible party of government probably owed a lot to impressions of Tony Blair as a strong and capable leader. Rather than scrutinizing the party's policies or personnel, many voters instead judged it by its leader. Put another way, leaders are a crucial element of the 'reality' in Figure 5.1 and thus are a key source of party image.

It is worth clarifying a couple of points about this process of judging parties by their leaders. First, it comes with no guarantee of accuracy. Leaders may appear more competent, moderate or compassionate than they actually are; moreover, even if a leader does have those characteristics, his or her party may well lack them. Equally, parties that pick the 'wrong' leader could find themselves unfairly tarred by association if voters simply project that leader's perceived deficiencies on to the party. Second, there is an important distinction between judging a party based on its leader and recognizing a leader's impact on that party. The example of New Labour in 1997 is again useful here. As noted above, some voters will simply have *assumed* that Labour was a competent and moderate party because Tony Blair showed those characteristics. Others will have *acknowledged* changes made by Blair within Labour that made it, in those voters' eyes at least, a more competent and moderate party. In that latter case, leadership has a strong but an indirect effect on voting behaviour (see King, 2002a): people were not voting for Tony Blair as such, but for the Labour Party as he had shaped it. Such indirect effects are very common and very important, since leaders can influence all of those features of a party – rhetoric, ideology, policy positions, economic record, image, and so on – that determine its electoral appeal. Having dealt with those matters in previous chapters, however, we focus here on direct effects: votes won by a leader's personality rather than by his or her record or policies.

How voters evaluate party leaders

Figure 5.1 outlined the process by which voters form images of the parties. A very similar model, shown in Figure 5.2, captures the way in which voters reach judgements about the party leaders. Each element can be illustrated with reference to Gordon Brown and David Cameron, outgoing and incoming Prime Ministers at the most recent general election. Leader images have their origins in reality in the sense that there are certain established facts about party leaders that might shape judgements of them. These include the most basic physical characteristics like age, sex, facial appearance and height, as well as aspects of personal and political biography. Some of the latter are of clear political relevance: for instance, Gordon Brown entered the 2010 election having spent thirteen years as Chancellor or Prime Minister while David Cameron had experience only of opposition. However, less obviously political characteristics can still influence voters. Being married with children, the major

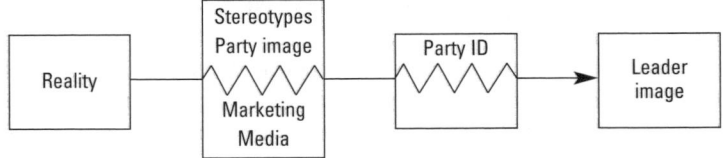

Figure 5.2 A model of leader image formation

party leaders in 2010 fulfilled what are sometimes seen as almost necessary conditions for electoral success. And there was at least the potential for political significance in the fact that Cameron is an Old Etonian and that Brown is (audibly) Scottish.

Whether this potential is realized depends, of course, on the way that such facts are presented to and interpreted by voters. A first thing to note is the pervasiveness of stereotypes which lead people to infer personality traits from demographics or background. It is well established, for example, that male and female candidates for office are assumed by voters to have different qualities. Such stereotyping can work for or against a candidate. Cameron's exalted educational background will have weakened his claims to be 'in touch with ordinary people' but may also have won him credit from deferential voters. Similarly, Gordon Brown's Scottishness may at one time have boosted his reputation for financial prudence (although the near-collapse and eventual bail-out of Scottish banks during the financial crisis of 2008 has probably weakened that particular stereotypical association).

The inclusion of party image in Figure 5.2 highlights the point that parties themselves are another source of stereotyping. People's impressions of a party are likely to rub off on its leader, especially if that leader is relatively unfamiliar. Given his party's reputation in the early 2000s, David Cameron was liable to be regarded as out of touch regardless of where he went to school. However, leaders are not helpless victims of social and party stereotypes. Usually with extensive public relations assistance, they actively seek to create and to develop – and, where necessary, to rescue – their own image. Brown was coached on how and when to smile, rather as Margaret Thatcher in the 1970s had received voice coaching to soften her strident tone (Atkinson, 1984: 113). Cameron used photo opportunities relating to the environment – being driven by husky dogs to visit a melting glacier and, more mundanely, cycling to work each day – in order to present himself as a modern and caring leader, in contrast to his party's rather reactionary image. Once leaders have established an image distinct from their party's, they can then attempt to drag that party image towards their own.

This process of image creation need not be an exercise in deception. Leaders typically refer to it in terms such as 'showing the voters who I really am'. The implicit accusation is that their image has been misrepresented and that brings us to the role of the media. Like parties, leaders have reason both to thank and fear the mass media. While broadcasters and the press are the main means through which leaders present themselves to the electorate, neither is a passive transmitter of the desired image. This is obvious in the case of partisan newspapers but the broadcasters can also shape public impressions of a leader as well as undermining his or her attempts at image formation. Merely by broadcasting Gordon Brown's speeches and appearances at Prime Minister's Questions, television revealed the failure of his smile coaching. And, when it was revealed that an official car, carrying David Cameron's shoes and papers, was following him on his daily cycle to work, the extensive coverage will not have boosted his green credentials.

The final stage of the process reflects the filtering effect of voters' own partisan sympathies. These predispositions not only influence voters' initial reactions to party leaders; they also shape the way that voters react to the attempts at image formation described above. Party identifiers are highly receptive to positive portrayals of their own leader and negative portrayals of their opponents' leaders. While Tony Blair and David Cameron are both strong television performers, the tendency among Labour and Conservative supporters was to regard one as genuine and engaging but the other as a more or less plausible confidence trickster. The result is to reinforce the earlier conclusion that leadership effects will be minimal among strong identifiers. Moreover, while dealignment has increased the scope for such effects, the kind of partisan bias described here is not confined to those who retain a strong party loyalty. Anyone with reason to like or dislike a party will be predisposed to like or dislike its leader.

In order to answer the question 'how do voters judge leaders?', we need – as with party images – to consider not only the sources but also the contents of these evaluations. King (2002a: 42–3) suggests numerous leader attributes that might be thought to influence voters and sorts them into four broad categories: physical appearance, native intelligence, character or temperament, and political style. All four are a matter of choice – or manipulation – to at least some extent but, especially in an era of intense media scrutiny, there is a limit on what self-presentation can conceal. So voters probably have quite accurate perceptions of all four attributes, at least for leaders who have been in the public eye for some time. The earlier items in the list, especially physical appearance, are less directly political, and as such it might be thought that they would weigh less heavily in voting decisions. However, it is at least possible that they could have an effect, not least by influencing the evaluations of character and personality that are more obviously relevant for leadership. Nevertheless, attempts to measure leader evaluations have focused on personality and political style. Respondents in the 2001 BES were asked to rate the leaders of all three major parties on seven aspects of leader image: 'capable of strong leadership', 'keeps promises', 'decisive', 'sticks to principles', 'caring', 'listens to reason', and '(not) arrogant'. Responses to those questions suggested that voters, rather than having complex and multi-faceted impressions of the leaders, instead basically rate them on two dimensions: competence, measured by the first four aspects in the list, and responsiveness, measured by the remaining three. (This distinction is best illustrated – and was clearest in voters' minds – in the case of Margaret Thatcher, whose robust style of 'conviction politics' won her much more credit for capable and decisive leadership than for caring and responding to voters' concerns.) Measures of leader images in subsequent BES have been simplified accordingly and respondents in the 2010 survey were asked to rate four aspects of leader image on a 0 to10 scale. They were also asked to report their overall feelings about the leaders on a dislike–like scale, also from 0 to 10. The average ratings for the three major party leaders on all five questions are shown in Figure 5.3.

The results illustrate the two key points about leader evaluations. First, there is some sign of the distinction between competence and responsiveness. David Cameron scores relatively well on the first two questions, gauging competence, while Nick Clegg enjoys a clear lead on the next two which have more to do with responsiveness. Second, the broad pattern is usually similar across different aspects of image and is consistent with overall feelings about the leaders. While there was some grudging acknowledgement that Gordon Brown might know what he was talking about, he was overall an unpopular leader in 2010 and this was reflected in all of his ratings. Put another way, the correlations (see Chapter 2 and the Glossary) between a leader's various ratings are usually very strong: people who like (dislike) that leader tend to give favourable (unfavourable) scores across the board. This simplifies the analysis of leadership effects because it means that general measures – such as the like–dislike scale above, or the pollsters' staple question 'which of these leaders would make the best Prime Minister?' – capture leader images quite efficiently.

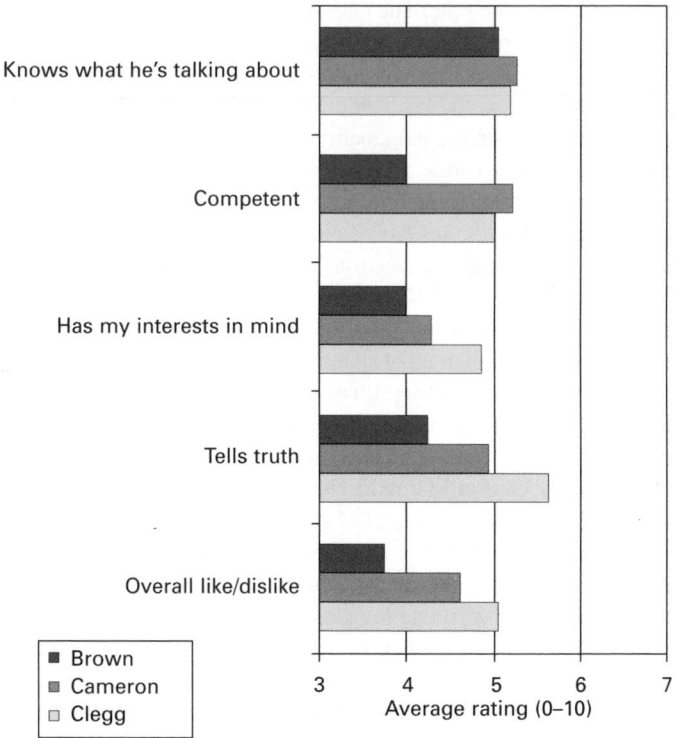

Figure 5.3 Average image ratings for major party leaders in 2010

Source: 2010 BES pre-election internet survey.

Evidence of party leader effects

It is not difficult to find data that look like strong evidence of leadership effects. Table 5.3 reports the relative popularity of the party leaders in elections from 1979, based on poll questions asking respondents which leader they thought likely to be the best Prime Minister. In all but one case, that leader's party won the election in question. The only exception is 1979 and even that is not a glaring exception because, while Labour's James Callaghan was popular in 1979, Margaret Thatcher was not very unpopular. (When not forced to choose between the two, voters gave Mrs Thatcher good ratings.) Moreover, the electoral landslides occurred in those contests – such as 1983 and 2001 – in which there was a big gap between the leaders of the major parties in the prime ministe-

Table 5.3   Best person for Prime Minister, 1979–2010 (%)

1979		1983		1987		1992	
Callaghan	44	Thatcher	46	Thatcher	46	Major	47
Thatcher	33	Steel	35	Kinnock	22	Ashdown	22
Steel	24	Foot	13	Owen	12	Kinnock	21
		Jenkins	6	Steel	11		
1997		2001		2005		2010	
Blair	38	Blair	52	Blair	37	Cameron	32
Major	28	Hague	20	Howard	25	Brown	26
Ashdown	15	Kennedy	15	Kennedy	19	Clegg	22

Note: The percentages do not total 100 as figures for 'don't know' are not shown.

Sources: Data from Gallup, *Political Index, Political and Economic Index,* Nos 226, 274, 322, 380, 441 and 489; YouGov final pre-election polls 2005 and 2010.

rial stakes. In the 2010 election, responses to the 'best Prime Minister' question are strikingly similar to the overall pattern of vote shares. Indeed, a recent study of opinion poll trends shows that the electorate's views about which party leader would make the best Prime Minister have tracked voting intentions very closely (Sanders, 2005). All of this is entirely consistent with the claim that these leadership evaluations drive party choice. And BES data from 2010 seem to reinforce the point. Of those nominating Brown as best Prime Minister, 76 per cent reported voting Labour, while 82 per cent of those preferring Cameron went on to vote Conservative, and 71 per cent of those choosing Clegg voted Liberal Democrat.

The problem, of course, is the recurring question of causal direction. We have seen that it is difficult to disentangle electors' views about the leader of a party or Prime Minister from views about the party or the government as a whole. It is possible that voters' feelings towards party leaders are consequences of their party choice rather than causes. Any plausible attempt to estimate the effects of leadership on voting must take this partisan bias into account. The standard method of doing this is through what King (2002a) calls the 'improved prediction' method. People's general loyalties to and attitudes about the parties give us a good basis for predicting their voting behaviour. However, our predictions will be confounded in the case of those voters who are led away from their 'usual' party by some short-term factor. One such factor could be leader images. The question here, then, is whether we become more accurate in predicting party choice when we know voters' leader evaluations as well as their partisan predispositions.

A simple version of the improved prediction approach was used by Butler and Stokes (1974, ch. 17). They compared voters' attitudes to the parties and to the party leaders and were thus able to analyse the voting behaviour of those who were, on balance, favourable to one party but more favourable to the other party's leader. Predictably, given the effects of partisan bias on leader evaluations, only relatively small proportions of Butler and Stokes' sample fell into this category: 14 per cent in 1964, and 12 per cent in both 1966 and 1970. Among those who favoured one party but another party's leader, it was attitudes to parties that were decisive. Those who were pro-Conservative in terms of attitude to the parties, but pro-Labour in their assessment of leaders, voted Conservative by three to one; those who were pro-Labour but preferred the Conservative leader voted Labour by two to one. This suggests that leadership offers some but quite limited improved prediction. Most of those who favour a party also favour its leader, and most of the minority that prefer a rival leader go with their preferred party nonetheless. However, a small number of votes at each of those elections do seem to have been swayed by attitudes by the leaders.

A similar conclusion is suggested by a slightly different kind of analysis of voting in the 2010 general election. The results are reported in Table 5.4. Here, it is party identification rather than more general attitudes to the parties that is held constant. The approach to improved prediction is also slightly different. We calculate support for each major party among two groups: first, those who chose its leader as best Prime Minister; second, those who preferred one of the other two party leaders. Since this is slightly complicated, it is helpful to go through an example. The first pair of figures shows that, among Conservative identifiers, there was 93 per cent support for the party among those who deemed Cameron the best bet for Prime Minister, but that this fell to 63 per cent among those who preferred Brown or Clegg as Prime Minister. That suggests quite a strong effect of leadership, as do the figures in the next row. Conservative voting was quite common (45 per cent) among Labour identifiers who preferred Cameron, but virtually unheard of among those (1 per cent) without that leadership pull. However, there is a danger of overstating leadership effects here. Party still seems to trump leadership in most cases where the two conflict. Among those Labour identifiers who preferred Cameron as Prime Minister, less than half voted Conservative (and there are even clearer examples elsewhere in the table). Besides, there remains the key point that such conflicts are relatively rare because most people prefer their party's leader. Since only 7 per cent of Labour identifiers nominated Cameron as best Prime Minister, even that high rate of defection to the Conservatives still amounts to relatively few votes that are being swung by leadership. Perhaps the most convincing evidence of leadership effects, therefore, is in the bottom row of the table which contains the results for non-identifiers. They were split much more evenly in terms of who they nominated as best Prime Minister and so each of the figures here represent substantial numbers of voters (many of them, of course, the coveted floating voters). And the differences are very large. To take the most striking example, Conservative support was at 75 per cent among non-partisans preferring Cameron, but only at 10 per cent among those who opted for a different leader as best Prime Minister.

A more sophisticated version of this approach involves holding constant a wide range of other variables – ideological position, issue priorities, economic evaluations, and so on – in addition to party identification. All of these variables boost the accuracy of our predictions of voting behaviour; the aim is then to see whether leadership can improve it still further. In Chapter 8 we show that, in 2010, evaluations of the party leaders had the power to predict party choice even when an array of other factors is taken into account. For previous elections, more advanced analyses have gone further than this, sometimes even estimating the effect of leaders on vote shares. Bartle and Crewe (2002) calculate that the direct 'Blair effect' in 1997 was rather smaller than had been generally supposed, accounting for just 1.5 percentage points out of an overall lead over the Conservatives of 11.9 points. The implication is that the landslide victory was largely the party's (although, of course, the

Table 5.4 Party choice by preferred Prime Minister controlling for party identification, 2010

Party ID	% Con vote by preferred PM		% Lab vote by preferred PM		% Lib Dem vote by preferred PM	
	Cameron	*Other*	*Brown*	*Other*	*Clegg*	*Other*
Conservative	93	63	25	0	27	3
Labour	45	1	87	42	46	11
Lib Dem	25	2	23	2	93	72
None	75	10	51	6	67	20

Source: Data from 2010 BES internet surveys.

indirect effects of Blair's leadership were probably a major reason for Labour's surge in popularity). Perhaps surprisingly, evaluations of Tony Blair played a larger part in Labour's 2001 win (Andersen and Evans, 2003). With the party's popularity waning, it needed Blair's personal appeal – and the unpopularity of his opponent, William Hague – to deliver a second landslide. By 2005, the picture had changed abruptly. Tony Blair had become far less popular, due in large part to events surrounding the war in Iraq. Overall, according to Evans and Andersen (2005), he became an electoral liability rather than an asset for Labour. They estimate that, if Blair had maintained his 2001 level of popularity, Labour would have won 40 per cent rather than 36 per cent of the vote.

While the extent of leadership effects has been the subject of dispute among academics, the evidence is actually rather uniform. Most voters' preferred leader comes from what is already their preferred party. This punctures any myth that leaders decide elections. The reason why the most popular leader usually wins (see Table 5.3) is because he or she is usually leading the most popular party. That said, leader images can and do swing votes. A popular leader attracts support from non-partisans and can even win over some of those who identify with other parties. This can widen a party's margin of victory and could, in a close election, be enough to swing the outcome. All of this is consistent with the conclusion on leader effects reached by Butler and Stokes (1974: 367–8). They say that if there is a marked imbalance in the public's estimation of party leaders, if one is clearly preferred or more disliked than another, then leadership will have considerable impact on voting behaviour. This was the case in 2001. If there is no great imbalance – as in 2005 following the slump in Blair's popularity – then the overall impact of leaders is likely to be small.

Conclusion

We begin this conclusion as we ended the previous section: commending the prescience of Butler and Stokes, whose conclusions about elections and voters in the 1960s continue to apply decades later. They wrote: 'In the 1960s, as for a century past, the behaviour of the electorate was shaped by generalized attitudes and beliefs about the parties far more than by any specific policy issues. People respond to the parties to a large extent in terms of images they form from the characteristics and style of party leaders and from the party's association, intended or not, with the things that governments may achieve' (1974: 338). This neatly summarizes the valence or 'performance politics' model of voting behaviour that has been developed by the team running the recent BES (Clarke *et al.*, 2009). However, it also emphasizes a crucial point about this model, namely that judging performance is difficult and subjective. If reading a handful of party manifestos every five years is a commitment too far for most voters, we can safely assume that even fewer are diligently maintaining a detailed record of government performance across issues and throughout the term. Even if they did, they would still have to judge how the opposition might have performed. Hence voters use their broader images of the parties and the leaders in order to assess past and estimate future performance. Voters' reliance on images gives greater power to the key players in image formation, notably the media and the parties themselves in their campaigning. Those are the subjects of the next chapter.

Meanwhile, we should acknowledge that it is easier to assert than to demonstrate the electoral importance of party and leader images. Such images are difficult to measure, partly because they are often quite hazy – especially with unfamiliar leaders and parties with no recent record in government – and partly because we never know whether survey questions are asking about those aspects of a party or leader that really matter to voters. Separating the effects of party and leader images is particularly difficult because the two are so closely intertwined: an appealing leader generates support for his or her party; a party's success spills over into a liking for its leader. There is also the particular difficulty of separating indirect and direct leadership effects. It is hard to judge whether voters opt for a party because they like its leader or because they like what that leader has done to his or her party. And, of course, there are the perennial concerns about causal direction given that prior feelings about parties do much to shape party images as well as being powerful drivers of voting behaviour.

Despite all these difficulties, however, there is clear evidence that party and leader images have a considerable influence over voting in Britain – an influence only likely to grow if dealignment continues. It is also clear that images belong at the heart of the valence approach to party choice. The point is vividly illustrated by the role of the Iraq war in the 2005 general election. While Iraq cost Labour support, this was mainly because of the damage to Blair's reputation as a leader (particularly his perceived trustworthiness). Labour actually lost relatively few votes due to straightforward opposition to the war. In other words, it was leader image rather than policy positions that explained Labour's losses. One obvious retort is that things might have been different if the major opposition party, the Conservatives, had opposed military action. As it was, those hostile to the war had few options. This underlines the point that image comes to the fore when there are fewer concrete differences in policy or outlook between the parties. It is no coincidence that the early peak of interest in party and leader images was during the 1950s, another era of ideological consensus. Butler and Rose (1960: 23) quote a political journalist's remark about the 1959 election: 'I am sure that people care much less about future programmes just now than about choosing which side will give the better and friendlier service under roughly the present rules. Or to put it another way, which side has the nicest competent fellows.' Performance politics is nothing new in British elections.

6

Campaigning and the Mass Media

For as long as there have been contested elections there has been election campaigning: that is, those standing for election and their supporters have endeavoured, by a variety of means, to persuade the relevant electorate to vote for them. Until well into the nineteenth century the main means of persuasion were 'treating' (providing electors with alcohol and other forms of largesse) and bribery. The earliest reference to treating was in 1467, while the first authenticated case of outright electoral bribery occurred in the reign of Elizabeth I (O'Leary, 1962: 6–7). Campaigning remained overwhelmingly a local-level activity until the start of the twentieth century when the introduction of the first of the mass media – cheap, mass circulation, national newspapers – along with steady increases in the sizes of constituency electorates led to the development of national campaigning. Local campaigning continued, of course and, as we shall see, has recently been taken much more seriously by the parties. For much of the latter half of the twentieth century, however, the parties' efforts and the attention of the media were mainly focused on the centrally directed and managed national campaign.

National campaigning

In Britain, the period of the election campaign is legally defined. It must cover at least three weeks before polling day, but usually lasts four weeks. It is only during the legally defined campaign period that the various rules regulating candidates' spending, broadcasting and other campaign activities apply. During this period there is a massive increase in political activity. Media coverage reaches saturation point with the progress of the campaign being charted day by day. Over the past 50 years, however, the nature of the national campaign – what the campaigners do – has changed very dramatically (see Kavanagh, 1995; Scammell, 1995; Rosenbaum, 1997; Bartle and Griffiths, 2001; Fisher and Denver, 2008).

During the 1950 general election campaign the then Prime Minister, Clement Attlee, undertook a 1,000-mile tour around Britain. He travelled in his pre-war family saloon car and was accompanied by his wife (who did the driving) and a single detective. If they were ahead of schedule they stopped by the roadside and Mrs Attlee would catch up with her knitting while the Prime Minister did a crossword puzzle and smoked his pipe (see Nicholas, 1951: 93–4). The idea of a Prime Minister or major party leader travelling around in this way would be inconceivable today. During modern election campaigns party leaders are whisked hither and thither by jet, helicopter, battle-bus or car with an entourage of personal staff, security personnel, newspaper reporters, television crews and assorted other hangers-on. This partly reflects the fact that campaigns are now focused more on the party leaders. Campaign managers have to ensure that the leaders project a good image. Their itineraries are planned in detail, the meetings they address carefully controlled, they are coached on how to perform well on television, advised on how to dress, how to have their hair cut, what to say in public speeches and television interviews, and so on.

Modern national campaigns have five main characteristics. First, as has just been seen and as noted in the previous chapter, they are highly focused on the party leaders. The media follow the leaders everywhere, lengthy set-piece television interviews with the leaders are key events in the campaign and there are also programmes in which the leaders answer questions from members of the public. In 2010 the leaders became an even greater centre of attention with the introduction of the leaders' debates. Gordon Brown (Labour), David Cameron (Conservatives) and Nick Clegg (Liberal Democrats) met three times to debate the key issues of the campaign. These debates became media spectacles, with the television networks vying for the flashiest ways of covering them – from focus groups of undecided voters using instant response trackers to instant public opinion surveys – and, as quickly as possible, determining the 'winner'. Second, campaigning is not restricted to the formal campaign period. Pippa Norris (1997b) goes as far as to say that campaigning is now 'permanent' and plans are certainly made well in advance. For at least a year before an election is due (the precise date being determined by the Prime Minister), the parties clearly engage in campaign activity. Indeed, party officials routinely assert that on the day after an election they start preparing for the next one. But of course, these activities increase in intensity as the anticipation of an election being called increases. In 2010 the Conservatives went so far as to launch their draft health manifesto on 4 January, a full four months before they guessed the election would be held. Third, the parties use modern methods to find out what the voters are thinking and feeling about issues, events and personalities. Between the wars the Prime Minister, Stanley Baldwin, famously consulted his local station master if he wanted to find out what the people were thinking, and as late as 1979 a senior Labour figure preferred to consult his local constituency activists (Kavanagh, 1995: 110, 132). Nowadays, however, the major parties engage polling firms and other professionals to monitor public opinion through conventional polling and focus group research, which involves getting small groups of voters together to talk at length about their political opinions and reactions. Fourth, the parties employ a variety of professionals, specialists and consultants for campaigning purposes. The campaign is conceived of as an exercise in marketing (see Scammell, 1995) and advertising agencies are employed to design posters, suggest slogans, advise on election broadcasts and so on. 'Spin doctors' make every effort to ensure that the party and its personalities get the best possible media coverage. Indeed, the parties have employed political consultants from the United States and Australia to help craft and execute their campaign strategies. In the 2010 general election, political consultants who worked for the Obama campaign in the US were hired to serve as advisors by both Team Cameron and the Brown Campaign. This professionalization of campaigning is one of the most important recent developments in British elections (Denver, Hands, Fisher and MacAllister, 2003). Finally, many campaign events are stage-managed for the benefit of television. It used to be – as late as the 1960s and 1970s – that party leaders would address large public meetings at which they would be interrupted by hecklers. Nowadays there are no such meetings. They have been replaced to a limited extent by 'rallies' of the party faithful to which admission is by ticket only, but generally large meetings are avoided. The daily press conferences, the leaders' tours and activities, the timing and locations of speeches, and the issues to be talked about are all carefully planned in advance. Unscripted events received massive publicity: during the 2001 campaign John Prescott punched a demonstrator who had hit him with an egg, and a week before the election in 2010, after talking on the street to a woman complaining about immigration policy, Gordon Brown was caught on tape referring to her as 'a bigoted woman'. But it is the fact that this sort of thing now happens so rarely – because every aspect of campaigns is so carefully scripted – that makes these incidents so newsworthy.

These developments have made modern campaigns expensive. Before 2001 there was no legal limit on the amount of money that the parties could spend on national campaigning. The parties do not have to pay the broadcasting organizations for election broadcasts on television and radio (a major expenditure item in other political systems) but, nonetheless, in the 1992 election the Conservatives spent about £10 million, Labour about £7 million and the Liberal Democrats about £2 million (Butler and Kavanagh, 1992: 260). Campaign expenditure in the twelve months preceding the 1997 election reached around £28 million for the Conservatives, £26 million for Labour and £3.5 million for the Liberal Democrats (Fisher, 2001). Under the Political Parties, Elections and Referendums Act passed in 2000, however, a stop was put to the spiralling costs of campaigning. For the first time national campaign expenditure was 'capped' and for 2001 parties were not allowed to spend more than £16.3 million on campaigning between the Act coming into force in February and the election in June. This, of course, made little difference to the Liberal Democrats, who are permanently plagued by relative poverty and spent only around £1.4 million during the 2001 campaign. The Conservatives, on the other hand, spent £12.8 million and Labour £11.1 million (Electoral Commission, 2001a). By 2010 the permitted expenditure for a party contesting all seats across the UK had risen to £19.5 million. In total, all political parties spent a combined £31.4 million – about £10.8 million *less* than was spent in 2005. Almost all of this drop can be accounted for by a significant decline in Labour spending (down £9.9 million from 2005 levels). The Conservative party accounted for 53 per cent (or almost £16.7 million) of all party spending in 2010, whilst Labour spent about 25 per cent (about £8 million) of the total and the Liberal Democrats just 15 per cent (or £4.8 million) of all party spending (Electoral Commission, 2010). Yet even in 2010 with its diminished spending, national campaigns do not come cheap.

Is it worth it? Do campaigns have any effects or are they four weeks 'full of sound and fury, signifying nothing', as Pippa Norris (1987) asked in the title of an article on the 1987 campaign? She goes on to suggest (p. 458) that, at least as far as that election was concerned, it is arguable that 'for Labour and the Alliance, no matter how professional the presentation, how effective the grassroots organisation, how persuasive the party political broadcasts, how convincing the leader's speeches, how enthusiastic the rallies, they could not win against the Conservatives'. Similarly, Worcester and Mortimore (1999: 98) argue that in 1997, 'by the time the strategic phase was played out, the election about to be called and the short-term tactics of the campaign itself begun, the election was already effectively lost' (by the Conservatives).

As before, however, the shift from aligned to dealigned voting provides a context within which the effects of campaigns can be considered and, a priori, this would lead us to have different expectations. With aligned voting, the election campaign is merely one other short-term factor which might marginally affect the voters. When the great majority of voters had enduring party loyalties they were unlikely to be deflected from them by any incidents occurring in a short campaign. Compared to the deep-seated influences of class and party identification, campaigns paled into insignificance. As these enduring ties have loosened, however, it seems likely that voters have become more open to influence during campaigns. Fewer will have their minds already firmly made up when the campaign begins.

Some support for this interpretation has already been seen in Chapter 3 in the discussion showing that there has been increased 'campaign swithering' since 1964, and the figures quoted there are certainly consistent with the view that there are now plenty of voters open to persuasion during campaigns. In 2010, according to the polling firm Ipsos MORI, the proportion of voters heading to the polls who had yet to decide how to vote was larger than ever before. Even on the day before the poll, 30 per cent still said that they might change their mind on how they might vote, an increase of 3 percentage points on 2005 and 9 points on 2001 (Ipsos MORI, 2010).

Given the fact that throughout general election campaigns there are almost daily opinion poll reports of voting intentions, it is relatively easy to trace changes in the levels of support for the parties as campaigns progress. Figures 6.1 to 6.3, displaying the polling trends for the last three elections, show that campaigns can be very different: some are rather dramatic, whilst others are humdrum. Figure 6.1 presents the trends in the 2001 election. Four pre-election polls at the start of May constitute the starting point and the chart then shows the average share of voting intentions in each week of the campaign and the parties' actual shares of the vote in Great Britain in the election itself.

Media reporting of the 2001 election generated a widespread impression that the campaign made no difference to the outcome. It is certainly true that Labour won easily, as expected, and the Conservatives 'flatlined', but Figure 6.1 suggests that there was some slippage in Labour's fortunes: having had more than 50 per cent of voting intentions in early May, support fell to around 45 per cent in the last week of the campaign. In addition, there was a clear upward trend in support for the Liberal Democrats. A similar increase in Liberal Democrat support occurred in 1997 (although not in 1992), and in part this simply reflects the fact that general election campaigns give the party (and its leader) more exposure

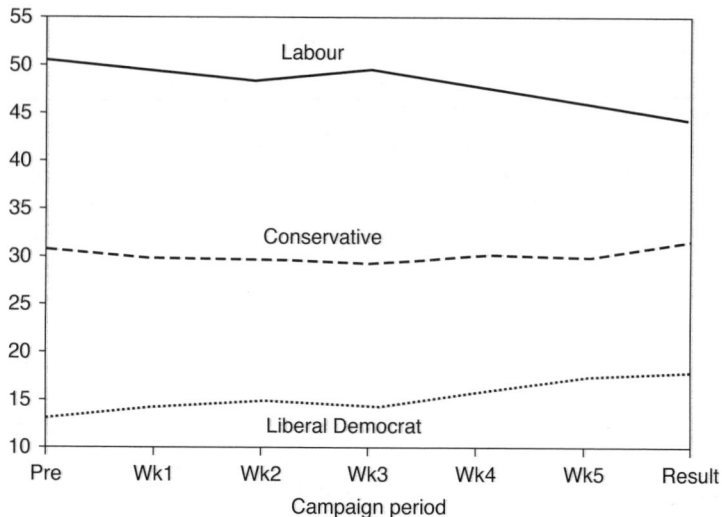

Figure 6.1   Voting intentions in campaign polls, 2001

Note: The calculations – the simple mean in each case – are based on the 'headline' figures reported by the polls, whether these were adjusted or unadjusted. Each poll is assigned to the week in which the majority of the fieldwork was carried out.

Source: Results of published national polls.

than they can get in the periods between elections. In part also, however, the 2001 figures reflect the fact that the public increasingly warmed to the Liberal Democrat leader, Charles Kennedy. During the campaign, Gallup conducted a rolling series of polls on behalf of the British Election Study in which respondents were asked to indicate how much they liked each of the party leaders by giving them a score on a scale running from 0 (strongly dislike) to 10 (strongly like). When the series began on 14 May, Conservative leader William Hague's mean score was 3.9, Blair's 5.6 and Kennedy's 4.9. By the end of the campaign Hague was still on 3.9 and Blair had increased to 5.9, but Kennedy made the biggest advance, scoring 5.4. Whatever interpretation is put on the figures, however, it seems clear that it is wrong to suggest that nothing changed over the weeks leading up to polling day in 2001.

Figure 6.2 shows the chart for the 2005 election. In this case, four pre-election polls at the start of April constitute the starting point. Campaign changes are not nearly as clear as they were in 2001. In the initial stages Labour support increased a little while the Conservatives

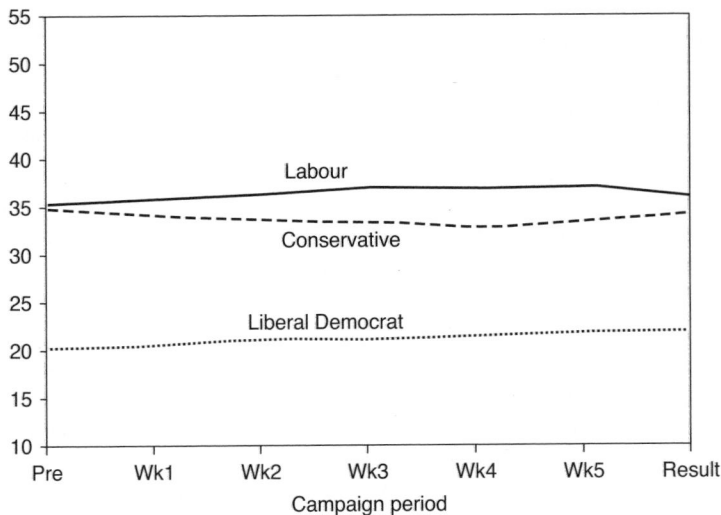

Figure 6.2   Voting intentions in campaign polls, 2005

Note: The calculations – the simple mean in each case – are based on the 'headline' figures reported by the polls, whether these were adjusted or unadjusted. Each poll is assigned to the week in which the majority of the fieldwork was carried out.

Source: Results of published national polls.

fell back somewhat; towards the end support for the Conservatives steadied while Labour's popularity eased downwards. As in 2001 the Liberal Democrats improved their position during the campaign, although not as markedly as in 2001 (in part, no doubt, because their starting point was higher). The likeability of Charles Kennedy may again have been a factor. On the same scale described above, he went from a score of 5.2 at the start to 5.5 at the end. Meanwhile, Tony Blair went from 4.0 to 4.1 and Conservative leader Michael Howard from 3.7 to 3.4.

Figure 6.3 presents an entirely different sort of campaign. Whereas there was little movement in the polls in 2005, in 2010 there were dramatic changes in the parties' relative positions – for a time the Liberal Democrats polled more favourably than the Labour Party. From their starting positions in early April, we see that the Conservatives dropped quite a bit, Labour slipped as well, but the Liberal Democrats rocketed past Labour. The weekly averages here actually somewhat obscure the fact that much of the dramatic increase in the intention of people to say they would vote Liberal Democrat occurred at the beginning of the second week. It was then that Nick Clegg was hailed as the winner of the first of the leaders' debates and the Liberal Democrats' position in the polls reflects their leader's debate success. Brown's 'dour' performance in the first debate is similarly reflected in the polls, where Labour is seen to trail the Liberal Democrats for most of the campaign period. Neither Labour nor the Liberal Democrats, however, managed to come terribly close to David Cameron and the Conservatives. After a poor showing in the first debate, Cameron performed better in the subsequent debates and his party's position gradually recovered. In the end, both the Conservatives and Labour received a slightly smaller percentage of the vote than their poll numbers reflected at the beginning of the campaign. Nick Clegg's Liberal Democrats only ended up around 4 percentage points above where they polled in early April. It seems that the much discussed shift to the Liberal Democrats was actually quite 'soft'; whether that is because people who told pollsters they would vote Liberal Democrat stayed at home or, when looking at their ballot papers, they reverted to the party they usually voted for is still a bit unclear (but see Curtice *et al.*, 2010).

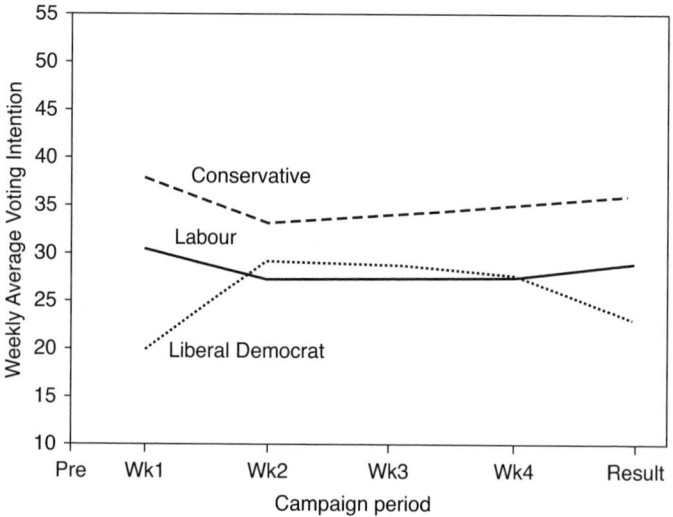

Figure 6.3   Voting intentions in campaign polls, 2010

Source: Results of published national polls.

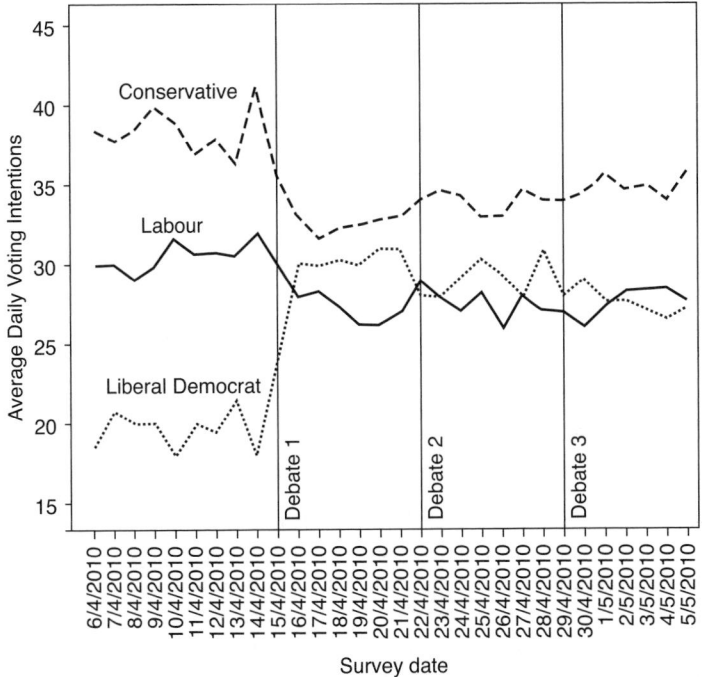

Figure 6.4 Daily averages of voting intentions in campaign polls, 2010

Source: Results of published national polls.

Whilst Figures 6.1 to 6.3 present the averaged polling figures for each week in the campaigns, Figure 6.4 presents the daily average of polling results for the 2010 campaign. Recall that in Chapter 1 we discussed the fact that **aggregate data**, or data that presents information generalized to groups, may obscure interesting information across individuals. **Means**, or averages, while providing a summary of complex information, may hide interesting variation as well. For example, the 'smoothed' Figure 6.3 provides a good picture of the broad trends, yet it does not show that support for the Conservatives (and to a lesser extent Labour) spiked to its highest point right before the first leaders' debate. Means are useful summaries of information, but it is important to pay attention to what information is being averaged.

The data in these figures could also understate the case that campaigns make a difference. Party campaigns have three main aims: to *reinforce* voters who are inclined to support them but who may be wavering or not strongly committed, to *recruit* people who are genuinely undecided at the start of the campaign and to *convert* those who start off with a preference for another party. Reinforcement does not show up in opinion poll figures, but campaign panel polls suggest that there is some conversion and a good deal of recruitment from indecision. However, voters move to and from all of the parties and, if no one party does much better than the others at converting and recruiting, then the effects of all the campaign movements will be to leave the net levels of party support relatively unchanged. In other words, the aggregate figures can and do conceal much individual change during campaigns.

The mass media

During an election campaign only a tiny percentage of voters will actually see a party leader in the flesh or attend a rally to hear him or her speak. Even when party leaders visit particular constituencies, security concerns are such that they flash in and out without most local people even being aware that they have visited until they read about it in a local paper. Overwhelmingly, voters' awareness of the national campaign and their experience of it is obtained from the media, in particular the national press and television. Modern campaigns are, therefore, media campaigns; they are a form of spectator sport. Most people do not participate in campaigns but watch them on television or read about them in the newspapers. Just after the 2010 election 57 per cent of respondents to the British Election Study (BES) said that they had seen some party election broadcasts on television, a drop of around 13 per cent from those who said they saw some of the party election broadcasts in 2005. The leaders' debates seemed to be a greater media attraction, with 68 per cent of BES respondents saying they saw some of the debates. Almost everyone must have seen something of the campaign reports on television news. More generally, in a study for the Electoral Commission in 2001, MORI found that 88 per cent of respondents said that they used television as a source of information and news about politics while 74 per cent used daily newspapers for the same purpose (Electoral Commission, 2001b: 58–61).

There are clear differences, however, between the national press and television in respect of their reporting of politics and these are summarized below:

National Press	*Television*
Partisan	Balanced
Not trusted	Trusted
Segmented audience	Mass audience
Active audience	Passive audience
Printed messages	Audio/visual messages
Secondary source of information	Most important source of information

First of all, most national newspapers are partisan; they usually have a preference for one party or another and state it clearly. Television, on the other hand, is required by law to be impartial in its coverage of politics. In practice this is interpreted as meaning that coverage must be balanced between the parties in terms of time, and current practice is that the details are agreed by an informal committee on party political broadcasting, involving party and broadcasting representatives. The Electoral Commission (2003) has proposed, however, that somewhat more formal arrangements should be put in place. Second, partly because they are overtly partisan, newspapers are not greatly trusted to tell the truth whereas television news (especially the BBC) is trusted to do so. In May 2010, for example, Ofcom, the independent regulator of UK communications industries, found that radio was actually the most trusted source of news, with 66 per cent of survey respondents saying they agreed with the statement, 'When I listen to radio news I tend to trust what I hear.' Interestingly, internet news websites were the next most trusted source of news (58 percent trusting), followed by television news (54 per cent). Only 34 per cent of survey respondents generally trusted print journalists (Ofcom 2010).

Third, the audience for newspapers is 'segmented': different sorts of people read different papers. Readers of broadsheets (such as *The Daily Telegraph* or the *Guardian*) are generally better educated and better off than readers of tabloids such as *The Sun* and the *Daily Mirror.* By contrast there is a mass audience for television. In this context 'mass' does not refer to the size of the audience (although it is, of course, enormous) but to the fact that it is relatively undifferentiated: all sorts of people watch television news, for example. Fourth, it is easy to ignore political coverage in the press; readers can simply turn to the sports pages or gossip columns or whatever it is that they are interested in. Only those who are actively interested in politics will look at the political coverage. The same is no doubt true of 'heavier' political coverage on television programmes such as *Newsnight,* but people watching the main news programmes will find themselves exposed to political news whether they are interested or not. It is this ability of television to reach a largely politically passive audience that makes it such an attractive medium to politicians. Fifth, television is also a much richer medium of communication than the press. The latter provides printed reports and some photographs. On television we can see and hear politicians: how they speak, move, interact with others and respond to questions; what gestures they use, whether they sweat under pressure, whether or not they seem sincere. Finally, and unsurprisingly, most people now regard television as their most important source of information about politics. At the start of the 2005 election campaign MORI found that 78 per cent of voters said that they regularly watched BBC1 as a source of information about news and current affairs. Newspapers remain an important secondary source but, in election campaigns or at other times, when voters want political information it is to television that they mostly turn.

These differences have important consequences for the roles played by the press and television in election campaigns and for their potential impact upon voters. Before considering this in more detail, however, it is helpful to make a brief digression to discuss media effects on attitudes and behaviour more generally. Since the national campaign and media coverage of the national campaign are all but indistinguishable, examining the impact of the campaign on voters effectively means examining the degree to which they are influenced by what they read, hear and see in the mass media.

Media effects

The question of the extent to which people's attitudes, opinions and behaviour are influenced by the mass media, especially television, is one that has provoked an enormous amount of research in a variety of fields. People worry, for example, about the implicit and explicit messages transmitted through the media; for example we may be concerned about the effects of presenting violent or obscene material, about the way women are sometimes portrayed in advertisements or about the effect of showing people smoking cigarettes. Early media theorists, impressed by the apparent power of the media to influence ideas, posited what is called a *direct effects* or *hypodermic needle* model. This is illustrated in Figure 6.5. The source or sender (S) communicates information by a particular 'channel' (print, film, television or whatever) to a receiver (R). The receiver receives the message directly, accepts it and is influenced by it. In a sense, the traditional advertising industry is based on this assumption, although modern marketing would recognize that it is very crude.

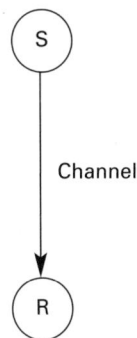

Figure 6.5 Direct effects of model of media influence

Note: 'S' refers to the source or sender and 'R' to the receiver.

Empirical research on political attitudes quickly concluded that this model was far too simplistic (see Trenaman and McQuail, 1961; Blumler and McQuail, 1967). Voters did not come to mass media with empty minds available to be filled with media-provided information; instead, they already had opinions, values, experiences and predispositions which affected their perceptions and interpretations of media messages. The direct effects model was, therefore, replaced by the *filter* model, which is illustrated in Figure 6.6.

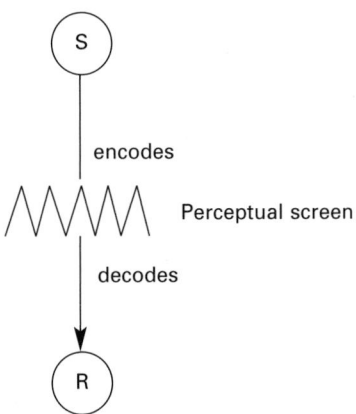

Figure 6.6 Filter model of media influence

Note: 'S' refers to the source or sender and 'R' to the receiver.

An important psychological theory underlies this model, known as the theory of *cognitive dissonance* (Festinger, 1962). Cognitive dissonance is a psychological state of unease or tension which occurs when an individual encounters facts or arguments that are at variance with his or her beliefs or attitudes. Thus a strong Labour supporter would feel uneasy if presented with evidence that ministers in a Labour government were not doing a good job. Subconsciously people want to avoid this sort of unease and do so by 'screening out' some information while being receptive to other information. Generally, people seek reinforcement of their own position from the media, and seek to avoid communications which contradict their views. This is done in three ways:

1 *Selective exposure*. We can't read all the newspapers or watch all television programmes. According to the model, we tend to read and watch material that supports our political viewpoint. Indeed, many people avoid 'political' material altogether and concentrate on sport, entertainment, soap operas and so on.
2 *Selective perception*. Even when we come across hostile media material, we reinterpret it to fit in with our preconceptions or don't even perceive its hostility. Thus David Cameron's opponents might see him as an ideological conservative set on shrinking the size of government, while his supporters may view him as someone who has the courage of his convictions in the face of difficult economic times; just as Tony Blair might have been seen by his supporters as very sincere, while opponents might have perceived him as duplicitous.
3 *Selective retention*. We remember selectively. We remember things that fit in with our views and quickly forget things that don't.

People employ these mechanisms subconsciously in 'decoding' the communications that have been 'encoded' by the sender. In doing so they erect a 'communications barrier' or 'perceptual screen' between themselves and the mass media. Despite all the propaganda efforts of the newspapers and of the parties in campaign broadcasts, the main effect of the media, as interpreted by this model, is to reinforce the voters' pre-existing predispositions. An interesting example of these processes at work occurred in December 2001, although it had nothing to do with elections. The United States government released a video in which Osama bin Laden appeared to demonstrate at least prior knowledge of the previous September's terrorist atrocities in New York and Washington. The reaction of some of those opposed to subsequent

American action in Afghanistan was to claim that the video was somehow faked. A letter-writer to the *Guardian* asked: 'May I be the first to nominate for an Oscar the actor who played bin Laden?' (see Harris, 2001). The evidence of the video was thus interpreted to accord with, rather than challenge, existing views.

The filter model of media effects has been very influential and it has been supported by plenty of evidence. Nonetheless, as we shall see, in the context of electoral behaviour it has increasingly been called into question in recent years.

Television

Television utterly dominates national campaigns. The activities of the party leaders are 'media events,' staged especially to be reported; photo opportunities are carefully arranged; schedules are timed to fit in with television news coverage. When leading politicians address meetings or rallies they do not really speak to their live audiences – who are occasionally glimpsed glassy-eyed with incomprehension – but to the television audience who will see clips from the speech ('sound bites') later in the evening. Indeed, speeches are deliberately constructed so that they contain plenty of sound bites for television producers to use. Similarly, when leaders visit different localities campaign managers try to ensure that they are always surrounded by enthusiastic supporters so that a good impression is created for the television cameras. If the advent of mass-circulation newspapers provided the original impetus for national campaigning, then the highly professional modern campaign described above can be seen as a slightly delayed reaction to the advent of television. The question is whether watching the news, party election broadcasts, interviews with party leaders and campaign reports affects the attitudes and behaviour of voters.

The two pioneering studies of the effects of television on British voting behaviour (Trenaman and McQuail, 1961; Blumler and McQuail, 1967) supported the filter model described above. They found that among a variety of sources of political information only television was able to overcome the 'communications barrier' between people and the media, but it did so only to the extent of increasing the voters' level of political information; it did not change political attitudes and opinions. Thus, Trenaman and McQuail (p. 233) concluded that 'in the field of attitudes a highly significant screening effect separates exposure to the campaign from changes in strength or direction of attitude'. They said

(p. 192) that there was 'a definite and consistent barrier between source of communication and movement of attitudes in the political field at the General Election'.

Many people find the conclusion that television has little effect on political opinions difficult to accept. It seems to fly in the face of common sense to suggest that such a pervasive and powerful medium has little impact upon political attitudes and behaviour. Moreover, if the medium has such little impact upon voters, why do the professionals in the political parties make such strenuous efforts to tailor their campaigns to the needs of television? Why are leading politicians extensively coached on how to come over well 'on the box'?

The first point to make is that both studies mentioned above focus on party election broadcasts (paying little attention to other political reporting) and tend to assume that these broadcasts only have an impact if they result in changes in voting intentions and attitudes (rather than, for example, reinforcement or recruitment). More importantly, however, it is simply the case that times have changed. Both of these studies were undertaken a very long time ago. Trenaman and McQuail's book is concerned with the 1959 general election, while Blumler and McQuail's deals with the 1964 election. At that time political television was in its infancy. The quantity of political coverage on television today is vastly greater than it was then and the quality has vastly improved. Television commentators, interviewers and presenters concerned with political coverage are much more professional and less deferential to politicians; coverage of elections (and of the House of Commons) is much more detailed and sophisticated. Finally, the emergence of a dealigned electorate has serious implications for the filter model. It was the existence of party identification which to a large extent created the 'communications barrier' in respect of party preferences. It was because most voters had strong pre-existing party loyalties that they employed selective processes in response to political messages in the media. If people were strongly Conservative they would screen out pro-Labour information and remember pro-Conservative coverage. Since there has been a notable decline in the strength of party identification it would seem reasonable to infer that the 'communications barrier' has become rather more permeable since the 1960s.

There has been no full-scale survey study of the effects of television on political attitudes and behaviour in the dealignment era. Miller's (1991) painstaking study, *Media and Voters,* pays hardly any attention to television's effect on attitudes, while the data reported by Norris *et al.* (1999) are based on experiments rather than surveys. In part, this absence of major survey studies on television effects is a product of the fact that researchers have come to realize that demonstrating such effects is hugely difficult. There are three major problems.

First, a major criticism of the early studies mentioned above is that their focus is very much on short-term change. They concentrate on the election campaign period and it seems unrealistic to expect to find marked changes in political opinions in such a short space of time, especially in a situation where voting was highly structured by class and party identification. Effects could be long-term, slow and subtle, but nonetheless significant. Party election broadcasts during campaigns might not convert people but that does not mean that attitudes might not be shaped over a long period by broader reporting of politics. The problem is that it would be difficult (and expensive) to construct a research programme to study the long-term effects of television.

Second, apart from party election broadcasts – which are clearly designed to persuade voters – television coverage of politics, as we have seen, is required to be balanced. Moreover, it is very diffuse, ranging from specialized regular features such as *Newsnight* and *Question Time* to documentaries, comedy and news broadcasts several times a day. Given this, it is difficult even to imagine how researchers could keep track of what information about politics viewers receive in order to try to measure its impact on their attitudes.

Third, as well as receiving information from television, voters are constantly exposed to a multiplicity of other influences, including family, friends, colleagues, newspapers, propaganda literature, websites and so on. The mind simply boggles at the complexity of trying to separate out the effects of television from all of these other influences. This is related to the final difficulty: the perennial problem of demonstrating causal connections. It is well established that people who watch – or remember watching – a particular party's election broadcasts tend to vote for that party, but it is arguable that this is not because they are influenced by the broadcast; rather, they are supporters of the party in the first place and are using television to reinforce their views.

There is no doubt that television has profoundly affected the conduct of politics in general and of election campaigns in particular. Simple observation suggests that it has led to a greater concentration on personalities rather than policies or issues and, in particular, on the party leaders. Leaders who come across well on television appear to be at an advantage. Parties devote far more resources to presentation and to media management than they used to. National campaigns revolve around television.

Finally, what remains unresolved and difficult to demonstrate, however, is the extent to which television affects voters' attitudes and hence their choice of party. Certainly the conditions for increased influence exist. Party identification, which previously filtered voters' perceptions of political communications, has declined in importance while voting on the basis of evaluations has become more prevalent. A precondition of making evaluations is possession of the requisite information, and television is by far the main supplier of political information (even if this amounts to little more than the impression created by a party leader when interviewed on *This Morning* or *The One Show*). More generally, the image that leaders project is largely communicated to the voters via television.

It is also frequently suggested that television has an important role in setting the agenda for political discussion, by choosing to highlight certain issues and not others. Television producers and commentators, it is said, rather than politicians or voters, determine the campaign agenda – what people will think about – by choosing the issues to be discussed and which events will be reported. In fact, however, both Miller (1991: 164–5) and Norris *et al.* (1999: 182–3) suggest that the agenda-setting role of television is modest, at best. No matter what topics are being discussed on television, the electorate generally continues to believe that 'bread and butter' issues, such as prices, employment, the NHS and so on, are the most important.

Suggestive evidence that how politics is reported on television news does affect attitudes is provided by Norris and colleagues (Norris *et al.*, 1999, ch. 9). During the 1997 election they conducted an innovative experiment in London in which they asked people to view a specially compiled 30-minute video of news items. One of the videos was neutral so far as the parties were concerned but others included material favourable to, or not favourable to, one of the parties. It was found that, after viewing the videos, those who had been exposed to pro-Conservative messages were more likely to intend to vote Conservative, and those who had seen pro-Labour messages were more likely to intend to vote Labour.

This evidence can only be 'suggestive', however, as it was not based on a scientifically selected sample and the respondents' views were ascertained immediately before and after viewing the videos. It is not clear whether the effect demonstrated by Norris *et al.* would still be evident after even only a few days. It would appear that, in general, the influence of television is so pervasive, long-term and mixed up with other factors that it is simply beyond the current ability of social science methods to measure it empirically.

The national press

Unlike television, the national press in Britain has traditionally been overwhelmingly and clearly partisan. On election day in 1992, for example, the whole of the front page of the *Daily Mirror* was taken up with Labour's red rose logo, a picture of Labour's leader, Neil Kinnock, and the slogan 'The Time Is Now – Vote Labour'. It would be difficult to be more clearly partisan than that! Similarly, during the 2005 election a *Mirror* headline read: 'Vote Labour – There's Too Much At Stake'. In 1997, the whole of the front pages of both *The Sun* and the *Mirror* consisted of a picture of Tony Blair and a banner headline: 'It Must Be Him' (*Sun*) and 'Your Country Needs Him' (*Mirror*). On the other side, in 2010 the *Sun* front page was devoted to a picture of David Cameron in the style of the US Barack Obama 'HOPE' posters, with the bold headline, 'Our Only Hope,' whilst the *Daily Express* exclaimed, 'D-DAY David Cameron is our ONLY hope' followed by the warning that 'Clegg could keep Brown in power'.

Deacon, Golding and Billig (1998) suggest, however, that in recent elections simply categorizing papers as pro-Conservative or pro-Labour has become more problematical. Some papers tend to give out mixed or unclear opinions, and partisanship has been much less strident than previously. They argue, therefore, that it is now better to think of papers' stances as falling at different points on a continuum from 'strong Labour' through to 'strong Conservative' rather than categorizing them on a dichotomous, either/or basis. Following this line, Deacon and Wring (2002) used campaign news reporting and comment, as well as editorials, to describe the overall partisan stance of the various papers in 2001 and their summary for national dailies (together with similar classifications for 2005 and 2010) is shown in Table 6.1.

Until 1992 there was a strong pro-Conservative bias in national daily newspapers. In 1992, for example, the circulation of pro-Conservative papers totalled 8.9 million, and all the rest only 4.8 million (Harrop and Scammell, 1992: 181–2). This historic advantage for the Conservatives vanished in 1997 when papers calling for a Conservative victory had a combined circulation of around 4.5 million while the rest totalled 9.2 million (Scammell and Harrop, 1997). By 2001, on Deacon and Wring's assessment, the Conservatives could count only on the support of *The Daily Telegraph*. In 2005, press support for the Conservatives increased somewhat but, even so, the preponderance of opinion among national dailies was still skewed in Labour's favour. The Conservatives were the

Table 6.1   Party 'supported' by national daily newspapers, 2001, 2005
           and 2010

	2001	*2005*	*2010*
Mirror	Strong Labour	Strong Labour	Strong Labour
Guardian	Moderate Labour	Weak Labour	Moderate Lib Dem
Star	Moderate Labour	None	None
Express	Moderate Labour	Strong Conservative	Strong Conservative
Sun	Weak Labour	Weak Labour	Strong Conservative
Times	Very weak Labour	Weak Labour	Weak Conservative
Financial Times	Very weak Labour	Weak Labour	Weak Conservative
Independent	None	Moderate Lib Dem	Moderate Lib Dem
Mail	None	Strong Conservative	Strong Conservative
Daily Telegraph	Strong Conservative	Strong Conservative	Moderate Conservative

Sources: 2001: Worcester and Mortimore, 2001; 2005 and 2010: Wring, Mortimore and
Atkinson, 2011.

preferred party of most of the papers in 2010, however, with just the
Daily Mirror, having endorsed Labour in every election since 1945,
continuing to do so, the *Guardian* backing the Liberal Democrats and
The Independent pushing for voters to vote tactically to defeat David
Cameron.

The fact that only two of the national daily papers gave strong
support to a party in 2001 led Deacon and Wring to argue that there has
been a dealignment of the national press (see also Seymour-Ure, 2002).
Just as voters' commitments to parties have weakened, so fewer newspapers now give strong, almost unquestioning, support to one of the
parties. Readers can easily detect the partisan bias of papers that make
their position very clear. In 2001 readers of the *Mirror, Guardian, Daily
Telegraph* and *Mail* had little difficulty in describing the stances taken
by these papers. In line with the dealignment argument, however, readers of other daily papers had rather less clear-cut opinions about where
the papers stood on the merits of the respective parties (Worcester and
Mortimore, 2001: 161). No comparable data are available for 2010 but
it is worth noting that, in general, respondents found it more difficult to
identify partisan bias in their newspapers in 2001 than they had done in
1997.

As with television, parties set great store by getting favourable coverage in the press – especially, perhaps, the mass circulation tabloids – and
politicians certainly believe that the press can be highly influential in
elections. After the 1992 election the former Conservative party trea-
surer, Lord McAlpine, wrote:

The heroes of this campaign were Sir David English [editor of the *Express*] and Kelvin McKenzie [editor of the *Sun*] and the other editors of the grander Tory press. Never in the past nine elections have they come out so strongly in favour of the Conservatives. Never has the attack on the Labour party been so comprehensive ... This is how the election was won. (*Sunday Telegraph*, 12 April, 1992)

The Sun itself was not slow to claim credit, asserting in a famous headline two days after the election, 'It's The *Sun* Wot Won It'. Whether this was actually true is debatable, to say the least (Curtice and Semetko, 1994), but after he became Labour leader Tony Blair made great efforts to court Rupert Murdoch (the paper's owner) and was rewarded with ringing endorsements in both 1997 and 2001 (and rather more qualified support in 2005).

As with campaigning in general, we have to ask whether this matters. Does what people read in the papers influence their opinions or voting behaviour? It is certainly the case that there is an association between the papers people read and the party they support. Table 6.2 shows the party preference of readers of the various papers in 2010. Although only quite small minorities of *The Times* and *Financial Times* readers followed their papers' advice and voted Labour, in broad terms voters tended to support the party supported by their paper (or, at least, not to vote for the party opposed by their paper). The relationship is far from perfect – there are, it seems, even some *Guardian*-reading Conservatives and non-Conservative *Daily Telegraph* readers – but it is fairly consistent and clear, and similar figures have been reported regularly at British elections.

What is not clear, however, is how these data are to be interpreted. They might indicate either that readers' political views are shaped by the paper they read or that they choose to take a paper that reinforces previously held political opinions. People may read the Guardian and vote Labour or Liberal Democrat, but that does not mean that they don't vote Conservative because they read the Guardian; rather, they may read the Guardian because they have anti-Conservative views in the first place. In other words, the data may reflect selective exposure. In fact, this has long been the standard interpretation of the relationship between newspaper readership and party choice. In the 1960s, Butler and Stokes (1974) noted that there was a strong relationship between newspaper reading habits and party choice but concluded (p. 118) that, in general, the relationship was spurious:

The correlation is most likely to have been produced by the family's passing on a partisanship which the child has matched by his choice of paper, or by its passing on a more general social location to which both paper and party are appropriate ... it is clear that newspapers often profit from, rather than shape, their reader's party ties.

There was evidence that the press helped to conserve or reinforce party loyalties and had a minor role in creating a party preference where readers were previously uncommitted, but little to support the hypothesis that people switched parties as a result of reading a paper with a particular partisan bias.

A similarly careful analysis of the political effects of reading different newspapers at the time of the 1983 election is provided by Martin Harrop (1986). He too finds some support for the view that papers can help to shape a party preference where readers previously had none, but he concludes that the main effect of the press is the reinforcement of existing party loyalties and finds no consistent evidence that newspapers convert their readers to the party supported by the paper.

When they were written, these interpretations represented the consensus among political scientists on the role of the press in influencing party choice and they are clearly in accordance with the filter model of communication. As with television, however, the weakening of party identification implies that voters could now be more open to persuasion by the press. Since they do not have a strongly entrenched pre-existing

Table 6.2   Party choice by daily newspaper read, 2010 (row percentages)

	Conservative	*Labour*	*Liberal Democrat*
Mirror	18	59	17
Guardian	9	46	37
Independent	14	32	44
Sun	43	28	18
The Times	49	22	24
Star	22	35	20
Express	53	19	18
Mail	59	16	16
Daily Telegraph	70	7	18
None	32	30	28

Note: Rows do not total 100 as votes for 'others' are not shown.

Source: Data from Ipsos MORI, 'Voting by Newspaper Readership 1992–2010', 24 May 2010.

preference for a party, they are less likely to filter information; lacking the 'anchor' of party identification they may be more likely to drift with the tides of opinion in the newspapers that they read. Proponents of the dealignment thesis would predict, therefore, that suitable research would find more positive evidence of press effects than hitherto, and in recent years some suggestive evidence has emerged.

As noted above, one of the problems that has bedevilled research on media influence is that it has tended to focus very much on the short term. Miller (1991), in the first major post-dealignment analysis of media effects, sought to overcome this problem by re-interviewing the same panel of respondents at widely different points in time. His results relating to readers of tabloid papers were impressive. Over the year between the summer of 1986 and the election of 1987, the change in the Conservatives' lead over Labour among Miller's panel as a whole was +10 per cent. Among readers of the *Express* and *Mail* it was +17 per cent, for *Sun* (then rabidly pro-Conservative) and *Star* readers it was +34 per cent, while among readers of the *Mirror* it was a mere +2 per cent. This suggests that the tabloids did influence their readers over this period. When Miller divided the readers of the different newspapers into those who were committed to a party (party identifiers) and those who were not, he found that the influence of the tabloids was particularly strong among the latter. When it is remembered that levels of political commitment in Britain have steadily declined, the message of Miller's analysis seems to be that there has been a corresponding increase in the scope for the national press to influence political attitudes and opinions and party choice.

Similar analyses using panel surveys from 1987 to 1992 and from 1992 to 1997 have been reported by Curtice and Semetko (1994) and Norris *et al.* (1999) respectively. Curtice and Semetko concluded that while newspapers had little influence on voters during the 1992 campaign, they had a small but significant effect over the longer term. Norris *et al.* remain more sceptical, however. They agree that newspapers 'can make a difference in mobilising their more faithful readers by playing them a familiar tune' but conclude that 'the partisanship of British newspapers is clearly part of the structure of British voting behaviour, but whether they can explain the flux is very much open to doubt' (pp. 168–9). On the other hand, Newton and Brynin (2001) suggest that newspaper effects are likely to be smaller in 'landslide' elections (such as 1997) than in closer contests, when voters may find it harder to make a decision. In addition, they find that when they take account of the 'selective exposure' argument by controlling for party identification and political attitudes (as well as a number of other relevant variables), newspaper readership has a statistically significant impact on party choice. Reading a paper that was consistent with respondents' party sympathies and attitudes significantly increased the likelihood of voting for the party in 1992 and 1997; reading a paper that was inconsistent with basic loyalties decreased the likelihood of voting for the party. In addition, in line with Miller's analysis referred to above, respondents with no party identification tended to follow their paper's politics even more closely than those who did identify with a party.

As with television, the conditions are ripe for increased press influence on voters' opinions with the development of a more free-floating and easily mobilized electorate. It is also true to say that both media cover much more than politics, especially outside election campaigns. Political scientists are highly interested in the political content of newspapers but the great majority of readers may give it scant attention, preferring to concentrate on sports coverage, celebrity news and so on. In that case, we should not be surprised that the influence of newspapers in shaping political opinions is easily exaggerated. It is worth saying again that it is extremely difficult to isolate the effects of one specific factor upon voting behaviour. As well as reading a newspaper, voters are exposed to a multiplicity of other influences upon their opinions: television, family, friends, colleagues at work and so on. It is impossible to control for all of these at once and so measure newspaper influence. Even so, some of the recent research discussed above suggests that the filter model no longer gives an adequate interpretation of the effect of press partisanship upon party choice.

Opinion polls

Public opinion polls are now a familiar feature of general election campaigns. (Accounts of the history and methodology of political opinion polls can be found in Broughton, 1995, and Moon, 1999.) They are closely related to media campaign coverage, since it is newspapers and television programmes which commission many of the polls, and the voters read and hear about polls in the press and on television. Different types of poll are published during campaigns (polls in specific regions, in marginal seats, of specific groups of voters and so on). In addition, the major parties regularly commission private polls, the results of which are not published. Most attention focuses, however, on the regular nationwide polls tracking voting intentions: Table 6.3 shows the number of such polls published during the campaign period in elections since 1959. To some extent the numbers are affected by the length of the campaign concerned, but there was clearly a slow increase in the number of campaign polls from 1959 to 1979. The number then increased sharply in 1983, increased further in 1987 and reached 57 polls in 1992. In the 1997 and 2001 elections, however, there was a falling-off in the number of polls undertaken. This was probably a product of the fact that in advance of these elections the outcomes were not thought to be in doubt. In addition, some people's faith in the polls had been shaken by their relatively poor performance in predicting the result of the 1992 election. While the expectation of a closer contest led to a resurgence in the number of polls conducted during the 2005 campaign, the 2010 campaign period saw an explosion of polling activity, with a whopping 91 surveys conducted between 6 April and 6 May. Obviously this rise had much to do with the closeness of the contest – with the final outcome in doubt, the last day of the campaign saw no fewer than 19 polls published. Additionally the increase in the number of polls can probably be in part attributed to the decrease in the relative cost of conducting a survey. With an ever-growing number of surveys conducted online by such firms as YouGov, the expense associated with measuring public opinion and voting intentions has greatly diminished in the last decade or so.

Although a number of smaller companies are involved from time to time, political polling in Britain is dominated by a few major firms: ICM, Ipsos MORI and YouGov (which, as we noted, conducts polls via the internet). Several more recent arrivals, such as Populus and

Table 6.3   Number of nationwide polls published during the campaign period, 1959–2005

Election	N (polls)	Election	N (polls)
1959	20	1979	26
1964	23	1983	46
1966	26	1987	54
1970	25	1992	57
1974 (Feb)	25	1997	44
1974 (Oct)	27	2001	36
		2005	52
		2010	91

Sources: Data from Crewe (2005) and UK Polling Report (http://ukpollingreport.co.uk).

Angus Reid, also conduct regular political polls. Although political polling is a high-profile activity, it is a very small part of the business of these companies and they do it neither on their own behalf nor in the public interest. Rather, they are commissioned (and paid) by clients – mainly in the media – to conduct political polls. In the 2005 election, YouGov worked for *The Daily Telegraph, The Sunday Times* and Sky Television, while ICM polled for the *Guardian,* Ipsos MORI mainly for the *Financial Times* (with occasional polls for other papers) and Populus for *The Times.* National Opinion Polls (NOP), having virtually withdrawn from political polling, returned to conduct campaign polls for *The Independent.* On polling day in 2005 and again in 2010 an exit poll (see below) was undertaken jointly by Ipsos MORI and NOP on behalf of the BBC and ITN (and Sky in 2010). In addition to print and broadcast media, blogs and websites, such as UK Polling Report (http://ukpollingreport.co.uk/), regularly dissect the latest polling results.

Campaign poll results are sometimes portrayed as predictions of the outcome of the election in question; this is not the case. As we have seen, opinion fluctuates over the course of campaigns and what campaign polls actually provide is a snapshot of the electorate's voting intentions at a particular point in time, not a prediction of how they will vote at a later date. Nonetheless, the polling firms themselves treat their final polls as election forecasts and it is legitimate to assess the accuracy of polls by comparing the result of the final poll produced by each company with the actual election result. Here again we need to be careful. First, what the final polls estimate is the share of votes that each party will obtain in the election and each of these estimates is subject to a margin of error (usually plus or minus about two percentage points). Thus if, from a sample of around 2,000 respondents, the Conservative vote is estimated at 30 per cent then there is a very strong chance that it will actually be between 28 per cent and 32 per cent. Clearly, if we move from estimates of individual party shares to estimating the gap between them then there is a much larger margin of error (plus or minus four points). Second, poll figures are sometimes used to predict the number of seats that the parties will win. While this is an interesting and important exercise it has little to do with polling, since it involves making judgements about how the electoral system will translate votes into seats.

The fairest way to assess the accuracy of final polls is to compare their estimates of each party's share of the vote with the actual shares obtained, and Table 6.4 shows how the polls have performed in these

Table 6.4 Average error in final campaign polls' prediction of party vote shares, 1964–2010

Election	Mean error	N (polls)	Election	Mean error	N (polls)
1964	1.0	4	1983	1.5	7
1966	1.3	3	1987	1.3	7
1970	2.0	5	1992	3.0	4
1974 (Feb)	1.0	6	1997	2.0	6
1974 (Oct)	1.5	5	2001	1.8	5
1979	0.3	5	2005	0.8	6
			2010	2.2	9

Sources: Data from Crewe (2005: 39), with 2010 update from UK Polling Report 2010.

terms in elections since 1964. Overall, the record up to 1992 was very creditable. Although in some elections some individual polling firms were less accurate, the mean errors were well within the margins expected in any poll. This was not enough to prevent embarrassment for the pollsters in 1970, however. In a close election, four of the five polling firms involved at the time predicted that Labour would win but, when the results came in, it was the Conservatives who came out on top. Post-mortems generally agreed that polling had finished too early – some days before the election – and that there had been a swing to the Conservatives in the last few days of the campaign.

In 1992, however, the polls came seriously unstuck. Only one of the four polls published on election day put the Conservatives ahead of Labour, and then only very slightly, and yet the Conservatives had a comfortable victory. This resulted in a series of post-mortems in which various explanations for the failure of the polls were suggested and investigated (see, for example, Butler and Kavanagh, 1992, ch. 7; Crewe, 1992a). There may have been a *very* late swing to the Conservatives; the methods used by the pollsters may have been faulty; the electoral register may have been more inaccurate than usual; Conservative supporters may have refused to answer questions ('shy Tories') or else deliberately lied to interviewers because they were ashamed to admit that they intended to vote Conservative; people may have realized that there is a qualitative difference between stating a preference in a poll and actually putting a cross on the ballot paper. As David Sanders (1992) pointed out, however, it is extremely difficult to determine what really went wrong without using survey-based data, and there is no guarantee that these do not suffer from the very same problems that led to misleading poll predictions. In any event, it seems likely that the widespread criticism of the performance of the polls in 1992 was part of the reason for the decline in the number of campaign polls commissioned in the two subsequent elections.

In 1997 and 2001, predicting the election winners was not difficult and all polls correctly did so. Even so, the polls came in for criticism, in particular because they mostly overestimated Labour's vote and underestimated that of the Conservatives, especially in 2001 (Crewe, 1997, 2001). Although Labour's vote share was again overestimated by most pollsters in 2005, the average error in predicting the parties' shares of votes was very small (0.8 percentage points). The average error across the polling companies increased somewhat in 2010 (to 2.2 percentage points). Whilst most of the firms (and certainly the major firms) were within ± 2 percentage points of the Conservative and Labour vote, they all overestimated support for the Liberal Democrats (by 2 to -5 percentage points). The error in predicting Liberal Democrat support is probably due to the fact that polls have a difficult time coping with (increased numbers of) 'late deciders' and 'waverers', as well as the more fragmented party system. Support for the Liberal Democrats seemed rather 'soft', for example, with Ipsos MORI reporting that on the eve of the election 40 per cent of respondents who said they would vote for a Liberal Democrat also said that they might change their mind before they voted (UK Polling Report, 2010). In addition, low turnouts make prediction more risky as it is difficult to know which poll respondents will actually turn out to vote, although all polling companies now have techniques for dealing with this (by counting only people who say that they are certain to vote, for example).

Exit polls – polls conducted on the day of the election, usually on behalf of the television channels, by interviewing voters as they leave polling stations – are of relatively recent vintage, being first used by ITN in October 1974 but not fully adopted by the BBC until 1992. These are not campaign polls and their main purpose *is* to predict the election outcome, although they also sometimes provide data on the characteristics and opinions of voters for the various parties. Given that the problems caused by late swings and differential turnout are eliminated, exit polls ought to be more accurate than 'final' polls and, indeed, they are. In 2001, for example, the mean error of the two exit polls was -1.2 per cent on the Conservatives' vote share, +2.0 per cent on Labour's and -0.8 per cent on that obtained by the Liberal Democrats. In 2005, the joint MORI/NOP exit poll slightly overestimated Labour's share (+1.0 per cent) but otherwise was pretty accurate. In 2010 the polls (on average) were almost spot on predicting the Conservative and Labour shares of the vote (being one and two percentage points off the mark, respectively) but overestimated the share of the Liberal Democrat vote. It seems that the Liberal Democrat surge in the polls following Nick Clegg's debate performance disappeared, or faded away, on polling day. Whether Liberal Democrat supporters stayed at home, there was a sudden swing away from Clegg's party or the intensity of support for the Liberals was just far softer when voters actually put pencil to the ballot paper is not yet clear.

Public opinion polls play a major part in election campaigns. Prime Ministers use them to help decide on an election date; the political parties closely monitor public polls and employ firms to do private polls on their behalf; campaign strategies are built around and adjusted in the light of what public and private polls are reporting. Party professionals, candidates and election workers can be encouraged or discouraged by poll results. Throughout campaigns, poll findings are regularly reported and the results analysed in depth.

It is more difficult to know whether the publication of poll results during campaigns influences voting behaviour. Certainly many voters say that they remember seeing the results of opinion polls: the figure was 89 per cent in 1992 and 63 per cent in 1997 (Worcester and Mortimore, 1999: 179–80). In 2005, around 39 per cent described themselves as very or fairly interested in what the polls were saying (Worcester, Mortimore and Baines, 2005: 212). On the other hand, very few voters (4 per cent in 2001 and 3 per cent in 2005) say that opinion polls influence the way that they intend to vote (Worcester, Mortimore and Baines, 2005: 207).

There have been two main hypotheses about the possible impact of polls on voters: one suggests that there is a 'bandwagon' effect, the other that there is a 'boomerang' or 'underdog' effect. The first suggests that when one party is seen to be in the lead some voters will 'jump on the bandwagon' and its support will increase, while supporters of the losing party will lose heart and may not vote. The 'underdog' hypothesis says exactly the opposite: supporters of the leading party become complacent, the resolve of supporters of the losing party is stiffened and there is a growth in sympathy for the underdog. The effect is to produce an upsurge of support for the trailing party. Early investigations of the question concluded, however, that there was no consistent pattern supporting either hypothesis (Teer and Spence, 1973, ch. 6). In four of the last five general elections, however – 1992, 1997, 2001 and 2005 – the polls consistently overestimated the level of support for the party that was reported to be leading during the campaign. In each case the underdog has done better than expected. Also in each case, however, it was the Conservatives that were the trailing party. It remains an open question, therefore, whether the pattern of the polls in recent elections indicates an underdog effect or reflects problems with the pollsters' methods which cause them to include too many Labour supporters in their samples.

It is sometimes suggested that the publication of opinion poll results should be banned during election campaigns in Britain, as it is in some other countries. The Speaker's Conference on Electoral Reform recommended this in 1967 but the proposal was not accepted by the government; nonetheless, the issue continues to be raised from time to time. Those who favour banning them believe that polls do affect voting behaviour and also argue that they 'trivialize' elections by reducing them to 'horse races', deflecting the attention of the voters from the serious issues at stake (see Whiteley, 1986).

If the publication of polls were banned, however, they would merely be replaced by leaks from private polls, rumour and deliberate disinformation campaigns. Local parties and candidates are not above referring to 'polls' of doubtful validity, or even inventing 'poll' results in their campaign literature. We are all familiar with the campaign organizer who claims that canvass returns show that his party is doing 'very well' and support is 'holding up', when the election result turns out to be a disaster. It seems better, on the whole, to have polls conducted by firms with no political axe to grind. More positively, reliable information about the relative support for parties is something that voters may wish to take into account before deciding how to vote, and why should they be denied it? Opinion polls by reputable companies should be counted as a benefit to the electoral process, not a problem. The electorate seems to agree with these arguments as a declining minority (down to 15 per cent in 2005) think that the publication of polls should be banned during campaigns (Worcester, Mortimore and Baines, 2005: 210).

Constituency campaigning

For most people, the national campaign is *the* election campaign. It impinges most persistently and directly on their consciousness as it is played out before their eyes on television and, although the vast majority of the electorate are mere spectators, it generates a considerable degree of interest and excitement, even in supposedly lacklustre elections. Another kind of campaigning goes on at general elections, however, and that is local campaigns in the constituencies. These are inevitably much more humdrum affairs, largely concerned with canvassing the electorate for support, delivering leaflets and get-out-the-vote efforts on polling day. It is at constituency level, however, that voters have direct contact with the election campaign. In the 2005 election, 21 per cent of BES respondents remembered being canvassed on the doorstep by a party, 7 per cent being canvassed by telephone and 6 per cent being 'knocked up' by party workers on polling day, while 89 per cent of MORI' s respondents remembered getting leaflets through the door (Worcester, Mortimore and Baines, 2005: 196). Most people are probably aware that there is a local campaign going on, but locally these campaigns rarely arouse much interest, let alone excitement. Nonetheless, in recent years constituency campaigns have played an increasingly significant part in elections.

Up to at least the 1980s the local campaigning strategies and techniques adopted by the political parties were, whether they knew it or not, based on the model of aligned and stable voting developed by Butler and Stokes. The main purpose of the campaign was to identify known or likely supporters and ensure that they voted. Each party knew where its supporters were to be found – in council estates and other working-class areas for Labour, in private housing estates and middle-class suburbs for the Tories – and concentrated their attention there. Party workers were actively discouraged from 'wasting time' by trying to persuade opponents or 'doubtful' voters of the merits of their candidate. The underlying assumption was that party loyalties were more or less fixed and the aim of the campaign was to maximize the turnout of supporters on election day. Constituency campaigns were not primarily intended to alter the party choice of electors but to mobilize known supporters. Even in this limited respect, however, the general view of electoral analysts was that, apart from rare special cases, constituency campaigns made no significant difference to election results. The consensus was that in general elections local campaigning was little more than a sideshow. It was frequently described as an anachronistic ritual and received scant attention from psephologists.

During the 1990s, however, constituency campaigning was transformed (Denver, Hands, Fisher and MacAllister, 2003). There were four main developments as outlined below:

1 Central party headquarters began to play a greater role in planning coordinating and managing local campaigns. In part this was

because the approach of headquarters staff to all aspects of campaigning became more professional. Partly also, however, it was due to a realization that the voters had changed and that effective campaigning could bring electoral rewards.

2 Resources and effort were increasingly concentrated on 'key' or 'target' seats. Parties had always known that some seats (those that might change hands) were more important than others (those that were safe or hopeless); they drew up lists of targets but this had little practical effect. From the 1990s, however, targeting was ruthless and highly effective, and extended to targeting specific types of voters as well as constituencies.

3 Technology began to be exploited to improve campaigning. In particular, the development of computers and the use of telephone 'banks' to canvass the electorate greatly increased the sophistication of local campaigns, allowing the parties, for example, to build a profile of individual voters and send them appropriate communications. Another innovation was the distribution of campaign videos and (in 2005) DVDs.

4 Campaigning began far in advance of the election. Whereas local activity used to be crammed into three weeks before polling day, many activities – including telephone canvassing and leafleting – now began a year or more before.

The Labour Party was in the forefront of these developments. In elections from 1997, indeed, it is not going too far to say that Labour's whole campaign strategy was built around the constituency campaigns (especially those in target seats). Other parties quickly learned the the appropriate lessons and, by 2005, nationally directed local campaigns targeted on key seats, telephone 'voter identification', communications targeted at individual voters, nationally produced local literature, nationally appointed constituency organizers and conscious attempts to 'localise the national message' were commonplace (Fisher *et al.*, 2006). Making use of software that allowed Labour members to set up 'phone banks' in their homes, in 2010 the party doubled the number of contacts in made in marginal seats. That was partly motivated by the fact that, as discussed above, Labour was severely outspent by the Conservatives (Wintour, 2010). Although they do not necessarily perform any better than traditional campaigning methods, the more 'modern' campaigning methods, relying on phone banks and information and communications technologies, have become increasingly central to constituency campaigns (Fisher and Denver, 2009).

The traditional view that local campaigning made little difference to election results was largely based on a single piece of evidence: the fact that swing tended to be uniform. In the 1950s and 1960s, it appeared that even if some local parties made great efforts and others did little, the outcome was just about the same. We have seen, however, that swing has become less uniform (Chapter 1) and this raises the possibility that differential local campaigning may explain the differences between constituencies. To investigate this possibility, however, researchers needed to devise some way of measuring campaign intensity across parties and constituencies. In the 1990s, three groups of researchers came up with different ways of doing this. Whiteley and Seyd (1994) used surveys of party members to estimate the activism of local parties; Pattie and colleagues (Pattie, Johnston and Fieldhouse, 1995) used campaign expenditure as a surrogate indicator of the level of campaign activity; Denver and Hands (1997a) undertook surveys of election agents and, based on these, derived direct measures of campaign intensity. When these different measures are compared with election results – which involves some rather advanced statistical techniques – then in most cases it is found that variations across constituencies in the intensity of campaigns mounted by the parties have been associated with variations in their electoral performance. The better the local campaign, the better the result. In addition, the more intense the campaign in a constituency the better is the turnout (Denver, Hands and MacAllister, 2004).

It should be emphasized that these studies find effects that are *statistically* significant. The authors would not claim that local campaigning is a *major* influence on election results; it is more a matter of stemming or accentuating a national tide. Denver, Hands and MacAllister (2004) estimate, for example, that in 2001 the gap in turnout between constituencies with the weakest and strongest campaigning was just over 4 percentage points. In the same election the best Conservative campaigns produced a share of the electorate that was 0.8 percentage points greater than their worst campaigns (after taking account of a large number of other variables), while the figures for Labour and the Liberal Democrats were 2.0 and 3.2 points respectively. These are not huge figures but are not to be sniffed at. The fact that Labour had very strong campaigns in their key seats in both 1997 and 2001 gave the party a clear advantage over the Conservatives, and the gains made by the Liberal Democrats in these two elections were clearly the products of highly targeted and effective local campaigning.

The new media campaign

The election of 1992 was dubbed the 'fax' election (Denver and Hands, 1997b); in 1997's 'telephone election' Labour used telephone banks to identify key groups of voters (Denver *et al.*, 2003) and since 2001 commentators and scholars alike have been waiting and watching for the first 'internet election' (Gibson *et al.*, 2010). As momentum started to build toward the formal campaign period, many observers thought that 2010 would be the year in which the internet would not only play a major part in campaign strategies, but would also be a way for party supporters to share information and build support for their candidates. Many of these expectations were, of course, based on witnessing the great success that the Obama campaign had mobilizing support – and fundraising – through new media sources in the 2008 US presidential race. Yet, before the election in May of 2010 analysts and commentators were already writing off the internet as a major campaign tool in the UK (Gibson *et al.*, 2010).

In a survey of all election agents who helped manage candidate campaigns in the 2010 election, Fisher, Fieldhouse and Cutts found that candidate campaigns were quite limited in their use of new media (2010: 7). In fact, they found that when they asked election agents to rate how much 'effort' the campaigns put into thirteen different campaign activities, ranging from traditional means of leafleting and doorstep canvassing to modern methods such as emailing voters and using social networking sites, the new media methods of campaigning were regularly rated as having the lowest priority in candidate campaign strategies. On average, emailing voters, using social networking sites and using video/image sharing sites received the lowest priority across all the parties. Instead of e-campaigning, Fisher and his colleagues found that, 'direct mail was the prevalent technique, with telephone canvassing also playing a significant role. Only in the case of the Liberal Democrats do we see the use of new media approaching that of other modern voter contact techniques (and only then in respect to Twitter)' (Fisher *et al.*, 2010). When aspiring MPs did make use of Web 2.0 tools – internet-based interfaces, such as Twitter, Facebook and other social networking resources, designed to foster dialogue, conversation and exchange of information – it seems that most candidates adopted a 'broadcast' approach rather than a 'conversational' mode (Williamson, 2010).

This is not to argue, however, that new media did not have an important role in the 2010 campaign. Williamson, for instance, argues that, 'the value of the internet for the parties in 2010 lay not in the public face of their official campaign sites, but "behind the scenes" in the management tools used to organise their campaigners, candidates and supporters. The internet was a vital way of keeping members and supporters connected to the campaign at large' (Williamson 2010: 18). Beyond its use as a campaign tool, new media formats such as blogs and social networking sites dramatically increase the pace at which news is disseminated. Events, including Brown's 'bigoted woman' comment mentioned above, are quickly broadcast through Twitter's 'tweets' and Facebook's 'status updates', dramatically accelerating the speed at which the public become aware of events that may have gone all but unnoticed years ago.

Whilst the 2010 election may not have been the 'internet' or 'e-campaigning' election that was predicted, it may be possible to argue that it was the 'app election'. It is highly unlikely that the parties' iPhone and Blackberry apps (or 'applications') did a great deal to influence the outcome of the election; however, they did garner a bit of attention in the traditional media (Carrell, 2009; Coates, 2010; Crabtree, 2010). The Conservatives' app directed at voters included features that attempted to mimic some of the techniques used by the Obama campaign, especially one that encouraged supporters to call friends in their address book, ask them how they intended to vote, then report that information back to Conservative headquarters through the app itself. The Conservatives also purpose built Blackberry and iPhone apps for their candidates that, according to *The Times*, provided them with a searchable database containing manifesto commitments, policy information, 'regional anti-Labour data', and even prepared attack talking points (Coates, 2010). Apps were not only the province of the large parties. The smaller parties

Figure 6.7   Conservative, Green Party and UKIP iPhone apps, 2010

also produced apps aimed at voters and, perhaps, the media in an attempt to grab some attention. The Greens' app presented a quiz to see how well a prospective voter's opinion matched with the party, whilst the UKIP app provided information on the party, links to social networking interfaces, videos and photos, information on events and a donation button.

The evidence consistently suggests that the parties are still adjusting to modern forms of campaigning and they are especially still trying to work out how to best make use of new media and social networking techniques. It does seem that the parties with more constrained pocket books, such as the Liberal Democrats and the smaller parties, are looking a bit harder at innovative uses of websites and Twitter as a way of overcoming some of their financial disadvantage. So far this seems to have had a relatively limited impact. That said, Gibson *et al.* do report that there was a 'striking increase' in the number of people saying they visited party or candidate online material in 2010 (Gibson *et al.*, 2010: 9).

Conclusion

With a dealigned electorate more open to change in the short term, election campaigns and the mass media are, potentially, more likely to influence voters and election outcomes. Identifying, measuring and demonstrating the extent of such influence, of course, is fraught with difficulties. There is solid evidence that local campaigning makes a difference to election outcomes – which is in tune with the kinds of developments anticipated by dealignment theorists – but as far as the impact of the national campaign as transmitted by the mass media is concerned, things are less clear-cut. It seems likely that if all parties run careful, professional national campaigns then short-term instability among the voters is unlikely to be markedly to the benefit or disadvantage of any one of them. On the other hand, the campaign is decision time for increasing numbers of voters and, as the example of Charles Kennedy and the Liberal Democrats in 2001 showed, a vigorous and fairly distinctive campaign can have an impact. Even when there is little change in aggregate voting intentions during a campaign, however, this can be deceptive. Beneath the surface appearance of stability, voters are switching, hesitating and moving between decision and indecision. For that reason the parties' campaigns remain very important and worth spending money on, as any party which did not campaign seriously and well would soon find out.

7

Electoral Geography and Electoral Systems

Electoral geography focuses on spatial variations in electoral behaviour: that is, variations across regions, constituencies, wards or neighbourhoods (see Johnston *et al.*, 1998). There is nothing new about this approach. Indeed, comparing election results from one place to another is probably the oldest form of electoral analysis and is something which all psephologists do, not just those with specialist expertise in geography. Comparing turnouts in different constituencies, for example, involves examining spatial variations. In this chapter the focus is on variations in party choice and, in this respect, where people live is an important part of the context within which voters make their decisions; it is a contextual variable.

Another important contextual variable is the electoral system that is used to collect and tally votes to determine which lucky candidates are elected. From childhood we learn that the rules of the game have a large impact on who wins and who loses. The importance of the rules is particularly important when considering how elections are conducted. In May 2011 people across Britain voted to keep the rules the same and retain the traditional first-past-the-post method for electing Westminster MPs instead of switching to the 'alternative vote' electoral system. While voters will continue to elect MPs the same way, they will have to use several other electoral systems in elections across the UK.

Regional variations

In analysing regional voting patterns, students of elections generally use regions (based on the previous 'Government Office Regions') for statistical purposes. The boundaries of these census regions change from time to time and in the most recent definition (revised in 1998) England is divided into nine regions – North East, North West and Merseyside, Yorkshire and the Humber, East Midlands, West Midlands, Eastern, London, South East and South West – while Scotland, Wales and Northern Ireland are also defined as separate regions. Dividing up the country in this way is inevitably rather arbitrary and it is unlikely that everyone living in these regions feels a distinctive regional identity (excepting, of course, Scotland, Wales and Northern Ireland, where people would probably resent the use of the term 'region'). People living in Newcastle upon Tyne, for example, would consider themselves 'Geordies' rather than inhabitants of the North-East region, and it is unlikely that many people would describe themselves as 'East Midlanders'.

Despite the artificiality of official regional boundaries, however, very clear regional voting patterns have been reproduced in election after election throughout the post-war period. This is illustrated, first, in Table 7.1 which shows the Conservative shares of the vote in the various regions (as they were then defined) in 1955 and in 2010. Already in 1955 there was something of a 'North–South divide' in patterns of party support. The Conservatives' vote share was larger than the national average in the South East, East Anglia and the South West and smaller in Wales, the North, and Yorkshire and Humberside. Scotland and the North West stand out as distinctive, however, in that the Conservative share there was greater than the national average. By 2010, the North–South divide was clearly defined. Conservative support was markedly lower in Scotland, Wales and the three regions in northern England, and clearly higher in the South outside London (South East, Eastern, South West) than in the country as a whole. While the average Conservative party vote in the South (outside London) was 46.6, in Scotland, the Conservative vote was almost 30 percentage points lower.

A summary picture of what happened between 1955 and 2010, in terms of regional voting patterns, is given in Figure 7.1. This shows, for each election, how the Conservative 'lead' (in some cases negative) over Labour deviated from the national (Great Britain) figure in Scotland, Wales, the three southern regions outside London and the three northern regions. From 1959 to 1987, slowly at first but then more rapidly in the 1980s, Scotland and the North deviated more and more away from the Conservatives while the South swung more and more to the Conservatives. After 1987 the gap closed a little (although widening again in 2005) and then quite a bit more in 2010 with the Conservatives gaining the largest share of the national vote. In 2010 we see that the North (including Yorkshire and The Humber) and Wales particularly show a marked increase in support for the Conservative party, so that it

Table 7.1   Conservative share of the votes in regions, 1955 and 2010

1955		2010	
South East	58.2	South East	49.9
North West	52.2	Eastern	47.1
East Anglia	51.8	South West	42.8
South West	51.5	East Midlands	41.2
Scotland	50.1	West Midlands	39.5
Greater London	49.5	London	34.5
West Midlands	49.4	Yorkshire and The Humber	32.5
East Midlands	46.8	North West	31.7
Yorkshire/Humberside	44.3	Wales	26.1
North	43.0	North East	23.7
Wales	29.9	Scotland	16.7
Great Britain	49.3	Great Britain	36.1

Source: Data from Rallings and Thrasher (2000), updated by the authors; region name differences reflect 1955–2010 classification changes.

was almost on par with the overall national figure. Scotland, though, continued to be a cold country for the Conservatives.

Figure 7.1 focuses on relative support for the Conservatives and Labour and so gives no information about two other distinctively regional features of elections during this period. The first was the distribution of support for the Liberals and their successors, which was markedly higher than average in the South West of England, in the Highlands and Borders of Scotland and in some parts of rural Wales. This continued their reputation as the party of the 'Celtic fringe'. Second, in the late 1960s there was an upsurge of political nationalism in Scotland and Wales and the SNP and Plaid Cymru emerged from the fringes of electoral politics in their respective countries. Thereafter, the two parties gained significant support in elections, further heightening the electoral distinctiveness of Scotland and Wales.

To an extent, regional differences in voting behaviour reflect differences in the social composition of the electorate. People living in the South are generally more affluent, more middle-class and more likely to be home owners than those in Scotland, Wales and the North so that the Conservatives would be expected to do better there in any event. Survey data show, however, that even when social characteristics are taken into account regional differences persist. In the mid-1960s Butler and Stokes (1974: 129) showed that among both working-class and middle-class

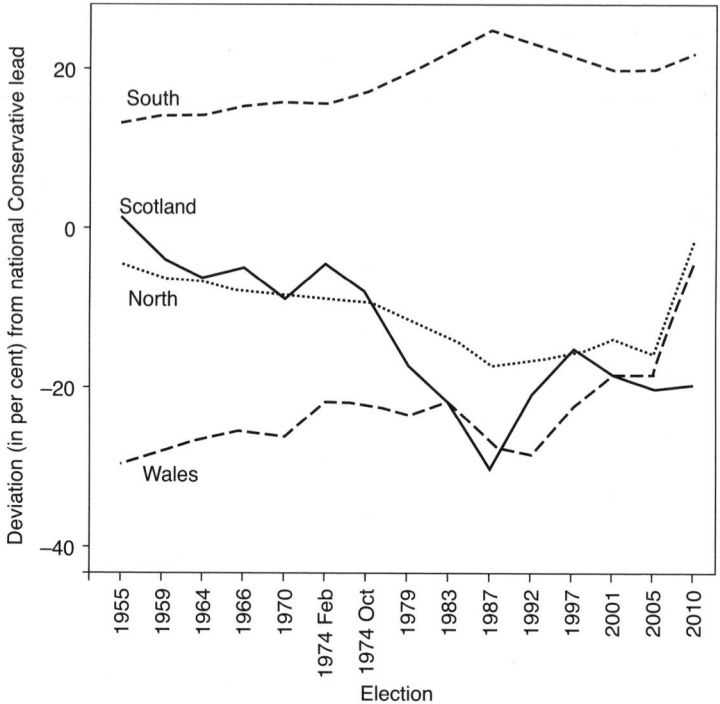

Figure 7.1   Regional deviations from national Conservative lead over
             Labour, 1955–2010

voters greater proportions voted Conservative and smaller proportions
Labour in the South than in Scotland, Wales and the North. Table 7.2
compares voting patterns in the South (outside London) and the North,
Wales and Scotland in the 2010 election, controlling for occupation, age
and housing tenure. Within each category voters in the South were more
likely to vote Conservative and Liberal Democrat and less likely to
support Labour than their counterparts in the North, Wales and Scotland.
It seems clear, then, that even in a year when the national vote swung
back toward the Conservatives there is some regional factor at work –
over and above simple social composition – which needs to be
explained. It should be said, however, that there is an alternative (and
minority) view which argues that apparent regional differences in voting
disappear when a variety of controls are introduced (McAllister and
Studlar, 1992). A problem with this analysis is that political attitudes are
controlled before regional differences are considered and these attitudes

Table 7.2 Party choice in the 'North' and 'South' in 2010 (row percentages)

	Conservative	Labour	Liberal Democrat
	%	%	%
Non-manual occupation			
North, Wales and Scotland	32	31	27
South	56	14	28
Manual occupation			
North, Wales and Scotland	19	56	15
South	41	22	30
Aged 65 and over			
North, Wales and Scotland	39	37	16
South	54	13	27
Owns home			
North, Wales and Scotland	33	32	24
South	55	15	27
Rents home			
North, Wales and Scotland	14	60	16
South	32	24	35

Note: Rows do not total 100 because votes for 'others' are not shown.

Source: Data from BES 2010 face-to-face survey.

are, of course, strongly related to party choice. The point is, of course, that people in the different regions have different political attitudes.

Urban–rural variations

The widening gap between regions in elections since 1955 has been accompanied by a less frequently noticed development: an increasing divergence between more urban and more rural areas. This is illustrated in Figure 7.2, which is based on a conventional definition of constituencies as very urban, mainly urban, mixed and rural, according to the number of electors per hectare and derived from Curtice and Steed (1992: 346). As can be seen, over time very urban areas have moved sharply away from the Conservatives (although there was a slight reversal of the

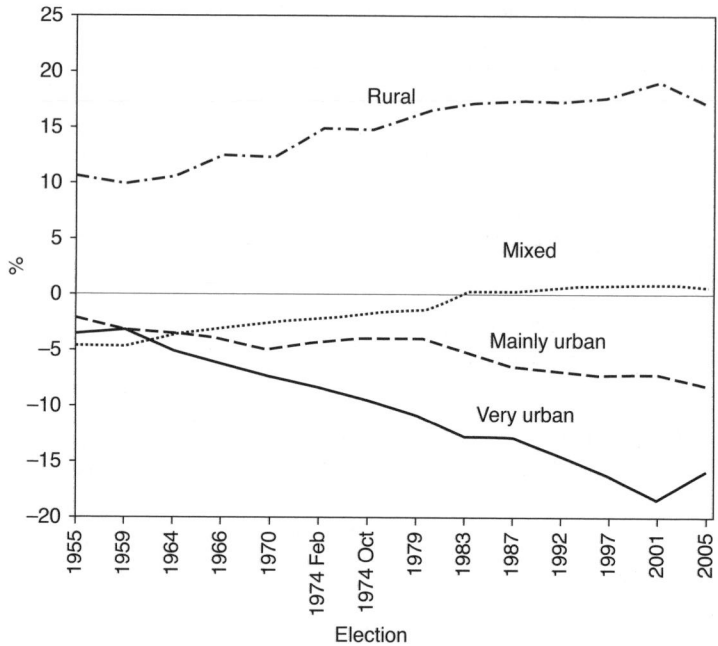

Figure 7.2 Urban–rural deviations from national Conservative lead over Labour, 1955–2005

trend in 2005, mainly due to the large swing away from Labour in London). Mainly urban constituencies have also moved against the Conservatives while, relative to the national results, mixed areas have become somewhat more Conservative and rural areas decidedly more so. The effect of this on party representation has been dramatic. Whereas in 1955 the Conservatives won 33 seats out of 74 in the ten largest British cities outside London – Birmingham, Bristol, Edinburgh, Glasgow, Leeds, Liverpool, Manchester, Newcastle, Nottingham and Sheffield – they won none at all (out of 51) in the same cities in 2005. And in 2010, the year the Conservatives won an additional 97 Westminster seats and secured a five per cent swing in the vote from Labour, the Conservative party still only managed one seat (out of 46) in those same cities.

When the urban–rural divergence is overlaid on the regional divergence then the extent of change in British electoral geography over the past 40 years or so is dramatic. Comparing 1966 and 2005 (both elections won by Labour), the Conservative lead over Labour in the rural south more than doubled–from 12.0 to 25.3 percentage points–while Labour's lead in the very urban parts of northern England rose from 21.5 to 37.4 points.

Explaining regional variations

The North–South electoral divide, which opened up so spectacularly in the 1980s, has generated a large literature (see, for example, Johnston, Pattie and Allsop, 1988; McAllister and Studlar, 1992; Pattie, Johnston and Fieldhouse, 1993; Johnston *et al.,* 1998; Johnston, Pattie and Rossiter, 2005). Like most generalizations, the suggestion that there is an electoral dichotomy between the north and south of the country is an oversimplification – party support in London, for example, is very different from the pattern across the south as a whole – but it does highlight a major feature of the geography of party support in Britain. How can it be explained?

At the start of the 1980s, Curtice and Steed (1982) suggested that the long-term trend to increased regional polarization could be explained in three main ways. First, there had been slow changes in the distribution of socio-economic characteristics among the electorate. The proportion of broadly middle-class people tended to increase more quickly in the South (and in rural areas) and, relatively speaking, to decrease in the North and Scotland (and in urban areas). In part this could be due to migration, but research on the electoral effects of patterns of migration within Britain suggests that population movement has not in fact contributed significantly to the growth of the regional and urban–rural divides (see Denver and Halfacree, 1992a). Second, differential regional behaviour was a product of regional variations in economic wellbeing; put crudely, Scotland and the North have simply not been as prosperous as the South. Third, Curtice and Steed offered a purely political explanation. As the Liberals and their successors (and the nationalists in Scotland and Wales) increased in popularity from the 1970s onwards, this was generally at the expense of the locally weaker major party. Since the Conservatives were already weaker in the North and Scotland (and urban areas) they suffered more from the increase in support for 'minor' parties, and so performed more poorly relative to Labour. In the South and rural areas the picture was reversed, with Labour being the party to suffer.

Johnston and his colleagues have written extensively on this issue and they have argued that the growing regional electoral divide during

the 1980s was closely related to uneven regional economic development. Areas which generally did less well under the Conservatives
moved away from the party, while those which prospered deserted
Labour. They suggest that government policy had a differential regional
impact, making for differences in such matters as changes in levels of
unemployment, in the occupational and industrial structure and in property values. Survey data showed that these changes resulted in regional
variations in satisfaction with the country's economic performance and
in optimism about the economic future. In turn, this was reflected in
divergences in regional voting patterns. Subsequently, the slight narrowing of the divide after 1987 is again explicable in terms of reactions to
regional economic circumstances.

Much of the literature on the North–South divide – especially explanations couched in terms of the rise of third parties or uneven economic
development – is mainly directed towards explaining changes in
regional patterns of party support since 1979 and certainly sheds a good
deal of light on these changes (see Field, 1997, ch. 3, for a critical review
of contemporary explanations). It is worth remembering, however, that
regional differences were clear in 1955 and, indeed, long before that.
Rose (1974: 490) demonstrates that the regional pattern of Conservative
support in 1970 was very similar to that in every election stretching right
back to 1918, while Field (1997: 37) shows that there was also a
North–South divide in Conservative support in elections from 1885 to
1910. This suggests that a more general explanation is required than the
regional effects of the policies of particular governments. Field himself
suggests that such an explanation is provided by a version of
'core–periphery' theory (see also Steed, 1986). Put simply, this theory –
which has been applied in a variety of disciplines – argues that Britain,
like most other societies, is divided into a 'core' and a 'periphery'. The
geographical core (London and the South East in this case) dominates
the periphery culturally, economically and politically. Peripheral regions
are poorer, suffer more in times of economic depression, have worse
housing conditions, and so on. People living in these regions tend to
resent the domination of the core. As a result, voters in the periphery
tend to favour radical, non-establishment parties. This theory certainly
does not fit the British case perfectly but it does offer some clues to
understanding the long-term geographical pattern of voting in Britain.
Nonetheless, in trying to explain regional electoral differentiation,
analysts often invoke even vaguer ideas such as distinctive social, religious and political traditions or distinctive cultures. At root, as Curtice
and Steed (1988: 333) imply, broad and long-lasting regional differences

in party support are likely to be a product of 'cultural or historical differences and defy economic interpretations'.

Constituency variations

It hardly needs to be said that the pattern of party support varies across constituencies. Elections would be rather boring if it didn't! In general terms there is also nothing very surprising about how it varies. Given what we know about the parties and their supporters, it would raise few eyebrows to find that in the 2010 election the Conservatives performed worst in Rhondda (6.4 per cent) and best in Richmond, Yorkshire (62.8 per cent), while Labour's best show was in Liverpool Walton (72.0 per cent) and their worst in Westmorland and Lonsdale (2.3 per cent). Until the late 1960s, however, the analysis of aggregate election statistics was normally confined to the election results themselves (as in the statistical appendices to the Nuffield studies). There were very few examples of analysis that attempted to relate the distribution of party support in constituencies to their socio-economic characteristics in a systematic way. The ability of psephologists to undertake aggregate data analysis of this kind was greatly increased when census data for parliamentary constituencies were compiled and published following the 1966 sample census. Constituency data are now also available for subsequent censuses (1971, 1981, 1991 and 2001).

In general terms, as suggested above, the results of these sorts of analysis are not exactly news to any observer of British electoral politics. Most people know that middle-class and rural areas usually return Conservative MPs and that working-class areas in cities tend to be Labour. With the availability of census data, however, analysts were able to bring a new precision to knowledge of this kind. Correlation coefficients enable us to tell exactly how strongly certain characteristics of constituencies are related to levels of party support; regression equations clarify the nature of such relationships and enable us to identify constituencies in which the pattern of party support deviates from what would be expected on the basis of their social composition. In short, the availability of appropriate social, demographic and economic data allows more subtle and sophisticated analysis of election results than had been possible before. Even though censuses usually take place only once every ten years, so that the data are somewhat out of date if applied to an election that is distant in time from the census date, the fact is that in terms of their main characteristics most constituencies change only very slowly. However, it is not only time that can undermine the utility of using census data to examine the effects of constituency social composition on patterns of party support. As pointed out previously, in 2010 new constituency boundaries for England, Wales and Northern Ireland, some representing significant changes from previous boundaries, came into effect, whilst the boundaries in Scotland were changed in 2005. For now, we present an analysis of the 2005 election on the basis of 2001 census data as it is most likely to give us an accurate picture of the relationships between social composition and constituency voting patterns in modern Britain.

Table 7.3 shows correlation coefficients measuring the strength of the association between, on the one hand, the shares of the vote gained by the Conservatives, Labour and the Liberals/Liberal Democrats across constituencies in 1966 and 2005 and, on the other, variables relating to the social characteristics of the constituencies. (For an exhaustive analysis of the social correlates of constituency voting patterns in the 1966 general election see Miller, 1977.) The coefficient of 0.71 for the Conservative share in 1966 and percentage of professional and managerial workers, for example, means that the greater the proportion of the latter in a constituency, the bigger the Conservative share of the vote. On the other hand, the greater the proportion of households with no car, the smaller was the Conservative share of the vote (coefficient is negative).

In 1966, the pattern of support for the Conservatives and Labour across constituencies was clearly structured by the socio-economic characteristics of the constituencies. The class variables provide the strongest correlations but all of the others, except the percentage of residents belonging to an ethnic minority, are statistically significant and in the expected direction. The absence of a significant association between major-party support and the proportion of a constituency's population belonging to ethnic minorities is a useful reminder of the pitfalls of inferring individual behaviour from aggregate statistics. We know from survey data that, as a matter of fact, ethnic minority voters disproportionately supported Labour. In most constituencies, however, they constituted such a small fraction of the electorate that variations in their numbers had no impact on the votes received by the parties and hence the correlations are very weak. The correlations between Liberal support in 1966 and these social characteristics are only moderate. The coefficients suggest that in general the pattern of Liberal support was a sort of pale reflection of that of the Conservatives but the level of Liberal support in a constituency was much less predictable on the basis of social characteristics than was support for the Conservatives or Labour.

Table 7.3 Correlations between socio-economic characteristics of constituencies and party shares of vote, 1966 and 2005

	1966			2005		
	% Con	% Lab	% Lib	% Con	% Lab	% Lib Dem
% professional and managerial	0.71	−0.82	0.24	0.57	−0.57	0.32
% manual workers	−0.68	0.71	−0.03*	−0.62	0.63	−0.33
% owner-occupiers	0.45	−0.49	0.18	0.61	−0.46	0.04*
% council tenants	−0.43	0.48	−0.13	−0.69	0.64	−0.23
% in agriculture	0.20	−0.46	0.55	0.31	−0.50	0.22
% households no car	−0.53	0.65	−0.30	−0.73	0.65	−0.16
% ethnic minority	0.01*	0.06*	−0.27	−0.22	0.24	−0.05*
Electors per hectare	−0.16	0.28	−0.34	−0.32	0.33	−0.03*
(No. of constituencies)	(617)	(617)	(310)	(625)	(625)	(625)

Notes: Asterisks indicate non-significant coefficients. The Speaker's seat is excluded in both cases and Staffordshire South (delayed election) and Wyre Forest (no Liberal Democrat) from the 2005 analysis. In 1966, 'ethnic minority' was measured as percentage born in the New Commonwealth and Pakistan.

Although the 2005 election was almost 40 years later, variations in party support across constituencies were patterned in much the same way as in 1966. The only major difference is that percentage ethnic minority was now significantly associated with variations in Conservative and Labour support (positively for Labour, negatively for the Conservatives). In 2005, variations in support for the Conservatives and Labour were less strongly related to the occupation variables, but most of the coefficients for the other variables are larger – indicating stronger associations – than they were in 1966. This reflects the divergences in the geography of party support discussed above. It is also the case that although the pattern of Liberal Democrat support across constituencies in 2005 was still similar to that for the Conservatives, it remained very weakly associated with variations in the socio-economic characteristics of constituencies.

The table shows that at the aggregate level there remain very strong associations between the class make-up of constituencies (measured by occupation and other class-related variables such as housing tenure) and the level of support for the Conservatives and Labour. This seems, at first sight, to contradict the argument advanced in previous chapters that, at the individual level, voting behaviour in Britain after 1970 was characterized by a loosening of the relationship between social class and party choice. In fact, however, the discrepancy between aggregate and individual data is more apparent than real. Although the strong positive correlation between the percentage of professional and managerial workers in a constituency and the percentage of Conservative voters means that the larger the proportion of these sorts of people in a constituency the greater is the Conservative share of the vote, this might reflect the fact that the more professionals and managers there are, the more *everyone,* irrespective of their class, votes Conservative. It tells us nothing about the extent of individual class voting.

In his work on this issue, Miller (1977, 1978, 1979) has shown that the relationship between the class character of constituencies and levels of support for the Conservative and Labour parties is stronger than would be expected on the basis of any given level of individual class voting. Where the Conservatives would be expected to do well on the basis of the class composition of the constituency, they do even better; where they would be expected to do badly, they do even worse. The same applies to Labour. Constituencies, in short, are more polarized politically than people. The correlations at aggregate level are stronger than the correlation at individual level. Once again this is compatible with individual dealignment. Indeed, if more and more working-class people vote Conservative in predominantly middle-class areas, and more and more middle-class people vote Labour in predominantly working-class areas, the effect would be to produce both increased polarization at the constituency level and decreased class voting at the level of the individual voter.

While the correlation coefficients shown in Table 7.3 are interesting and important, the various measures of social composition are themselves highly inter-correlated. Thus constituencies which have a large proportion of manual workers tend also to have large proportions of households with no car, council tenants and ethnic minority voters, as well as higher population density. As previously explained (Chapter 2), to sort out which variables are the most important influences on levels of party support and to assess the combined effects of different variables, we can undertake multivariate analysis by computing regression equations predicting party shares of the vote on the basis of the variables listed in Table 7.3. This form of analysis can select the combination of variables which gives the best prediction of the dependent variable. Remember that 'prediction' here has nothing to do with the future; what is 'predicted' is the share of the vote that the party concerned should have received in the actual election analysed, given its scores on the variables included in the equation. Equations for 2005 are shown in

Table 7.4   Multiple regression equations of party shares of vote in 2005

	% Conservative	% Labour	% Liberal Democrat
Constant	99.4	–111.1	65.4
% professional and managerial	–0.51	1.03	–
% manual	–0.82	1.35	–0.37
% owner-occupiers	–	0.57	–0.33
% council tenants	–0.16	0.45	–0.24
% in agriculture	1.14	–2.34	1.29
% households no car	–0.49	0.63	–
% ethnic minority electors per hectare	–0.07	0.10	–0.11
Scotland	–12.7	–4.96	–
Wales	–13.9	5.72	–3.9
R^2	0.755	0.715	0.201
(N)	(625)	(625)	(625)

Note: Only statistically significant coefficients are shown.

Table 7.4. Since the party system in Scotland and Wales is rather different from that found in England, due to the important role played by the SNP and Plaid Cymru, it would be helpful if that could be taken into account in the regression equations. The problem is that region (or in this case country) is a categorical variable. Different regions do not have different scores on 'regionality'. In order to overcome this problem, analysts frequently create what are called **dummy variables** by assigning scores of 0 to cases not in the category and 1 to cases which are. Here, for example, Scottish constituencies score 1 for the variable 'Scotland' and all other constituencies score zero. This is a somewhat artificial procedure and the created category has to be dichotomous (only two scores) but it does have the great advantage of allowing some categorical variables to be incorporated into ordinary regression analysis. In this case, two variables have been created: 'Scotland' and 'Wales'.

On the basis of each constituency's scores on the variables in the equations we can predict what each party's share of the vote should have been in 2005, given the constituency's characteristics. Thus, the Conservative percentage is predicted as:

99.4 – 0.51 (% professional and managerial) – 0.82 (% manual workers) – 0.16 (% council tenants) – 0.49 (% no car) – 12.7 (Scotland) – 13.9 (Wales)

The variables for which coefficients are shown in the table are significant: they make a contribution to explaining constituency variations in support for the relevant party, even when the other significant variables are taken into account. Where no coefficient is given the variable in question is not significant. The R^2 statistics show that 75.5 per cent of the variation in the Conservative share of the vote across constituencies is explained by the equation; for Labour the figure is 71.5 per cent but for the Liberal Democrats only 20.1 per cent. The first two figures are respectable but even in these cases it is clear these regional and socio-economic factors are not the whole story (about a quarter of the variation remains unexplained) in accounting for spatial variations in Conservative and Labour support; for the Liberal Democrats they are a relatively small part of the story.

Having established the equation that best predicts a party's share of the vote across constituencies we can then calculate a predicted score for each constituency: what a party *should have* scored given the constituency's socio-economic characteristics. Comparing this with the *actual* share of vote obtained we have the **residual,** which is the difference in each constituency between the share of the vote predicted by the equations and the actual share in the election. Looking at the residual scores we can easily identify the constituencies where each party performed exceptionally well or exceptionally poorly. Thus, Labour underperformed most in Birmingham Sparkbrook, Blaenau Gwent and Bethnal Green and Bow while the Conservatives did so in City of Durham, Ceredigion and Hornsey and Wood Green. The Liberal Democrats overperformed most in Ross, Cromarty and Skye, Birmingham Yardley and Harrogate and Knaresborough. A look at the 2005 election results in these constituencies should reveal why they produced results which deviated sharply from the norm.

While examining residuals for individual constituencies is interesting, they can also be used to explore reasons for cross-constituency variations that are not captured by the variables in the original equations. In this case, the residual scores suggest that the particular electoral context in constituencies – the parties which are in contention – clearly causes levels of party support to deviate sharply from the levels predicted on the basis of social characteristics. This can be seen in Table 7.5, which presents the mean residual scores for each party in differing electoral contexts. The Conservatives did much worse than predicted in seats where Labour and the Liberal Democrats were in contention, and Labour much worse where the contest was between the Conservatives and Liberal Democrats. The Liberal Democrats themselves performed

Table 7.5 Mean residuals for share of vote in 2005 in differing electoral contexts

	First two parties in 2001		
	Conservative/ Labour	*Conservative/ Liberal Democrat*	*Labour/Liberal Democrat*
Conservative	1.5	−1.3	−7.4
Labour	2.2	−8.6	−0.3
Liberal Democrats	−3.5	10.5	9.5
(N)	(413)	(101)	(60)

much better than expected in these two contexts but rather worse when the Conservatives and Labour were the top two parties. If we add three dummy variables to the equations to take account of these electoral contexts then the R^2 figures increase significantly for the Conservative and Labour vote share (to 0.806 and 0.803 respectively) while the figure for the Liberal Democrat share jumps to 0.600. In each case, then, the ability to predict the party's share of the vote in constituencies is markedly increased.

With constituency-level analysis we do need to be careful not to ascribe broad, aggregate findings to individual voters, or, in other words, commit the **ecological fallacy** in describing our results. All that we can say with this sort of research is how particular constituency characteristics tend to predict broad voting patterns and electoral outcomes. For example, the fact that the British National Party polls more heavily in areas with higher immigration does not, of course, mean that immigrants are more likely to vote for the party. Such an aggregate-level tendency does not tell us about the kind of people who vote for the BNP; it tells us about the kinds of constituencies in which the party polls strongly.

Tactical voting

The data in Table 7.5 suggest that constituency variations are partly explained by what has come to be called 'tactical voting'. This occurs when voters do not vote for the party that they prefer most, usually because it has no chance of winning the particular constituency, but vote for their second preference since that party is in a better position to defeat the party which the voter dislikes most. An alert Labour supporter in Westmorland and Lonsdale in 2005, for example, would have been aware – or have had it drawn to his or her attention by the local Liberal Democrat campaign – that Labour had no chance of defeating the incumbent Conservative and that it might be more sensible, therefore, to vote for the Liberal Democrats who up to that point had regularly claimed second place. In Scotland and Wales, opportunities for tactical voting are even greater since the SNP and Plaid Cymru add an extra dimension to patterns of electoral competition.

Interest in tactical voting emerged in the 1980s and its extent is relevant to the main themes that we have discussed in previous chapters. We would expect voters to be more willing to vote tactically when they are dealigned rather than strongly aligned with one party or another (see Galbraith and Rae, 1989). In their report on the 1987 election, Heath *et al.* (1991, ch. 4) reported that in both 1983 and 1987 around 6 per cent of voters said that the main reason for their choice of party was tactical: that is, when asked in the BES surveys to indicate the main reason for their choice of party, they selected from the options offered: 'I really preferred another party but it had no chance of winning in this constituency'. (Other analysts, using more BES survey questions to classify voters as tactical or not, suggest that the proportion of tactical voters in 1987 was 17 per cent overall and was higher among those who were better educated, had weak party identification or lived in a constituency where tactical voting made sense: see Niemi, Whitten and Franklin, 1992.) Even on the somewhat narrow definition originally devised by Heath *et al.,* however, the proportion of tactical voters is creeping up: it was 9 per cent in both 1997 and 2001, 12 per cent in 2005 and slipped ever so slightly to 11 per cent in 2010. Moreover, these voters would have been largely concentrated in seats where the structure of electoral competition lent itself to tactical voting so that in these the percentages would have been much larger.

Tactical voting is clearly reflected in election results. Although it can and does involve switching between all competing parties, Curtice and Steed's analysis of the 1997 results showed that 'voters exhibited a striking tendency to opt for whichever of the two opposition parties appeared best placed to defeat the Conservatives locally' (1997: 309). In the 2001 election, tactical switching by former Liberal Democrats helped to explain Labour's relatively good performances in their most marginal seats (Curtice and Steed, 2001: 321–2). In 2005, however, there seemed to be an increased willingness on the part of Conservative supporters to switch to the Liberal Democrats in order to defeat incumbent Labour MPs (Curtice and Steed, 2005: 243–5). In 2010 Labour seemed to make an appeal for Liberal Democrats to vote tactically, with Gordon Brown declaring, 'If people don't want a Conservative government, then they must make sure that they don't allow the Conservative [candidate in their constituency] in' (McFarlane, 2010). On the Sunday before the election in 2010, *The Independent* was more explicit, suggesting that 'readers should consider voting tactically on Thursday...we are asking voters in 85 key constituencies to vote for the candidate best placed to frustrate David Cameron' (*The Independent*, 1 May 2010).

Localities and neighbourhoods

In their pioneering study of British voting behaviour, Butler and Stokes (1974: 130–7) provided survey evidence showing that the social composition of the locality in which people lived affected their party choice. Middle-class people living in mining communities were more likely to be Labour supporters, and those living in seaside resorts were more likely to be Conservatives, than the middle class as a whole; Labour support was stronger among working-class people in mining areas and weaker among the working class in seaside resorts than in the working class as a whole. Using NOP data, Butler and Stokes extended their analysis to cover a number of constituencies and showed that there was a tendency for local areas to become politically homogeneous. The more middle-class a constituency, the larger the proportion of the middle class which voted Conservative; the more working-class a constituency, the larger the proportion of the working class which voted Labour. Thus Butler and Stokes found evidence of a constituency effect at the individual level which was later demonstrated at aggregate level by Miller (see above).

Although Butler and Stokes described this as an effect of the local political environment, most constituencies are not natural communities; instead, they are simply slices of cities or other urban areas, combinations of towns and villages with little in common, or other contiguous areas which happen to include a convenient number of electors to form a constituency. The local political environment, it can be argued, is more local than the constituency and subsequent analyses have focused on neighbourhoods. Harrop, Heath and Openshaw (1992) used data relating to census enumeration districts (which typically contain about 190 households) to categorize the neighbourhoods lived in by 1987 BES respondents and found compelling evidence of a 'neighbourhood effect'. Whereas about 70 per cent of middle-class home owners living in 'select suburbs' voted Conservative, around 43 per cent of the same sort of people living in neighbourhoods characterized by working-class terraced housing did so. The effect of neighbourhood type persisted even when a variety of factors such as the voter's class, housing tenure, income and trade union membership were controlled. Indeed, Harrop, Heath and Openshaw's data showed (p. 105) that 'neighbourhood type proves to be just about the best single predictor of vote ... knowing a person's address tells us at least as much about how he or she will vote as finding out about his or her class or [housing] tenure'.

A similar, although more complicated and fuller, analysis of neighbourhood and party choice in the 1997 election was undertaken by Johnston *et al.* (2000). Johnston and colleagues were able to place BES respondents in a variety of 'neighbourhoods' ranging from their immediate vicinity (nearest 500 persons) to the constituency as a whole. They found that there was a neighbourhood effect at every level (even after controlling for a variety of individual characteristics and the electoral context). The lower the status of the 'neighbourhood' , the fewer people of all classes and types voted Conservative; the higher the 'neighbourhood' status, the more they voted Conservative. Johnston *et al.* suggest, however, that the strongest neighbourhood effect is found in 'neighbourhoods' comprising 2,500 to 5,000 residents. It is, therefore, very much a locality effect rather than a constituency-level effect.

Explaining the impact of the local political environment

In their original discussion of this subject, Butler and Stokes suggested that the tendency of localities to become politically homogeneous was caused by voters recognizing and conforming to local political values. The mechanisms by which this worked were informal: face-to-face contacts in pubs, clubs, shops, workplaces and so on. If almost everyone one meets appears to support the same party, then there is strong pressure on an individual to support that party too. A similar explanation relating to constituency effects was given by Miller (1977), who argues that the crucial feature of a voter's local environment is the concentration (or absence) of what he calls 'core' classes. These are 'controllers' (employers and managers) and 'anti-controllers' (manual workers who are trade union members). Concentrations of these classes set the tone, as it were, for an area and their influence is reinforced by personal contacts. As Miller (p. 65) puts it: 'Those who speak together vote together.' On the other hand, Dunleavy (1979: 413) poured scorn on the implication that 'political alignment brushes off on people by rubbing shoulders in the street' or that people picked up political signals in the bus queue or across the garden fence.

For some time the mechanisms by which people came to adopt locally dominant political norms remained a matter of speculation. In their 1992 article, however, Harrop, Heath and Openshaw went on to investigate various possibilities, including political discussion between neighbours, party activity in the locality, and parental partisanship. Their data do not offer much support for these suggestions but do suggest that there is evidence of neighbourhood self-selection. They say (p. 118) that 'consciously or not, the mobile minority migrate to politically congenial neighbourhoods'. In other words, when people move house they tend to move to areas which are predominantly of their own party colour. It is hard to believe that people weigh up the political complexion of an area to which they intend to move, however, and Harrop, Heath and Openshaw acknowledge that this pattern of behaviour is likely to be an unintended consequence of other consider- ations. They conclude (p. 118) that, while the evidence of a neighbour- hood effect is clear, 'when we look for the mechanisms of neighbourhood influence we are less successful'.

More recently, however, Pattie and Johnston (1999, 2001) have examined in detail BES data on political conversation, considering who talks to whom and what the effects are. As it turns out, not many people talk to their neighbours about politics (only 3 per cent) but they do with their spouses (48 per cent), other family (38 per cent), friends (24 per cent) and workmates (16 per cent) (see Pattie and Johnston, 1999: 887). In respect of vote switching between 1987 and 1992, Pattie and Johnston conclude (p. 889) that 'political conversation forms a distinct context within which people evaluate the parties and decide who to support. Conversations with supporters of a particular party encourage respondents to vote for it too.' In the context of the Labour landslide, the results for 1997 are less clear-cut but, even so, using panel data Pattie and Johnston (2001) show that conversations were associated with attitude changes and, to an extent, with vote changes. At last, it appears, we have evidence to support Miller's assertion that 'Those who speak together vote together'.

Examining the mobilization of minorities, Fieldhouse and Cutts (2007, 2008) have found evidence that as the diversity and size of the minority population increases, so does the proportion of those minori- ties registered to vote and actually turning out to vote. Looking specif- ically at British Asian communities, they find evidence for a 'mobilising effect', where people living amongst others of a similar ethno-religious minority background tend to be encouraged to participate in electoral processes: 'As the Asian population density increases, so to does their turnout' (2008: 545).

The neighbourhood effect underlies and helps to explain constituency effects, since constituencies are mostly collections of neighbourhoods. Arguably, constituency effects are then translated into regional and urban–rural divergences. This is, of course, not the whole story in terms of explaining the kind of regional variations and urban–rural differences discussed above; nonetheless it appears to be a significant piece in the puzzle of explaining long-standing spatial variations in party choice. In the next section, however, we turn from discussing the causes of spatial variation to a consideration of its consequences, particularly in relation to the operation of the electoral system.

Electoral systems in Britain

All voting takes place in the context of a particular electoral system. There has to be some agreed way of aggregating votes to produce a result. Votes indicate individuals' preferences and in public elections these have to be translated into seats (in Parliament, local councils or whatever) by some formula. There are many different electoral systems: in the 1990s, a cross-national study found 70 different systems in 27 democracies (Lijphart, 1994; for a useful introduction to the operation of different systems see Farrell, 2001). In evaluating electoral systems, or making an argument in favour of one system or another, it is important to consider what a particular (or an ideal) system is, or should be, for. What is it, or should it be, designed to achieve? There are at least four simple answers to this question:

(a) to enable the representation of voters' opinions in rough proportion to their strength in the electorate;
(b) to allow for the representation of geographically defined areas;
(c) to decisively confer power on a team of leaders or a party;
(d) to enable the electorate to hold a government accountable and replace it.

No system can do all of these at the same time, and ultimately a preference for one sort or another comes down to making a value judgement about which of these purposes should be given greatest priority.

In Britain, historically almost all public elections were conducted under what is formally known as the Single Member, Simple Plurality system (SMSP). Each electoral district (constituency) has a single representative and he or she wins by virtue of getting most votes (a simple plurality) in the area concerned. This is more commonly known – in an analogy with horse racing – as the first-past-the-post system (FPTP). For a long time, interest in the possibility of changing the British electoral system was confined to a small band of enthusiasts (who might be labelled 'anoraks' by unfriendly critics) and few took the possibility seriously. The Liberal Democrats, however, had long advocated for a public vote, or referendum, to be held on the question of whether to change the electoral system used for electing MPs. Following the May 2010 election, the Conservative–Liberal Democrat coalition agreement allowed for a referendum asking voters to decide whether they wanted to retain the traditional FPTP electoral system or switch to the alternative vote (AV) system. The AV electoral system allows voters to rank candidates contesting an election in order of preference and then allocates those preferences so that the candidate who wins the election has a minimum of 50 per cent of the votes cast. The AV referendum failed with a thumping 68 per cent voting to retain FPTP. Yet a variety of other electoral systems are in use across the UK. As part of its devolution programme, the Labour government elected in 1997 introduced new electoral systems for the Scottish Parliament and the Welsh and Northern Ireland Assemblies, and also brought in new

Table 7.6   UK electoral systems today

System	Body elected
Single Member, Simple Plurality	House of Commons
	Some English/Welsh local authorities
Multi-Member, Simple Plurality	Some English/Welsh local authorities
Additional Member System	Scottish Parliament
	Welsh Assembly
	London Assembly
Single Transferable Vote	Northern Ireland Assembly
	All Scottish Councils
Regional Party (Closed) Lists	European Parliament
Supplementary Vote	Mayors in England

electoral systems for the European Parliament and for electing mayors in England and the London Assembly. The various electoral systems now in operation in the UK are listed in Table 7.6.

Criticisms of first-past-the-post

Why has there been so much recent debate about, and activity in relation to, electoral systems in Britain? Two major reasons relate to how the FPTP system has operated in translating votes into seats, but other criticisms focus on the activities of the parties and effects on voters.

The first criticism is that FPTP is simply unfair. The shares of seats that parties receive do not reflect their shares of votes; in particular, the Liberal Democrats have been severely underrepresented. In the five elections from 1992 they won, respectively, 18.3, 17.2, 18.8, 22.6 and 23.0 per cent of the votes but only 3.1, 7.2, 8.1, 9.9 and 8.8 per cent of the seats. Put another way, in 2010 the number of votes cast for the Liberal Democrats per seat won was 119,944, while for the Conservatives it was 34,940 and for Labour 33,370. Compared to the Conservatives, the Liberal Democrats garnered 3.4 times as many votes for every seat they won. The next biggest party in terms of popular support (UKIP) won 919,546 votes but no seats at all.

These sorts of discrepancies between votes and seats occur because the geographical distribution of a party's support is almost as important as its level: the system rewards parties with concentrations of support and penalizes those whose support is more evenly spread. Thus the system regularly produces disproportionality between votes and seats and, indeed, on two occasions (1951 and February 1974) the party winning most votes did not win most seats and thus 'lost' the election. In the past few elections, this disproportionality has strongly advantaged Labour to the extent that commentators agree that the system has been biased in Labour's favour (see, for example, Blau, 2001; Curtice, 2001; Johnston *et al.,* 2001; Johnston, Rossiter and Pattie, 2006), yet this bias is by no means fixed and can vary over time as constituency boundaries are redrawn to reflect changes in population (but not necessarily to fix other problems underlying the bias in the FPTP system). In 2005, under the previous constituency boundaries, for example, the Conservatives polled more votes than Labour in England but won 92 fewer seats. If, at the election after 2005, the Conservatives had achieved a uniform swing across the country of 1.5 per cent then that would have brought them level with Labour in terms of votes, yet

Labour would have had 111 more seats in the Commons. In fact, the Conservatives would have had to be 6.4 points ahead of Labour before they would have drawn level in terms of seats (Curtice, Fisher and Steed, 2005: 251). Following the 2010 election Michael Thrasher examined the multiple sources of electoral bias under FPTP and found that with the redrawn constituency boundaries Labour still benefits from FPTP, but not nearly as much as it did previously. Thrasher and his colleagues found that the new constituency boundaries cut Labour's advantage by 20 seats, while the Conservatives improved to a positive advantage of 12 seats (they previously had a disadvantage of –30 seats). The Liberal Democrats saw their disadvantage increase to –76 seats (Thrasher, 2010). The bias of the FPTP system in favour of Labour arises for three main reasons. First, seats won by Labour tend to have smaller electorates than those won by the Conservatives. Second, turnout is generally lower – fewer votes are cast – in seats that Labour wins. Third, the Labour vote happens to be more efficiently distributed across constituencies in that they win quite a lot of seats by fairly narrow margins rather than piling up huge majorities in a smaller number of bastions. Paradoxically, the Conservatives are strongly opposed to electoral reform (at present) even though they are severely penalized – at least relative to Labour – by the current system.

Supporters of FPTP see its unfairness or disproportionality as a virtue. In particular, it is claimed that in translating votes to seats the system exaggerates the lead of the winning party in a predictable way and thus ensures that the winner has a clear majority. Critics have suggested, however, that the changes in the geographical distribution of party support discussed above have led to a situation in which the system cannot be relied upon to do what it is supposed to do (see Curtice and Steed, 1982, 1986). The 2010 result clearly demonstrates that FPTP with more than two parties does not always produce a clear majority in Parliament. However, in the 1950s and before, the share of seats that a party was going to obtain in the House of Commons, on the basis of a given share of the total national vote, could be predicted fairly well by using the 'cube rule' (sometimes also called the 'cube law'). If the share of votes between two parties were in the ratio A:B, then the share of seats would be in the ratio $A^3:B^3$. Thus, if the ratio of the two-party vote were 3:2, then the ratio of seats would be 27:8 (3 x 3 x 3:2 x 2 x 2). In other words, a party which obtained 60 per cent of the votes would get 77 per cent of the seats, while the other party with 40 per cent of the votes would get only 23 per cent of the seats. Clearly, then, the winning party's lead in terms of votes was greatly exaggerated by the electoral system when it was translated into seats, and it was widely assumed that the cube rule was an integral aspect of FPTP. In fact, the cube rule only worked if the votes of the major parties were geographically distributed across constituencies in a particular way, and regional and urban/rural divergence from 1955 to 1997 significantly changed the distributions. (For the cube rule to work, the distribution of the vote shares of each party across constituencies had to be close to a normal distribution with a standard deviation of 13.7.)

In general, the effect of regional divergence was to make Labour seats more safely Labour, and Conservative seats more safely Conservative. As a result, there were fewer and fewer marginal seats. In 1955, some 166 seats could be classed as marginal but by 1983 there were only 80 (Curtice and Steed, 1986: 214). There were thus fewer seats for a party to gain for each percentage point swing in its favour, and fewer to be lost by incumbents for each point of swing against their party. Much bigger swings in votes were now required for the party in opposition to gain enough seats to achieve a majority in the House of Commons. The exaggerative quality of the electoral system declined such that the ratio of seats to votes could no longer be predicted by a 'cube rule', or even a 'square rule'. Indeed, by the 1992 election the electoral system failed to produce any exaggerative effect at all. The ratio of Conservative to Labour votes was 55:45 and the ratio of Conservative to Labour seats won was also 55:45 (see Curtice, 1992). In the extraordinary circumstances of the 1997 Labour landslide, however, the ratio of Conservative to Labour seats was once again close to fulfilling the cube rule, while in both 2001 and 2005 there was an even greater disparity than the cube rule would imply. Clearly, the operation of the system is not predictable; in the last three elections it is not simply that there was a 'winner's bonus' but rather a clear bias in favour of Labour.

From the point of view of the voters, a major criticism of FPTP is that it results in many votes being wasted. In 2010, only around 47 per cent of voters voted for a winning candidate; the votes of the remaining 53 per cent could be said to have been wasted in that they did not help to elect anyone. If the definition of wasted votes is extended to include those which only serve to pile up large majorities for one party or another then the percentage of votes wasted would be even larger. It is undoubtedly the case that many voters have voted in general elections for all of their lives without ever voting for a winner. It could be argued that these voters are, therefore, unrepresented and that there is little incentive for people to vote in constituencies where the same party always wins. In addition, critics suggest that FPTP limits the choices that voters can make. They have to plump for one candidate or another (the one selected by local party members), whereas under some other systems they can rank their preferences or indicate their support for a particular candidate of their party.

The electoral system also affects how parties campaign. Increasingly campaigns are focused on target or key seats, and the major parties almost ignore constituencies in which they have little chance of winning (see Denver *et al.,* 2002). This sort of skewed campaigning would be avoided if all votes counted equally no matter where they were cast.

Two final (more general) points of criticism are worth mentioning. First, because FPTP produces even greater disproportionality at regional level than over the country as a whole, Conservative and Labour representation in the House of Commons is heavily weighted to specific areas. After the 2010 election, 66 per cent of Labour MPs represented constituencies in Scotland, Wales and the North of England, compared with 17 per cent of Conservative MPs. On the other hand, 53 per cent of Conservative MPs were from constituencies in the South of England outside London, compared with 4 per cent of Labour MPs. Second, it might be argued that although the system generally produces majority governments (but, again, not in 2010), which can then operate as almost an 'elected dictatorship', governments actually lack legitimacy since they have not been voted in by a majority. Indeed, in the elections of 1992, 1997, 2001 and 2005 the percentages of the eligible electorate in the UK as a whole (rather than of those who voted) that voted for the party which went on to form the government were, respectively, 32.6, 30.8, 24.2 and 21.6. Looking at 2010, even if we are extremely generous and combine the votes for the two coalition partners, only 38 per cent of the total electorate voted for one of the two governing parties (23 per cent voted Conservative and 15 per cent voted Liberal Democrat). That is not exactly a solid basis on which to govern.

In defence of first-past-the-post

Although these criticisms have persuaded many people that reform of the electoral system for Westminster is long overdue, FPTP still has its defenders among academics as well as practising politicians (Chandler, 1982; Hain, 1998). Five main points are frequently made in defence of the system.

First, it is easy for voters to operate and understand. Survey evidence relating to the use of the Additional Member System in the Scottish Parliament election of 1999 suggests that operating it was not much of a problem: only 10 per cent found filling in the ballot papers very or fairly difficult. On the other hand, the translation of votes into seats under other systems can be complicated, and 48 per cent of Scottish respondents found it very or fairly difficult to understand how the allocation of seats was worked out (Paterson *et al.,* 2001).

Second, the system maintains a clear link between MPs and their constituents. This link is particularly valued by MPs themselves and their attachment to it represents a major stumbling block to radical reform, since any change would have to be approved by MPs elected under the current system. It was for this reason that the Jenkins Commission's proposed alternative to FPTP still allowed the great majority of MPs to be elected directly from constituencies.

Third, FPTP tends to prevent 'fringe' or extremist parties gaining representation. Whereas a more proportional system might allow the BNP or UKIP to win a few seats, they are effectively excluded under FPTP, since the voters are encouraged to concentrate on the parties having a reasonable chance of winning their constituency. In addition, it is suggested that the major parties are forced by the system to be moderate since they are aware that dropping only a few points in vote share can result in the loss of many seats.

Fourth, alternatives to FPTP give too much power and influence to small parties. Since neither of the major parties would win a majority under a more proportional system, a small party for which not many people voted could effectively decide who formed the government. Thus FPTP militates against coalitions. A single party can form the government and thus the lines of responsibility are clear. The electors know which party to blame if things go awry or to reward if it is seen to be successful.

Finally, an associated argument claims that a strength of FPTP is that it enables the voters to choose the government. In proportional systems, which do not create majorities in legislatures where none exists among the voters, there is often a gap between an election and the formation of a government during which the politicians negotiate. Deals are struck without reference to the voters, and governments emerge which sometimes comprise surprising coalition partners.

Arguments about the electoral system go backwards and forwards (proponents of change could produce counter-arguments to the five listed in defence of FPTP), and there is certainly more interest in the subject than there used to be. As indicated above, however, coming to a decision about which electoral system is 'best', or whether the current Westminster system should be reformed, is ultimately a question of values. Is it more important to have a governing party with a majority or to give fair representation to various shades of opinion? Is it acceptable to make it difficult for fringe parties to win seats? Is maintaining the link between MPs and constituents more valuable than having a system which allows more voters to have an influence on who is elected? People will have different views on these questions and these views will lead them to different conclusions about the advisability or otherwise of retaining FPTP for Westminster elections.

Voting under different electoral systems

There have now been four rounds of elections to the Scottish Parliament and the National Assembly for Wales (1999, 2003, 2007 and 2011). In these elections a modified 'additional member', or mixed-member proportional, electoral system is used. Electors are asked to cast two votes. The first is to elect a constituency representative under the familiar FPTP rules. In addition, however, they vote for a party list within regions (eight in Scotland and five in Wales), and these votes are used to elect 'additional' or 'top-up' members after taking account of the number of constituency seats that each party has already won in the region concerned (see Curtice and Steed, 2000).

In both countries the electoral system has helped to make elections and the subsequent governing arrangements interesting. In Scotland in both 1999 and 2003 no party had an overall majority and a Labour–Liberal Democrat coalition was formed to govern the country. The 2007 election saw the Scottish National Party (SNP) beat Labour by just one seat, giving the SNP the opportunity to form a minority government. Having shown themselves to be a viable governing party, the SNP went on to win an unprecedented absolute majority in the 2011 election – something that was not supposed to be able to happen under the additional member system.

In Wales, a coalition was eventually formed after the 1999 elections but in 2003 Labour won exactly half of the seats in the Assembly and on that basis was able to govern alone. In 2007, while Plaid Cymru gained seats, Labour remained the largest party in the Assembly. After the dust settled on coalition negotiations, Labour and Plaid Cymru agreed to form a coalition government. The 2011 election again saw

Labour securing exactly half of the seats in the Assembly and forming a government on its own. The additional member electoral system, therefore, has importantly affected the outcomes of the elections and subsequent political developments in the two countries.

Surveys have found that electors in both countries rather like the AMS system and recognize its advantages, although in Scotland at least there was some decline in the popularity of the system between 1999 and 2003 (Curtice *et al.*, 2000; Curtice, 2004). Voting behaviour has also clearly been affected by the new system. In Scotland, about 20 per cent of voters 'split their tickets' in 1999 by voting for different parties in the constituency and list contests; the figure was around 29 per cent in 2003 and 27 per cent in 2007 (Carman and Johns, 2010). Clear evidence of the effects of this is that in 2003 there were 7 Greens, 6 Scottish Socialists and one Senior Citizens' Party representative elected on list votes. In addition, opinion poll evidence suggests that Scottish voters bring different considerations to bear when deciding which party to support in Scottish elections and UK-wide general elections. Scottish opinion polls regularly report that larger proportions intend to vote SNP and smaller proportions to vote Labour in the former than in the latter. Analysis of survey data leads Paterson *et al.* (2001, ch. 3) to argue that, in the context of Scottish Parliament elections, more voters are concerned to support a party (the SNP) which they think is more likely to 'stand up for Scotland', to promote and to advance the country's interests within the UK, than is the case at general elections. The same is true of Wales. Here, about 25 per cent of voters 'split their tickets' in 1999 and once again there is evidence that many voters did so for understandable reasons (Curtice and Steed, 2000). The surprisingly good performance of Plaid Cymru in 1999 and 2007 – although no doubt influenced by the immediate context of the election – seems also to indicate a willingness on the part of voters to desert their normal party in the context of Assembly elections. In summary, then, both the electoral system and devolution itself appear to have influenced the voting decisions of significant proportions of the Scottish and Welsh electorates.

Londoners have also had experience of using a novel electoral system in elections for a Mayor and Assembly in 2000, 2004 and 2008. In these cases three votes could be cast: one for the Mayor (in which voters could indicate a first and second preference among candidates), one for a constituency Assembly member and one for a party list for the Assembly. If turnout is a guide, then London voters have been less enamoured of the new way of voting than the Scots and Welsh, though Londoners seem to be warming to the city's elections: only 31 per cent voted in the Assembly election in 2000, 36 per cent in 2004 and 45 per cent in 2008. It should be remembered, however, that these are essentially local elections. In addition, significant proportions of those who voted did not appear to understand what they were being asked to do since in these elections there was a much larger number of rejected or invalid ballot papers than would be normal in first-past-the-post elections. Nonetheless, the mayoral results show, overall, perfectly logical patterns of first and second preferences. As far as Assembly voting is concerned, about one-third of voters chose different parties at constituency and list level in 2000 and about 40 per cent in 2004 (Dunleavy, Margetts and Bastow, 2001; Margetts, van Heerde and Dunleavy, 2005). The effect of using the system was to produce fairer results. The FPTP constituency elections in 2008 produced 8 Conservative and 6 Labour Assembly members but, as a result of the list votes, 3 Conservative, 2 Labour, 3 Liberal Democrat, 2 Green and 1 British National Party (BNP) members were added. In concluding their detailed study of the 2001 London elections, Dunleavy, Margetts and Bastow argue that the FPTP system has severely constrained the choices that voters can make and conclude (p. 32) that 'London voters have complex preference structures which they were able to signal in sophisticated ways … using the opportunities provided by the [new] electoral systems.'

Conclusion

These are, then, exciting times for electoral anoraks. The 2010 election saw the FPTP system produce a coalition government in Westminster; the 2011 Scottish Parliament election saw the Additional Member system produce a clear majority for the SNP. While we may be able to generalize about the outcomes usually produced under different electoral systems, we must remember that it is the voters who actually cast ballots – and sometimes voters do things that surprise us.

What is certain is that the context provided by the electoral system affects electoral behaviour. It is worth remembering that the influential Michigan model focusing on party identification, and the Butler–Stokes model derived from it, were both developed in the context of FPTP elections. When the electoral system does not require voters to plump for a single party then the usefulness of party identification in explaining party choice is likely to be reduced. With more choices to be made, more subtle explanations are required.

There is no doubt that the ways in which electoral systems – especially FPTP – translate votes into seats is strongly affected by the geographical or spatial distribution of party support. Changes in that distribution have also been one of the key features of British elections over the past 50 years. It is something of an exaggeration to say that 'Geography reigns - supreme!' , which is how Johnston *et al.* conclude their (2001) study of the operation of the electoral system in Britain. Nonetheless, in electoral studies, geography does matter.

Elections and Party Choice in Contemporary Britain

One of the pleasures – and, occasionally, frustrations – of studying elections is that they keep happening. No sooner, it seems, have the data from one general election been collected, analysed and pored over than people are looking forward to the next. In addition, once every five years there are elections to the European Parliament, and these tend to fall conveniently (for analysts, if not governments) between Westminster Parliament elections (2004, 2009 and so on). There are now also elections to the Scottish Parliament and Welsh Assembly and, if that were not enough, there are annual rounds of local elections. 'Elections galore!', one might say, and certainly more than enough to satisfy the keenest enthusiast and keep electoral analysts busy. The fact that there is always another election just around the corner means that there can be no 'last word' as far as explaining voting behaviour is concerned. Explanations of how individuals come to make their choices have to be refined; the outcomes of particular elections require explanation. The simple passage of time – with associated social changes and changes in the parties themselves – means that well-established theories have to be re-examined. In addition, the introduction of more proportional electoral systems has meant that voting decisions have become more complex; there is more to understand than there used to be.

In this concluding chapter, we review the theories of party choice introduced in Chapter 1 and suggest how election outcomes are best explained in modern circumstances. Before doing so, however, it is worth making a few comments about the role of theories in electoral analysis. These theories – frequently also called models – attempt to provide explanations as to why people vote the way that they do (and whether they vote at all). It is clear, however, that no theory can possibly account for the millions of individual decisions made in an election. Over the whole electorate there is an immense variety of motives for party choice; individual voters also frequently have a number of different considerations in mind when marking their ballot paper for one party or another. Models of party choice are bound, therefore, to be partial, to simplify and to generalize. Nonetheless, they provide a framework within which relevant data can be collected and interpreted. Thus the sociological model suggested that belonging to certain social groups importantly affects party choice. Consequently, voting surveys ask respondents for the relevant details and analysts can check whether or not the claims made by the theory are borne out by the data. Other models point to different questions that should be asked. Models offer, therefore, different perspectives on the same problem, but none is going to tell the whole story.

Explaining party choice

The sociological approach and the Michigan model

The basis for this theory is that people vote for a party because of their social location. Different groups have different interests and different parties seek to represent those interests. However, there is broad agreement among those who study elections that the link between the social characteristics of individual voters and their party choice has weakened over the past 40 years or so. In the BES study of the 2001 election, Clarke *et al.* (2004, ch. 3), having described the weakening of the alignment between class and party, show that there has been no corresponding increase in the explanatory power of other social and demographic characteristics and conclude that, overall, what they call the 'sociological approach' has declined in importance. 'Those wishing to understand electoral choice in present-day Britain', they say, 'must look elsewhere' (p. 123). Results from the 2005 survey gave Clarke and his colleagues no reason to revise this conclusion. Nonetheless, they did find evidence that some different social groups tend to vote in significantly different ways (2009, p. 164).

Table 8.1 shows, firstly, that in 2010 those with manual occupations were still more likely to vote Labour and less likely to vote Conservative than routine non-manual workers and those – the largest group – with professional and managerial occupations. There is also a class dimension to support for the Liberal Democrats, who were weakest among manual workers. These differences are much narrower than in the heyday of class voting but they are still appreciable – more, perhaps, than simply 'embellishment and detail'. At the same time, the results for

Table 8.1 Social characteristics and party choice in 2010 (row percentages)

	Conservative	Labour	Liberal Democrat	(N)
Occupational class				
Professional and managerial	40	26	26	(905)
Other non-manual	38	29	24	(524)
Manual	25	45	17	(570)
Housing tenure				
Owner-occupier	40	29	22	(1,734)
Tenant	21	43	22	(522)
Age				
18–24	25	30	35	(95)
25–34	29	38	24	(252)
35–44	32	33	25	(394)
45–54	32	32	26	(400)
55–64	37	30	21	(420)
65+	43	32	16	(708)
Sex				
Male	36	31	20	(1,066)
Female	35	33	24	(1,214)
Religion				
None	31	31	27	(1,000)
Anglican	50	26	18	(679)
Scots Presbyterian	23	39	19	(144)
Roman Catholic	28	45	18	(200)
Nonconformist	40	29	22	(98)
Non-Christian	26	47	20	(113)
Ethnicity				
White British	37	31	22	(2,095)
Indian	24	60	15	(409)
Pakistani	12	60	24	(459)
Bangladeshi	17	69	11	(191)
Black Caribbean	8	78	12	(371)
Black African	7	85	7	(300)

Note: Rows do not total 100 because votes for 'others' are not shown. The BES survey overestimated Labour's share of the vote (by 2.4 points) and slightly underestimated the shares obtained by the Conservatives and Liberal Democrats. What matters here, however, is not the precise shares of votes indicated but the differences between the various groups.

Sources: BES 2010 face-to-face surveys; EMBES 2010 (for the five ethnic minority groups).

housing tenure provide some support for the notion that a sectoral (public/private) cleavage has partly supplanted the occupational (manual/non-manual) cleavage. The great majority of voters own (or are buying) their homes and so it is not surprising that the voting of owner-occupiers in 2010 was similar to the overall outcome of the election. However, those who rent, either from the local council or privately (which includes many young people), are strongly anti-Conservative and pro-Labour.

The figures relating to age groups are a little more complicated but also show clear patterns. Labour's support was fairly uniform across these categories but support for the Conservatives tends to increase and that for the Liberal Democrats to decline with age. The likelihood is that the Liberal Democrats' strong showing in the youngest age group – in which they outpolled the Conservatives – reflected a particular appeal to students (an appeal that may well have waned sharply for reasons discussed in the conclusion to this chapter). The poor Liberal Democrat showing in the oldest age category is understandable given that these voters were socialized during the heyday of two-party politics and would be expected, as per the Michigan model, to be set in those ways. However, the fact that Conservative support increased with age in 2010, just as it did in 1970 (see Chapter 3, p. 60), suggests that this tendency is to be explained in terms of 'life cycles' rather than 'political genera-tions' since it has persisted over 40 years as different generations have moved through the electorate. Meanwhile, in line with recent trends, there is no sign of the traditional tendency for women to be more Conservative than men. The only perceptible sex differences concern the smaller parties: women were more likely than men to support the Liberal Democrats while men were particularly attracted by the minor parties.

Religious denomination continues to be related to party choice. The most strongly pro-Labour group is non-Christians, followed by Roman Catholics and Scottish Presbyterians (although in the latter case this probably has more to do with their national than their religious identity). The most Conservative group are Anglicans, while Liberal Democrat support is particularly strong among those with no religion. The strong showing for Labour among those of non-Christian religions is readily explained by the final set of results in the table which shows that members of all Britain's main ethnic minorities heavily favoured Labour in 2010. This is not a new development. For example, the 1997 BES survey included a special 'booster sample' of ethnic minority respon-dents and showed that 81 per cent of Asians and 89 per cent of black voters opted for Labour (Saggar, 1998: 35). If anything, then, the 2010 figures record a weakening of Labour's dominance among ethnic minority groups. This is partly because the party's performance across the board was much weaker in 2010 than in 1997. However, it probably owes in part to some ethnic minority voters, especially Muslims, objecting to Labour's stance on the Iraq war. The relatively strong support for the Liberal Democrats among Pakistani voters points in that direction, as does the fact that the Liberal Democrats polled especially well among non-Christians in 2005 (shortly after the war). Unfortunately, there was no ethnic minority booster sample in that year's BES and so the numbers are too small for detailed analysis. In 2010, there was a special Ethnic Minority British Election Study (EMBES) which includes analysable samples from the five most common minority groups. That survey provides the basis for the ethnic minority voting data in Table 8.1.

As explained in previous chapters, we can use logistic regression analysis to examine the combined effects of these variables on party choice. In particular, the results of this procedure tell us whether a particular variable has a significant independent effect while the others in the analysis are held constant. Table 8.2 reports the results of three such analyses. The first compares voting Conservative with voting for any other party, the second makes the same comparison for Labour voters while the third compares Conservative and Labour voters only. Summarizing all three analyses, it is clear that occupational class still makes some difference. Taking all the other variables into account, there were no significant differences between professionals and managers (the reference category) and the 'other non-manual' group, but manual workers were both more likely to vote Labour and less likely to vote Conservative – almost three times more likely to vote Labour than to vote Conservative (as shown by the odds ratio of 2.84 in the 'head-to-head' analysis). Housing tenure mattered, too, tenants being clearly more inclined to Labour than owner-occupiers. There is an effect of age but it is only really noticeable in the older age groups: those over 55 were significantly more likely to vote Conservative, other things being equal. As Table 8.1 leads us to expect, there are no significant differences between men and women. The figures for religious attachment confirm the Conservatives' particular strength among Anglicans and Labour's strength among Roman Catholics. It is noticeable that the coefficients for non-Christians are not only non-significant but are also very weak (not much different from 1). This is the effect of holding constant the ethnicity variable, which has a powerful effect in all three analyses. Table 8.1 reported that non-Christians vote disproportionately for Labour; Table 8.2 indicates that this has more to do with their ethnicity than with their religious affiliation.

222

Table 8.2 Logistic regression analysis of Conservative and Labour voting in 2010 (social variables)

	Conservative versus others	Labour versus others	Labour versus Conservative
Class (Reference = professional and managerial)			
Other non-manual	1.00	1.03	1.03
Manual	**0.50**	**2.37**	**2.84**
Tenure (Reference = owner-occupier)			
Tenant	**0.61**	**1.46**	**1.95**
Age (Reference = 18–34)			
Aged 35–44	1.27	1.14	0.97
Aged 45–54	1.12	1.20	1.08
Aged 55–64	**1.75**	0.84	0.60
Aged 65 +	**1.83**	1.06	0.71
Sex (Reference = male)			
Female	0.80	1.19	1.26
Religion (Reference = none)			
Anglican	**1.90**	**0.83**	**0.63**
Scottish Presbyterian	**0.49**	1.45	**2.26**
Roman Catholic	0.85	**2.01**	**1.89**
Nonconformist	1.01	0.87	0.89
Non-Christian	0.86	0.94	1.06
Ethnicity (Reference = white)			
Non-white	**0.59**	**3.00**	**2.72**
Nagelkerke R^2	0.11	0.10	0.16
% correctly classified (original)	64.5	67.6	52.3
% correctly classified (equation)	67.8	69.3	64.1
Change in % correctly classified	3.3	1.7	11.8
(*N* of cases)	(1,038)	(1,038)	(722)

Note: Significant odds ratios ($p < 0.05$) are shown in **bold**. The BES contains too few members of specific ethnic minorities to include these separately in the regression and so we can use only a basic white/non-white distinction.

Source: BES 2010 face-to-face surveys.

The figures at the bottom of the table summarize how accurately we can predict voting behaviour based on these social and demographic characteristics. These statistics are not easy to interpret in themselves but can usefully be compared with similar analyses. In particular, there is a telling contrast with equivalent analyses of BES data from the 1964 election. In that earlier case, the R^2 statistics for the three models (estimating the amount of variation in party choice explained by the equations) ranged from 0.25 to 0.33. Here, they are much smaller, as are the changes in the proportion of respondents whose party choice is correctly classified on the basis of the equations. Whereas in 1964 knowing voters' social characteristics improved our ability to classify them as Conservative or 'other' by around 12 points, as Labour or 'other' by 19 points and as Labour or Conservative by 20 points, the relative improvements in 2005 were only 3 points, 2 points and 12 points respectively. In short, social characteristics have become less useful in predicting party choice and so a simple sociological model is less useful in explaining voting behaviour. In many ways this is not at all surprising. One of the aims of the New Labour leadership in the 1990s was to broaden the party's appeal and make it into a 'catch all' party (see Heath, Jowell and Curtice, 2001). Nonetheless, as Table 8.2 indicates, Labour still retains an edge among its traditional sources of support.

These analyses give an incomplete picture of the sociological approach to voting behaviour, however. We also need to consider party identification: the enduring attachments that some voters have to one party or another. This was conceived in the 'Michigan model' as the central route through which social group membership drove party choice. Partisanship was also the central element in the model – itself a version of the Michigan model – used by Butler and Stokes to explain voting in Britain in the 1960s. At the time, it was widely accepted that party identification (together with class voting) provided a good explanation of party choice in Britain.

As time has passed, however, doubts have arisen. As we have seen (Chapter 3), one area of doubt concerns the survey question used to elicit party identification. When respondents are offered the opportunity to say that they do *not* 'generally think of themselves as' party supporters, fewer party identifiers are found. Another concerns the stability of identification over time. If identification really does relate to an 'enduring attachment' to a party then the identification of individuals should be very stable over time. Clarke *et al.* (2004, ch. 6) cite various panel survey studies which suggest that for a sizeable minority of voters this is not the case. In addition, monthly data collected by Gallup between

January 1992 and December 2002 showed that identification with the Conservatives ranged from 21 per cent to 37 per cent, with Labour from 30 per cent to 54 per cent and with the Liberal Democrats from 7 per cent to 19 per cent. These figures suggest either that many people do *not* have an enduring attachment to a party, which they stick to through good times and bad, or that the standard survey questions do not tap those attachments which do exist. Finally, of course, even on the basis of the standard question asked at each election we have seen that the strength of party identification in Britain has sharply declined (Figure 3.2). There are still some strong party identifiers around, for whom supporting their party at an election is more or less automatic, but they are thinner on the ground. The proportion of electors whose voting can be explained as being a consequence of their being socialized by their parents and other personal contacts into a specific party identity, which then colours their whole approach to politics, has diminished and looks likely to diminish further.

Nonetheless, it is essential to include party identification in our assessment of voting behaviour in 2010. For one thing, still around half of the electorate report either a 'strong' or a 'fairly strong' identification with a party. Another reason for including party identification is that, paradoxically, it may partly explain the weakening effects of sociological variables. Strong party identifications, instilled early in life, can survive social mobility and so some middle-class Labour voters or working-class Conservatives may be voting in line with family traditions rather than current circumstances (or even interests).

Simple cross-tabulations – of the kind reported in Table 8.1 – suggest that, as in previous elections, party identification had a predictably powerful impact on voting behaviour in 2010. Of those who said before the election that they identified with the Conservatives, 88 per cent reported after the election that they had voted that way. The corresponding percentage for both Labour and the Liberal Democrats was 75 per cent. The relatively disappointing figure for Labour is typical of parties at a low electoral ebb, indicating that they struggle not only to win over floating voters but also to hold on to their core support. Table 8.3 presents the results of adding party identification to the regression analyses reported in the previous table. The social characteristics were also included in the analysis (and thus held constant) but we do not repeat all of their coefficients – the table shows only the results for the added partisanship variables.

The results are exactly as would be expected based on the percentages mentioned above. Independent of their social characteristics, voters were fifteen times more likely to vote Conservative if they identified with the party, and Labour identifiers were ten times more likely to vote

Table 8.3 Logistic regression analysis of Conservative and Labour voting in 2010 (party identification with social variables controlled)

	Conservative versus others	Labour versus others	Labour versus Conservative
Party ID (Reference = none)			
Conservative	**15.09**	**0.11**	**0.05**
Labour	**0.19**	**9.94**	**12.12**
Liberal Democrat	**0.30**	**0.16**	0.47
Other	**0.32**	**0.54**	1.64
Nagelkerke R^2	0.60	0.57	0.72
% correctly classified (social variables only)	67.8	69.3	64.1
% correctly classified (adding party ID)	84.4	85.6	88.7
Change in % correctly classified	16.6	16.3	24.6
(*N* of cases)	(1,028)	(1,028)	(719)

Note: Significant odds ratios ($p < 0.05$) are shown in **bold**.

Source: BES 2010 face-to-face surveys

Labour. Equally predictably, those identifying with the Liberal Democrats or one of the minor parties were also much less likely to vote for one of the major parties. The key point to note about Table 8.3 is the very marked improvement in our prediction of party choice once we take into account party identification. Both the r^2 values and the percentages of correctly classified voters increase sharply, much more so than in the analyses in Table 8.2. This is not surprising given how closely related partisanship is to the vote. Nonetheless, it highlights the key point that, dealignment notwithstanding, party identification remains a crucial component in any explanation of voting in Britain (see Clarke *et al.*, 2009, chs. 3, 5). While the definition and measurement of partisanship are subject to dispute, its importance is not.

Models based on rational choice

It should go without saying that voters do not sit down before an election to comb through the manifestos and to make detailed calculations of the costs and benefits of voting for each party. Just in case it does not, we have made the point several times. We should also emphasize that such a process is not just unrealistic but actually irrational, and is certainly not what is implied by the term 'rational choice'. As noted in Chapter 2, the likelihood of an individual's vote changing the outcome of an election is extremely small. If it is irrational to spend fifteen minutes walking to and from the polling station on election day, then it is certainly irrational to spend hours deciding how to vote. Instead, rational choice theory has inspired a whole family of explanations for party support, each of which sees the voter as making a more or less conscious choice. The two key approaches are issue voting and valence voting. Neither involves complex calculations; indeed, the simpler versions of both approaches have fared better when confronted with the empirical evidence.

The *issue voting* approach suggests that voters make up their minds on the basis of what they perceive to be the key issues in an election. They have opinions about these issues, know the stances of the parties and vote for the one which, overall, advocates policies of which they approve most. A variant of issue voting suggests that it is not so much their preferences on issues of the day which influence voting choices but the more general political values or principles that voters hold. Proponents of this approach pay more attention to voters' stances on broader political questions that have been around a long time (nationalization versus privatization of industry, for example, or the balance between taxation and spending on public services) than to their opinions on contemporary issues.

As described in Chapters 4 and 5, *valence voting*, now sometimes referred to as 'performance politics', is basically about the voters making judgements. These relate to three overlapping areas. First, voters react to the performance of the government and, to a lesser extent, the opposition. In this view, elections constitute a judgement on a party's tenure of office, enabling the people to hold their governors accountable. Taking everything into account – including how well the alternative government (the opposition) might have performed – voters decide whether to confirm the government in office or vote to 'throw the rascals out'. Second, voters are influenced in particular by how well the government has managed the economy. They may consider their own situation or the situation of the country as a whole; they may focus on past performance or future prospects. For some analysts, however, economic considerations such as these are uppermost in the voters' minds when an election comes along. Finally – and unsurprisingly in a television-dominated age – judgements about party leaders now weigh heavily in the scales when voting decisions are being made. Indeed, making a judgement about the leaders can be seen as a short cut which avoids making more complex judgements. It may not be so much the details of the leaders' performances that are important but the general image that they convey: whether they seem likeable, honest, decisive, caring and have a strong personality, for example. The same is true of parties. Details of policy and performance can be secondary, especially for less informed voters, to general images of the parties.

These two approaches do not exhaust the kinds of explanation for party choice that have their roots in rational choice theory. Another obvious example is tactical voting. As noted in the previous chapter, tactical voters react in predictable and rational ways to aspects of local context. The 2010 election provided an instance of tactical voting based on the national context, too. As polling day approached, some of those seeking to avoid a hung parliament switched to the Conservative Party, the only plausible outright winner. On the other hand, some Labour supporters switched to the Liberal Democrats precisely in order to minimize the likelihood of a Conservative majority.

The impact of issues, performance and leader images in 2010 is illustrated in Table 8.4, which again reports the results of three logistic regression analyses. Three preliminary points should be made about the table. First, it is not intended to be a comprehensive analysis of party choice in the 2010 election but merely to illustrate the importance of electors' judgements. A whole variety of other variables could have been selected for inclusion but, for our purposes, there is no need to debate this at length or to explain in detail how the variables used were created from the original data. Second, as before, we retain the variables – in this case, both social characteristics and party identification – included in previous analyses. Thus the table shows the effects of various judgements while still taking account of the impact of social characteristics and party identification, although coefficients for the latter are not shown. As we have frequently stressed, it is crucial to take account of party identification when estimating the effects of variables, like government performance evaluations, on which those who already support or dislike the government are predisposed to take a particular view. Third, it is worth saying again that the coefficients listed are odds ratios, indicating the odds that a respondent in the category concerned voted for the first-named party in the column heading as compared to a respondent in the reference category, while holding all other variables constant. Thus, all things considered, compared with those who thought that the

Table 8.4 Logistic regression analysis of Conservative and Labour voting in 2010 (issue and valence variables with social variables and party identification controlled)

	Conservative versus others	*Labour versus others*	*Labour versus Conservative*
General economic expectations (Reference = same/don't know)			
Get worse	**1.97**	**0.52**	**0.40**
Get better	1.18	0.80	0.85
Best party if economic difficulties (Reference = neither/don't know)			
Conservative	**2.36**	**0.43**	**0.32**
Labour	**0.40**	**1.77**	**3.20**
Liberal Democrat	**0.40**	0.49	**0.41**
Position on tax–spending scale (Reference = midpoint/don't know)			
Cut taxes and spending	1.33	0.71	0.84
Increase taxes and spending	0.82	1.23	**1.91**
Opinion on Afghanistan war (Reference = neither/don't know)			
Approve	**2.13**	0.72	0.58
Disapprove	1.50	0.65	0.53
Feelings about party leaders (Reference = neutral/don't know)			
Dislike Brown	1.63	**0.56**	0.57
Like Brown	**0.55**	1.52	**2.87**
Dislike Cameron	**0.54**	1.24	**2.68**
Like Cameron	**1.83**	0.98	0.73
Dislike Clegg	1.43	0.84	**0.47**
Like Clegg	0.79	**0.52**	0.48
Nagelkerke R^2	0.70	0.63	0.82
% correctly classified (social and party ID)	84.4	85.6	88.7
% correctly classified (adding issue/valence)	87.4	86.7	93.0
% correctly classified (change)	3.0	1.1	4.3
(*N* of cases)	(1,028)	(1,028)	(719)

Note: Significant odds ratios ($p < 0.05$) are shown in **bold**.

Source: BES 2010 face-to-face surveys.

economic situation would stay the same, those who expected that the country's economic situation would get worse were twice as likely to vote Conservative rather than another party (1.97), just over half as likely to vote Labour rather than another party (0.52), and less than half as likely to vote Labour rather than Conservative (0.40).

Those results among economic pessimists are as would be anticipated. It is perhaps more surprising that the party preferences of optimists, those believing that the economy would improve, were not significantly different from those of the reference group (i.e., those who thought things would remain about the same). The lack of statistical significance is partly to do with numbers of cases: there were so few optimists amid the general economic gloom that any differences could be put down to chance. Another likely explanation is that the optimists include two groups: those impressed by Labour's handling of the economy, and those distinctly unimpressed but expecting a Labour defeat to usher in more competent economic managers. For both reasons, it is particularly useful to look at the next set of results which concern the party deemed best able to handle economic difficulties. Here, all the effects are in the expected direction and almost all of them are significant. In the Labour versus Conservative analysis, those who thought that one of those parties was best equipped for economic crisis were three times more likely to vote for that party. This is a strikingly strong effect considering that it is obtained while holding constant partisanship, economic expectations, leadership evaluations and so on.

The effects of economic variables therefore provide solid evidence of valence voting. There is rather less evidence of position issue voting. Although public spending was a prominent campaign issue, knowing where respondents stood on the trade-off between lower taxes and increased public spending was of some but limited use in predicting their vote. There was also only one significant effect in the results for attitudes to the war in Afghanistan, with those who approved of British military action being twice as likely to vote Conservative. It is worth restating the point that position issues can only be important in elections if the parties adopt different stances on them. In 2010, all three major parties supported continuing action in Afghanistan and, for all the heated rhetoric about the public finances, the parties' concrete offerings in terms of tax and spending were not all that different either. These results may, then, say as much about the parties as they do about the voters.

The last set of odds ratios relate to whether or not respondents liked or disliked the party leaders (or were neutral towards them: the reference category). The effects are mostly in the expected direction but they are not uniformly statistically significant, and one or two anticipated effects do not materialize. For example, those who liked Gordon Brown were significantly less likely to vote Conservative but not significantly more likely to vote Labour. In the Labour versus Conservative analysis, those who disliked Brown and those who liked Cameron proved not to be significantly different from those neutral towards those leaders. By contrast, and more in line with expectations, both liking Brown and disliking Cameron were associated with being nearly three times more likely to vote Labour rather than Conservative. There is also some evidence that Nick Clegg's popularity cost the other parties votes, although the effect is only significant in the case of Labour. (A separate analysis of voting for the Liberal Democrats as opposed to another party shows that liking or disliking Clegg had the expected and significant effects.) These leadership effects are, on the whole, rather weaker than the economic effects but clearly stronger than the position issue coefficients.

As noted above, the details of the analysis and interpretation of the results need not detain us here. The most important point to notice is the extent to which the addition of these issue and valence variables improves our ability to predict party choice. The answer is: not by very much, especially in the Labour versus others model where the proportion of cases correctly classified increases by barely one point. There is a more appreciable increase in the Labour versus Conservative analysis, taking the percentage of correct classification well into the 90s. Of course, it might reasonably be pointed out that the inclusion of party identification had already taken these percentages so high that there was limited scope for further improvement. If we focus on the 'pseudo' R^2 statistics instead, there look to be greater gains from adding these variables. Comparing Tables 8.3 and 8.4, and interpreting these R^2 statistics as proportions of variation explained, we see increases of 10, 6 and 10 percentage points across the three models. These judgements about the parties' performance, policies and leaders do add significantly to our ability to predict party choice.

By any yardstick, however, the major boost to predictive accuracy came with party identification. We should acknowledge that this is largely due to the sequence in which the batches of variables were added. Had we added the judgement variables to the social characteristics, then *they* would have generated the big increases in R^2 and correct classification, and adding party identification would simply have topped up the levels of predictive accuracy to those in Table 8.4. In short, whichever variables go in earlier will look like the more important for explaining voting behaviour. The question of which is the 'correct' order is a matter of theory, not a matter of statistical method. It depends on which way the causal arrow is thought to run between party identification and these political judgements. That brings us back to the controversy about the meaning of party identification mentioned in Chapter 3. Those favouring a traditional Michigan interpretation would endorse our approach here. For them, long-held party allegiances shape the way that voters see political events and personalities. Partisanship should therefore be introduced first and, in this way, held constant when examining the effects of variables such as leader evaluations. Otherwise, we will mistake correlation for causation, wrongly concluding that people vote for a party because they like its leader, when in reality it is partisanship that is driving both leader evaluations and voting behaviour. Those favouring the 'running tally' model regard party identification as continually reshaped by variables like leader images or economic performance. For them, such judgements are the real drivers of voting behaviour – even if their effects often work through party identification – and so introducing them into the model first would better reflect the real contribution to explaining party choice.

To sum up this section, explanations of party choice based on social location or social identities retain some value but are less successful than they used to be. Explanations based on party identification are still potent even if they apply to a steadily decreasing part of the electorate. In analysing the modern electorate, attention must also focus on their opinions, perceptions and attitudes. There is no definitive answer to the question of which opinions in particular are critical – this will change over time and probably also varies across different groups of voters. What is clear, however, is that in explaining party choice in modern British elections, two things are crucial: voters' opinions and judgements, and the partisan predispositions that remain a key influence on those judgements.

Explaining election outcomes

There is clearly an intimate connection between explaining how voters come to make their decision in a particular election and explaining the distribution of support for the parties in the election. The latter, after all, is simply the aggregated effect of millions of individual decisions. In fact, when the electorate was largely aligned, and 'social determinist' and party identification explanations predominated, it was quite difficult to explain election outcomes on this basis. Such models emphasized long-term influences on party choice and these changed only very slowly. The Conservatives might have benefited from the slow decline in the size of the working class, for example, but this would have taken a very long time to affect election results significantly. As would be expected under these models, electoral change was slow and small. Between 1950 and 1970 the Conservatives' share of the vote ranged between 41.4 per cent and 49.3 per cent, while Labour's was never higher than 49.4 per cent or lower than 43.9 per cent (Table 1.2). Most voters regularly supported the same party and short-term electoral change was produced by a small proportion of 'floating' voters who switched parties or (more commonly) in and out of non-voting.

Sometimes, it was difficult to determine what motivated 'floating' of this kind. Those who switched parties were found to be less concerned and less knowledgeable about politics, and less interested in the outcomes of elections, than were those whose voting pattern was stable. It was not those who were interested in and knowledgeable about politics and current affairs who determined which party won elections – such people were mainly loyal party supporters – but the less concerned, less interested and less knowledgeable. Butler and Stokes (1969: 437) suggested that switchers in some way acted 'as surrogates for those who, although they [did] not change, recognised in themselves the reactions which ... moved the less committed'. In other words, when an election came along the political wind would be blowing in a particular direction. All felt it and were inclined to move with it, but only those with weak class or party attachments were actually propelled into switching to the party in whose direction the wind was blowing.

By the 'political wind', we mean broadly the same kinds of short-term factors that have been shown in this book to influence voters today. They include, among others, assessments of economic performance, images of the parties as moderate or extreme, the popularity of the leaders and the effectiveness of the rival parties' campaigning. What has changed, then, is not the factors that drive election outcomes. Elections continue to be determined by voters' judgements of short-term factors, notably government (and estimated opposition) performance. The difference is that dealignment has made these short-term factors more important and, as a consequence, electoral change is more obvious and more rapid. This is well illustrated through explanations of the outcomes of the past three general elections: 2001, 2005 and 2010. The pattern of judgements made by the electorate provides good explanations for the results of these elections.

The 2001 election

Change in the context. Being in government can cause electoral problems for parties since some people are bound to be disappointed and some policy failures are inevitable. There are also advantages, however, since the Prime Minister can name the election date and an economic upswing can be engineered as the next election approaches. Between 1997 and 2001, the modernization of Labour continued and the moderation of the government was plain for all to see. Unsurprisingly, 72 per cent of 2001 BES respondents described Labour as 'moderate' and only 15 per cent as 'extreme'. Despite much internal organizational reform, soul-searching over their defeat and debate about the direction to be taken, the Conservatives in 2001 were seen as being broadly the same party that had lost disastrously in 1997 (Norton, 2002). One other potentially significant change in the electoral context concerned the Liberal Democrats. Having won more seats than ever before (46) in 1997, the party could anticipate benefiting from an 'incumbency effect' in those constituencies. Moreover, having been in government in Scotland and Wales, it could be argued that the Liberal Democrats could no longer be described as inexperienced or peripheral to the party battle (Denver, 2001).

Performance of the government. Although the Blair government disappointed some of its own traditional supporters and did not fill many with enthusiasm, the electorate was generally satisfied with its performance. Apart from a rocky period during 2000, Gallup's monthly polls consistently found that more people approved of the government's record to date than disapproved. In March and April 2001, approximately 55 per cent and 52 per cent of respondents respectively said that they approved of the government's record.

The economy. In stark contrast to previous Labour governments, the 1997–2001 government's handling of the economy was believed by many to be particularly effective. Unemployment fell steeply, interest rates were low and inflation was at lower levels than had been experienced for a generation. Pluralities of MORI respondents at the time thought that all five of the budgets introduced by Gordon Brown, the Chancellor of the Exchequer, were good for the country while his last pre-election budget was the best-received ever recorded by MORI (Worcester and Mortimore, 2001: 27). Unsurprisingly, 62 per cent of 2001 BES respondents thought that the government had 'handled the economy generally' well, while only 9 per cent thought that they had handled it badly.

Party images. The image of sleaze that had dogged the Conservatives in 1997 had been largely dispelled by 2001. In addition, fewer people saw the party as divided (71 per cent on Gallup's figures for May 2001) than had been the case in 1997, although this was still a historically high proportion and contrasted with 44 per cent seeing Labour as divided (Gallup, *Political Index,* Report 489). On the other hand, despite the efforts of William Hague to make the party seem more inclusive, youthful and even trendy – or perhaps because of them – Gallup data (Report 489) also show that the Conservatives were now seen as being 'out of touch with modern Britain' (69 per cent) and 'going on too much about Europe' (65 per cent).

Party leaders. Tony Blair's lead over William Hague as the preferred Prime Minister was huge and greater than any party leader's since 1979 at least (see Table 5.3). It was not just Hague personally who had a problem connecting with the electorate, however; the people around him in the leadership team also failed to impress. When MORI asked just before the election which party had the best team of leaders, only 9 per cent of respondents chose the Conservatives (47 per cent chose Labour, 5 per cent the Liberal Democrats and 33 per cent said none or didn't know; see Worcester and Mortimore, 2001: 78). At the same time, Gallup found an astonishing 81 per cent agreeing that the Conservatives did not have a strong team of leaders. In contrast, the new leader of the Liberal Democrats, Charles Kennedy, made a favourable impression on the electorate. Thirty per cent of BES respondents said that they liked him, 59 per cent were neutral and only 11 per cent disliked him. For comparison, 23 per cent disliked Tony Blair and 41 per cent disliked William Hague.

Key issues and policies. In 2001 Labour remained the preferred party on the key issues nominated by voters, although their lead was generally smaller than in 1997. On the other hand, their lead over the Conservatives as the party thought to have the best policies for the country as a whole (47 per cent to 17 per cent) once again increased substantially as compared with the previous election.

* * *

In the light of these evaluations it is again not difficult to understand why Labour won the 2001 election, if not as overwhelmingly as in 1997 (and also why the Liberal Democrats improved their position).

The 2005 election

Change in the context. The context of the 2005 election was markedly different from those of 1997 and 2001. Labour was very much on the defensive and the main reason for that was the Iraq war, which began in March 2003, and subsequent related developments. Although there were large anti-war demonstrations at the time, initially a clear majority of the public supported Britain's involvement (66 per cent to 29 per cent in April 2003, according to YouGov). As events unfolded, however, support waned. Among other things, the failure to find weapons of mass destruction, the impression that in making the case for involvement the government had been less than straightforward and the apparently unending chaos in Iraq itself all took their toll. By the start of 2005 only 35 per cent of YouGov's respondents were in favour of the war with 56 per cent opposed (see Quinn, 2006). Labour's difficulties on Iraq did not advantage the Conservatives – who had supported the invasion – but probably helped the Liberal Democrats who had opposed the war outright and picked up votes as a consequence, especially among Muslims.

Performance of the government. Quite unlike the period between 1997 and 2001, the electorate were generally dissatisfied with the performance of the government between 2001 and 2005. In every month from January 2003 (when the series started) to March 2005, YouGov reported large majorities saying that they disapproved of the government's record. Over the 27 months, the average figure for those disapproving was 59 per cent compared with 29 per cent approving.

The economy. On the other hand, Labour could take some comfort from the fact that it came to be seen as the party most likely to do a good job as far as managing the economy was concerned. YouGov data show that although the two major parties were virtually neck-and-neck on this issue for some time after January 2003, Labour's lead on the issue began to stretch in the early months of 2005. During the campaign itself, over five separate surveys, the proportion opting for the Conservatives as the party more likely to run the economy well averaged 28 per cent, while those choosing Labour averaged 47 per cent. The economy may not be the only thing that matters in an election, but it does matter a lot and Labour's record in this respect put the party in a strong position.

Party images. Labour's image in 2005 was less positive than it had been in 2001. On one set of measures produced by pollsters Ipsos MORI, indeed, positive attributes (such as 'has a good team of leaders') were outweighed by negative ones (such as 'out of touch with ordinary people'). However, the Conservatives, despite a slight improvement from 2001, had an even more negative image. On the other hand, the image of the Liberal Democrats was generally positive (see Worcester, Mortimore and Baines, 2005: 36–40). When the images of the two major parties were compared by YouGov, however, Labour clearly still had the edge. By more than two to one, respondents described the Conservatives rather than Labour as appealing to only one section of society, being stuck in the past, being old and tired and wanting to divide people instead of bringing them together (King, 2006: 168).

Party leaders. Following the 2001 general election, William Hague was replaced as Conservative leader by Iain Duncan Smith. The latter failed to make much of an impact with the voters and was replaced by Michael Howard in November 2003. YouGov data show that Howard scored better than Duncan Smith in terms of which party leader was thought to be the best person for Prime Minister but, even so, he did not challenge Tony Blair's lead for long. From mid-2004 through to the election Blair was clearly the preferred Prime Minister. YouGov continued to monitor opinion on this matter during the election campaign but little changed. Over five surveys, the proportion preferring Blair varied between 34 per cent and 37 per cent, while Michael Howard's scores were always between 23 per cent and 25 per cent and Charles Kennedy's between 15 per cent and 18 per cent. Blair's leads were much smaller than those he had recorded over William Hague in the 2001 election – and that, no doubt, helps to explain Labour's decline in popularity – but they were clear and sustained. Whatever their misgivings about the Labour leader and the fact that he was not particularly liked, the electorate clearly believed that he would be a better Prime Minister than either of his rivals and that goes a long way in explaining why Labour won.

Key issues and policies. Despite its importance in providing the context of the election and contributing to concerns about the extent to which the Prime Minister could be trusted, the Iraq war was not of itself particularly salient to the voters in the election. As already seen (Table 4.1), the three issues that concerned voters most were health, education, and law and order. Labour had handy leads as the most preferred party on the first two of these. BES data tell a slightly different story. In answer to a question asking what was the most important issue facing the country, the three most commonly referred to by post-election survey respondents were (in order) the NHS, asylum seekers and immigration, and law and order. Labour had a big lead on the NHS and a smaller one on law and order, while the Conservatives were clearly ahead on asylum seekers and immigration. Overall, however, Labour was named by 36 per cent of respondents as the best party on what they thought was the most important issue, compared with 20 per cent choosing the Conservatives and 7 per cent the Liberal Democrats. This certainly represented a narrowing of the 'issue gap' from 2001 (when the respective figures were 46 per cent, 16 per cent and 8 per cent) but still left Labour comfortably ahead of its rivals.

* * *

The judgements of the electorate in 2005 in respect of government performance, the economy, the parties, leaders and issues were decidedly more mixed than in the two previous elections. The government and the Prime Minister were clearly not very popular but the Conservatives had problems of their own and, despite a slight improvement in their performance, were not able to benefit as much as they could have. The main beneficiaries, it could be argued, were the Liberal Democrats and minor parties, in particular UKIP and the BNP.

The 2010 election

Change in the context.   If the 2001–2005 term had seemed at the time a turbulent period for the Labour government, by 2010 it looked like an era of tranquillity. A major financial storm, including banks on the brink of collapse until bailed out by the taxpayer, was coupled with the longest recession since the 1930s. Together, these generated both a general sense of economic crisis and a spiral in public debt such that 'the deficit', a concept of which most voters had for decades been largely and blissfully ignorant, became a central political issue. The other major change in the electoral context was in leadership, 2010 being the first time since 1979 that all three major parties were fielding debutant leaders. While the Conservatives and the Liberal Democrats had chosen young and (at the time) relatively unfamiliar leaders, Labour's new Prime Minister Gordon Brown was a very familiar figure. Initially, he proved quite popular among an electorate wearying of Tony Blair, so much so as to trigger rumours of a snap election in autumn 2007. This election did not materialize and Brown, accused of 'bottling it', saw his popularity decline quite steadily from that point. Since that political turning-point was quickly followed by the economic turmoil, Labour was forced on to the back foot and remained there, postponing the election until the very end of the five-year term.

Performance of the government. As in the previous parliamentary term, consistently large majorities of opinion poll respondents reported dissatisfaction with the government's performance. As reported in Table 3.6, there was, on average, a 38-point gap between the percentages of satisfied and dissatisfied voters, a gap around half as wide again as that recorded during the 2001–2005 term. There were some chinks of light for Labour in the approval ratings, however. At moments of emergency during the financial crisis, the party's handling of the situation won some credit. Also, and crucially, opinion polls revealed persistent doubts about whether the Conservatives would have performed better. Nonetheless, insofar as governments are rewarded for perceived good and punished for perceived poor performance, Labour went into the 2010 election with a very weak hand.

The economy. Predictably, the economy was far and away the most salient issue for voters in the 2010 election. It was all the more costly for Labour, then, that the party had lost both its reputation as an economic manager and its advantage over the Conservatives in this respect. This major difference between the 2005 and 2010 elections is almost certainly a key reason for their different outcomes. However, the Conservatives were unable to open up a clear lead in terms of economic competence. One reason seems to have been a lingering distrust of their ability – or perhaps their willingness – to deal with the fall-out from economic crisis. An ICM poll in March 2010 gave the Conservatives a 12-point lead over Labour on 'delivering economic growth' but only a 2-point advantage on 'dealing with recession'. Paradoxically, then, it was in the incumbent's interests to play up the macroeconomic difficulties (with frequent warnings about the risk of a 'double-dip' recession) while the Conservatives tried to refocus the debate on a different aspect of the crisis, the mounting public debt, on which their advantage over Labour was clearer.

Party images. Table 5.2 neatly summarizes the major changes in party image between 2005 and 2010. The Conservatives may not have been seen as in touch with ordinary people or even particularly trustworthy, but they were widely perceived as united and competent. Meanwhile, Labour's hard-won reputation as a party capable of strong government had been severely tarnished and they had no other clear image advantage over the Conservatives to fall back on. In contrast with the other two parties, the Liberal Democrats made their customary positive impression on voters according to pre-election polls. However, they were not widely seen as a capable alternative government – a point that became crucial as their poll rating soared following the first leaders' debate – and, by the time of the BES post-election survey following the formation of the coalition, they had already lost their reputation for unity and keeping promises.

Party leaders. Both David Cameron and Gordon Brown enjoyed honeymoons in the approval ratings, making their relative popularity difficult to assess, but Cameron had long held a clear and consistent lead by the time the election approached. Like his party, Cameron was regarded more as competent than as trustworthy. However, since Brown was regarded as neither, this was sufficient for a significant leadership advantage. The gap on the question of 'best Prime Minister' narrowed somewhat during the campaign, indicating a certain lack of enthusiasm for Cameron. Indeed, many voters told election-day pollsters that they still did not know who would make the best Prime Minister. This was costly for Nick Clegg who, again like his party, was widely liked but not seen by many voters as ready for office.

Key issues and policies. The economy crowded most other issues out of the election campaign and thus, to a large extent, out of voters' minds. There was a substantial minority of voters for whom immigration remained the key issue and, as in 2005, they regarded the Conservatives as better equipped than Labour to deal with it (although doubts about all of the major parties' commitment in this regard helped the BNP and UKIP, both of which took strongly anti-immigration positions, to their best ever general election showings). The Conservatives also enjoyed a small lead over Labour on crime. If Iraq was surprisingly low on voters' list of priorities in 2005, Afghanistan appears barely to have registered in 2010, and the reason is probably the same: consensus, at least among the major parties, about the war. It is also worth noting the low salience of health and education, usually trump cards for Labour, at this election. These, rather than immigration and crime, seem to have been the issues that were elbowed out by the economy in 2010. In any case, with all parties forced to concede that the upcoming parliamentary term was going to be one of spending cuts, it was much more difficult for Labour to portray itself as the party of investment in public services.

* * *

Looking at the trajectories in vote shares, the 2010 result looks like a continuation – perhaps also acceleration – of the trends visible in 2005. The Conservatives made further but unspectacular progress while Labour lost a large chunk of public support. Again, this can be readily explained looking at the balance of voters' judgements. Indeed, 2010 provides an excellent illustration of the need to look not only at the objective circumstances but also at voters' perceptions of them. Labour's defeat is easy enough to explain. The party was led by a deeply unpopular leader, had presided over a deep recession and accompanying financial mayhem, and had largely lost its reputation for competence. It is more difficult, at least on the face of it, to explain why the Conservatives were unable to secure a majority. One reason lies not in voting behaviour but in the electoral system, which continues to work to Labour's advantage. In 2010, the Conservatives had both a larger vote share and a bigger lead than Labour enjoyed in 2005; Labour won a clear majority in 2005 while the Conservatives fell short in 2010. Nevertheless, it is also worth wondering why, in very propitious circumstances, the Conservatives were only able to win 36.7 per cent of the popular vote. The likeliest answer lies in continuing doubts about their capacity to govern competently and in the interests of the broader electorate. A comparison with Labour in 1997 is instructive. Like Tony Blair, David Cameron had worked hard to transform a struggling party's image and to broaden its base of support. Blair was simply more successful at the task, however. New Labour were perceived more favourably than Cameron's Conservatives in terms of governing competence but also on key image criteria such as being 'moderate' and 'in touch with ordinary people'. Blair was also more personally popular than Cameron, perhaps in part because Blair himself was more widely seen as responsive to the concerns of ordinary voters.

It should be emphasized that the sorts of judgement made by the electorate that we have used to explain the outcomes of the last three elections do not, of course, tell the whole story. (For extended treatments of these elections, see Norris, 2001; Butler and Kavanagh, 2002; Geddes and Tonge, 2002; King, 2002b; Geddes and Tonge, 2005; Kavanagh and Butler, 2005; Norris and Wlezien, 2005; Bartle and King, 2006; Kavanagh and Cowley, 2010; Wring, Mortimore and Atkinson, 2011.) A fuller account would also include consideration of the role of the media, for example. In addition, while electors' judgements may give strong clues as to why votes are distributed as they are, to understand the election outcome in terms of seats won we also have to take account of the electoral system – as discussed just above – and the geographical distribution of support which is influenced by, among other things, local campaigning. Nonetheless, if we are to use the insights that studies of individual voting behaviour have provided in order to explain overall election results, it is clear that the best starting point is to focus on the judgements made by individual voters about government performance, the parties, issues, policies and leaders. And that is how it should be if elections are to fulfil the functions prescribed for them in democratic political systems.

Conclusion

We suggested at the beginning of this book that one reason for studying elections is that they are fun events. Turnouts in recent elections might suggest that fewer people are now finding them quite as much fun. Terms such as 'disengagement' and 'alienation' are now commonly used in discussions of the electorate's attitudes to the electoral process. Nonetheless, students of elections should find elections more interesting, and even exciting, than they used to be. They should do so because elections are now much less predictable. The electorate's judgements on relatively short-term matters have come to play a key role in determining party choice, and short-term judgements are subject to rapid change. As Mrs Thatcher found to her cost, the transition from being perceived as resolute to being perceived as pig-headed can be swift. When governments these days run into a bit of heavy weather, the absence of the anchor provided by widespread and strong party identification among voters means that they can rapidly become critical and withdraw their support. Thus, between 2001 and 2010, Labour fell from over 40 per cent to under 30 per cent of the popular vote as short-term factors moved against them. Electoral change can be much more rapid than that, too. During the 2010 election campaign, the likely result and even the rank ordering of the major parties changed almost by the day.

In line with this theme of flux, much had changed in British politics within a year of the 2010 general election. Indeed, there had been a major development within days of polling: the formation of the first formal coalition government since 1945 between the Conservatives and the Liberal Democrats. After the usual honeymoon period, during which the public registered approval not only for this particular government but for the notion of coalition government itself, the clouds began to gather. One question that invariably arises with coalition politics is that of how credit and (more often) blame will be shared among the partners and, during the first year of office, it was the Liberal Democrats – and their leader, Nick Clegg, in particular – who took much of the flak. The party will struggle to repeat its strong showing among younger voters following the tuition fees controversy that blew up in late 2010. Having very publicly pledged during the election campaign to abolish university tuition fees, the Liberal Democrats then found themselves defending their government's plan for a 200 per cent increase in the maximum chargeable fee. This not only alienated those who had voted for the party on the strength of its opposition to fees but also reawakened the objections of those – mainly on the left of the Liberal Democrats – who had been unenthusiastic about joining the Conservatives in government in the first place. However, these were mainly 'noises off' rather than discord within what has, to date, been a fairly harmonious coalition.

The broader question about the coalition government concerns public reactions to its programme of public spending cuts. Opinion polls show that the public is, on the whole, persuaded of the need to cut spending. However, support in the abstract is not the same as support for specific cuts – most announcements of planned reductions have been greeted with vociferous opposition from at least some quarters – and it is certainly not the same as continued support when the effects are being felt. Sluggish economic growth has created further doubts about the scale and timing of the planned cuts. As noted above, the public has lingering doubts about the Conservatives' capacity to deal with economic difficulties, notably unemployment, and so a sunnier macro-economic outlook is probably a precondition not only for successful deficit reduction but also for regaining public approval of the government.

The word 'regaining' is necessary because satisfaction with government performance has already declined quite sharply. The figures moved 'into the red' – that is, more dissatisfied than satisfied voters – in the autumn of 2010 and the gap quickly widened. An Ipsos-MORI poll in March 2011 recorded 36 per cent satisfaction and 59 per cent dissatisfaction. These are better ratings than those recorded in the closing stages of the previous Labour government and are far from beyond rescue, given the length of time until the next election. But the speed with which the honeymoon wore off is further proof of the volatility of public judgements and, by extension, voting intentions.

As if to prove the point, Labour has rebounded from its very poor election result to take a small but steady lead in the opinion polls. The party has been a particular beneficiary of the halving in Liberal Democrat support since, not surprisingly, it is those erstwhile Liberal

Democrats least sympathetic to the Conservatives that have deserted the party. Labour may also have benefited from public disquiet about spending cuts. (We mentioned that the public recognizes the need for spending cuts but tends to oppose specific reductions, and that accurately summarizes Labour's tactics in this parliament so far.) The party has had a change of leadership, too. A few months after the election, Ed Miliband was elected as Brown's successor by a wafer-thin margin over his older brother, David. Political commentators and the public alike have been underwhelmed by Ed Miliband's performance so far. In the March 2011 poll cited above, the Labour leader received slightly more negative than positive evaluations, leaving his approval ratings clearly behind those of Prime Minister Cameron (although some way ahead of Nick Clegg's). It is, of course, very difficult to predict how Miliband – or, indeed, any of the party leaders – will be perceived by the time of the next election. However, given the argument that the electorate's evaluations of party leaders now play an important part in determining party choice, these changes will clearly be electorally significant.

Given that all of these developments occurred within less than a year of the 2010 general election, it would clearly be foolish for anyone to attempt to predict what will happen in the next general election, which may be some years distant. A bill for fixed parliamentary terms (of five years) has recently gone through Parliament and that would at least reduce the uncertainty over the date of an election. Yet the electoral context and the personalities involved are always shifting and uncertain, and all sorts of unforeseen issues – such as the recent uprisings in North Africa and the deployment of British forces in Libya – can arise. (In the previous edition of this book, written after the 2005 election, one of us made the same point, noting that 'it is impossible to know whether economic storms will suddenly blow up'. This was prescient.) Combine these uncertainties with a fickle and judgemental electorate and it is easy to understand why British elections will continue to be exciting and the study of British elections and voters fascinating.

Glossary of Statistical and Technical Terms

These explanations of statistical terms used in the text are not instructions about 'how to do it' as no formulae are given. If that is what is required, readers should consult an appropriate statistics textbook (for example, Rose and Sullivan, 1996; Bryman and Cramer, 2001) but, these days, all the necessary calculations are done by appropriate computer packages such as SPSS. Neither are the following explanations given in technical language. Rather, the intention here is to provide non-specialist readers with a basic working knowledge of various statistical techniques and terms commonly used in electoral analysis. An understanding of what the various techniques measure and what the results mean is all that is required to engage with the electoral studies literature and even to undertake basic research. In what follows, terms in the text in bold type have their own separate entries.

Aggregate data

Aggregate data describes information referring to aggregates or collectivities rather than to individuals. Constituency data – such as election results or social composition figures – is a common example in electoral analysis. It is an important feature of aggregate data that they cannot be used to infer anything about the individuals comprising the collectivity concerned.

Binary logistic regression

Normal linear **regression analysis** can only be used with **continuous data**. Binary logistic regression enables the application of regression analysis methods, with their associated advantages, in cases where the **dependent variable** and associated **independent variables** are **categorical**. These advantages include being able to analyse a large number of **independent variables** simultaneously and to measure the separate independent effect of each, as well as the combined effect of all of them.

The dependent variable has to be reduced to two categories, such as voted Conservative or not (hence 'binary'), and for each independent variable a 'reference' category has to be specified with which other categories will be compared. The output produced by each analysis is voluminous and the initial coefficients difficult to interpret. The most important elements for interpretation are: the **odds ratios** given for each category of an independent variable (which show the extent to which cases in the category differ from the reference category); the **statistical significance** of each odds ratio (which shows whether the difference between the category and the reference group could have arisen by chance); the R^2 **statistics** (which estimate how much of the variation in the dependent variable is explained by the independent variables in the analysis) and the classification tables (which show the extent to which allocating cases to the categories of the dependent variable on the basis of the regression equation improves upon allocating all to the largest category).

Bivariate analysis
Analysis involving two variables.

Categorical variables
Sometimes called 'nominal variables', these are **variables** for which the information is such that each case can only be assigned to one of a number of discrete categories. Examples are party voted for, religion, sex and occupation group.

Chi-squared test
A test of **statistical significance** normally applied to **cross-tabulations**. The test indicates the probability that any difference between the categories could have arisen by chance; the lower that probability the more significant the difference. Normally a probability of 0.05 or less (usually reported as '$p < 0.05$') is taken to indicate a statistically significant difference. When the probability is larger, the difference found is normally interpreted as not being statistically significant.

Continuous data
When a **variable** is such that each case can be assigned a precise score on a scale, the resulting data are described as continuous. Examples for individuals could include height (the scale could be metres), weight (pounds), age (years) or score on a political quiz (marks out of ten). For constituencies, the parties' percentage shares of the votes, the percentage of manual workers in the workforce and persons per hectare would be examples.

Correlation (coefficients)
As most commonly used, these are measures of the strength of association between two **interval-scale** or **continuous variables**. The coefficients are signified as 'r' and can vary between -1 and + 1. A positive sign indicates that as the scores on one variable increase, so do the scores on the other. A negative sign means that as one increases the other decreases. The closer the coefficient is to zero, the weaker the association.

Cross-tabulation
This is the standard way of presenting and investigating the relationship between two or more **categorical variables**. Tables are created by defining categories for the column (**independent**) variable and the row (**dependent**) variable. Thus we could allocate survey respondents according to sex (two categories – independent variable) and party voted for (say, three categories –(Conservative, Labour, Liberal Democrat) – dependent variable). This defines a table of six cells and respondents are allocated to the appropriate one. The figures in each column are then usually converted to percentages. More variables can be incorporated, but two problems quickly arise: first, the number of cells multiplies rapidly so that tables become unwieldy, difficult to present clearly and hard to understand; second, the number of cases in each cell becomes very small so that the percentages become unreliable.

Dependent variable
A **variable** that is presumed to be affected by other factors: for example, in examining the relationship between age and vote it is clear that vote must be the dependent variable.

Dummy variables
Categorical variables can be converted into *quasi* **continuous variables** by being reduced to two categories and assigning scores (usually 0 and 1) to each. Because they are not truly continuous, the created variables are known as 'dummy' variables. Thus, region could be converted into a series of 'dummies' scored 0 = Not Scotland, 1 = Scotland; 0 = Not North East, 1 = North East; and so on. The advantage is that dummy variables can then be used as an independent variable in ordinary **regression analysis**.

Ecological fallacy
This is a logical fallacy committed in the interpretation of statistical

data. When committing the ecological fallacy the analyst uses **aggregate data** to make inferences about the characteristics or behaviours of individuals. While we can summarize **individual-level data** (through **means**, for example) to make inferences about groups, it is not appropriate to use group data to make inferences about individuals.

Independent variable

A **variable** that is presumed to affect other (dependent) variables: for example, in examining the relationship between age and vote, it is clear that age must be the independent variable.

Individual-level data

These are data which refer to individuals. Such data are most commonly collected by means of sample surveys and the individuals concerned are usually anonymous.

Interval-scale data

See **continuous data**.

Mean

The most common measure of the central tendency of a set of scores on an **interval-scale variable**. In everyday speech it is commonly called the average (although there are other relevant measures) and it is calculated by summing the scores and dividing the total by the number of cases. The mean can give a misleading impression if the number of cases is small and there are some extreme values (very high or very low scores compared to most cases).

Multiple regression analysis

Regression analysis involving more than one **independent variable**.

Multivariate analysis

Analysis involving two or more **independent variables**.

Nagelkerke R^2

This statistic gives an estimate of the proportion of **variation** explained by an equation produced by a **binary logistic regression** analysis.

Odds ratios

Odds ratios allow us to compare cases which have been allocated to a two-category **independent variable** in respect of a two-category **dependent**

variable. For example, if the **independent variable** is class (working versus middle) and the **dependent variable** is party voted for (Conservative versus Labour), then we can define the odds of voting Conservative (as opposed to voting Labour) for both working- and middle-class respondents. The odds can be expressed as probabilities (thus 50:50 equals 1; 60:40 equals 1.5; 40:60 equals 0.67) and the ratio between the figures for the two groups summarizes the comparison. In **binary logistic regression** odds ratios are produced comparing each category of each independent variable with the reference category in each case.

Panel surveys

These are survey designs in which the same respondents are surveyed at multiple times, enabling researchers to observe not only the amount of change in opinion or behaviour but also which types of people are changing. There are single-election panels, with respondents surveyed before and after polling day, or inter-election panels, with respondents surveyed at each election and often at multiple time points in between.

Regression analysis

This is a shorthand way of referring to ordinary least squares linear regression (OLS), a technique for analysing the relationships between **continuous variables**. Simple regression analysis involves estimating the line (the 'regression line') that best fits a distribution of points on a scatter diagram plotting the **dependent variable** (vertical axis) against an **independent** or 'predictor' **variable** (horizontal axis). In the most common analysis the line is assumed to be straight ('linear regression') and is the 'least squares line' (i.e., that line which minimizes the sum of the squares of the vertical distances from each point to the line). It can be described by an equation of the form $y = a + bx$, where y is the dependent variable score, a is a constant, b is a measure of the slope of the line and x is the independent variable score. By extension, **multiple regression** is used to predict a dependent variable on the basis of more than one independent variable. The goodness of fit of the regression line to the data is measured by R, the **correlation coefficient** (either simple or multiple) and the **R-squared** (R^2) statistic estimates the proportion of variation in the dependent variable statistically explained by the equation.

Residuals

On the basis of an equation produced by **regression** analysis, 'expected' scores on the **dependent variable** can be predicted for each case (the scores that would be expected given scores on the **independent variable**). The difference between this expected score and the actual score is known as the residual.

R-squared (R^2)

The square of the **correlation coefficient** (R) is a measure of the proportion of the **variation** in the values of one variable which is statistically explained by variations in the values of another (or others).

Standard deviation

This is a measure of the dispersion or spread of a set of scores on a **continuous variable**. The smaller the standard deviation, the more closely the scores are clustered together; the larger it is, the more the scores are spread out.

Statistical significance

Significance tests measure the probability that a statistical relationship found in analysis might have occurred by chance. There is a variety of such tests appropriate for different types of analysis. In all cases, however, the key indicator is the probability statistic and normally a probability of 0.05 or less (usually reported as '$p < 0.05$') is taken to indicate a statistically significant result. When the probability is larger the relationship found is not significant. It is important to remember that the *statistical* significance of a relationship does not necessarily imply that it is *theoretically* or *substantively* significant.

Variable

A variable is any characteristic, quality or other measure that varies. It can vary over time, from place to place, from person to person or across any other set of cases.

Variation

Any set of values on a **continuous variable** has a given amount of variation. The square of the **standard deviation** (called the 'variance') is a measure of this variation, and in **correlation** and **regression analysis** estimates can be made as to how much of the variation in a **dependent variable** can be explained or accounted for by variations in **independent variables**.

References

Albright, J. (2009) 'Does Political Knowledge Erode Party Attachments? A Review of the Cognitive Mobilization Thesis', *Electoral Studies*, 28, 248–60.

Alford, R. (1964) *Party and Society* (London: John Murray).

Andersen, R. and Evans, G. (2003) 'Who Blairs Wins? Leadership and Voting in the 2001 Election', *British Elections & Parties Review*, 13, 229–47.

Atkinson, M. (1984) *Our Masters' Voices* (London: Methuen).

Bara, J. (2010) 'The 2010 Manifestos: Was it Only "The Economy, Stupid"?' Paper presented at the Elections, Public Opinion and Parties conference, University of Essex, 10–12 September.

Bartle, J. (2001) 'The Measurement of Party Identification in Britain: Where Do We Stand Now?', *British Elections and Parties Review*, 11, 9–22.

Bartle, J. (2002) 'Why Labour Won – Again', in A. King (ed.), *Britain at the Polls 2001* (New York: Chatham House), 164–206.

Bartle. J. (2005) 'The Press, Television and the Internet', in P. Norris and C. Wlezien (eds), *Britain Votes 2005* (Oxford: Oxford University Press), 43–55.

Bartle, J. and Crewe, I. (2002) 'The Impact of Party Leaders in Britain: Strong Assumptions, Weak Evidence', in A. King (ed.), *Leaders' Personalities and the Outcomes of Democratic Elections* (Oxford: Oxford University Press), 70–95.

Bartle, J. and Griffiths, D. (eds) (2001) *Political Communications Transformed: From Morrison to Mandelson* (Basingstoke: Palgrave Macmillan).

Bartle, J. and King, A. (eds) (2006) *Britain at the Polls 2005* (Washington, DC: CQ Press).

Bealey, F., Blondel, J. and McCann, W. (1965) *Constituency Politics* (London: Faber & Faber).

Beer, S. (1982) *Britain Against Itself* (London: Faber & Faber).

Benney, M., Gray, A. P. and Pear, R. H. (1956) *How People Vote* (London: Routledge & Kegan Paul).

Berelson, B., Lazarsfeld, P. and McPhee, W. (1954) *Voting* (Chicago, IL: University of Chicago Press).

Birch, A. H. (1959) *Small Town Politics* (Oxford: Oxford University Press).

Blau, A. (2001) 'Partisan Bias in British General Elections', *British Elections and Parties Review*, 11, 46–65.

Blumler, J. G. and McQuail, D. (1967) *Television in Politics* (London: Faber & Faber).

Broughton, D. (1995) *Public Opinion Polling and Politics in Britain* (London: Prentice Hall).

Brewer, M. (2009) *Party Images in the American Electorate* (New York: Routledge).

Bryman, A. and Cramer, D. (2001) *Quantitative Data Analysis with SPSS Release 10 for Windows* (London: Routledge).

Butler, D. (1952) *The British General Election of 1951* (London: Macmillan).

Butler, D. (1955) *The British General Election of 1955* (London: Macmillan).

Butler, D. (1998) 'Reflections on British Elections and Their Study', *Annual Review of Political Science*, 1, 451–64.

Butler, D. and Kavanagh, D. (1974) *The British General Election of February 1974* (London: Macmillan).

Butler, D. and Kavanagh, D. (1975) *The British General Election of October 1974* (London: Macmillan).

Butler, D. and Kavanagh, D. (1980) *The British General Election of 1979* (London: Macmillan).

Butler, D. and Kavanagh, D. (1984) *The British General Election of 1983* (London: Macmillan).

Butler, D. and Kavanagh, D. (1988) *The British General Election of 1987* (London: Macmillan).

Butler, D. and Kavanagh, D. (1992) *The British General Election of 1992* (London: Macmillan).

Butler, D. and Kavanagh, D. (1997) *The British General Election of 1997* (London: Macmillan).

Butler, D. and Kavanagh, D. (2002) *The British General Election of 2001* (London: Macmillan).

Butler, D. and King, A. (1965) *The British General Election of 1964* (London: Macmillan).

Butler, D. and King, A. (1966) *The British General Election of 1966* (London: Macmillan).

Butler, D. and Pinto-Duschinsky, M. (1971) *The British General Election of 1970* (London: Macmillan).

Butler, D. and Rose, R. (1960) *The British General Election of 1959* (London: Macmillan).

Butler, D. and Stokes, D. (1969) *Political Change in Britain*, 1st edn (London: Macmillan).

Butler, D. and Stokes, D. (1974) *Political Change in Britain*, 2nd edn (London: Macmillan).

Campbell, A., Converse, P., Miller, W. and Stokes D. (1960) *The American Voter* (New York: John Wiley).

Carman, C. J. and Johns, R. (2010) 'Linking Coalition Attitudes and Split-ticket Voting: The Scottish Parliament Elections of 2007', *Electoral Studies*, 29, 381–91.

Carrell, S. (2009) 'Scottish Independence? The SNP have an App for that', *The Guardian*, 30 November, available online at: http://www.guardian.co.uk/politics/2009/nov/30/scottish-national-party-iphone-app (accessed 27 February 2010).

Chandler, J. (1982) 'The Plurality Vote: A Reappraisal', *Political Studies*, 30, 87–94.

Clarke, H. and Stewart, M. (1995) 'Economic Evaluations and Election Outcomes: An Analysis of Alternative Forecasting Models', in D. Broughton, D. Farrell, D. Denver and C. Rallings (eds), *British Elections and Parties Yearbook 1994* (London: Frank Cass).

Clarke, H., Stewart, M. and Whiteley, P. (2001) 'The Dynamics of Partisanship in Britain: Evidence and Implications for Critical Election Theory', *British Elections and Parties Review*, 11, 66–83.

Clarke, H., Sanders, D., Stewart, M. and Whiteley, P. (2004) *Political Choice in Britain* (Oxford: Oxford University Press).

Clarke, H., Sanders, D., Stewart, M. and Whiteley, P. (2006) 'Taking the Bloom off New Labour's Rose: Party Choice and Voter Turnout in Britain, 2005', *Journal of Elections, Public Opinion and Parties,* 16, 3–36.

Clarke, H., Sanders, D., Stewart, M. and Whiteley, P. (2009) *Performance Politics and the British Voter* (Cambridge: Cambridge University Press).

Coates, S. (2010) 'Tories Wired Up but not Fired Up for the First Blackberry Election', *The Times Online,* 18 March, available online at: http://www.timesonline.co.uk/tol/news/politics/article7066320.ece?print=yes&randnum=1268914311866 (accessed 18 March 2010).

Converse, P. (1964) 'The Nature of Belief Systems in Mass Publics', in D. Apter (ed.), *Ideology and Discontent* (Glencoe: Free Press), 206–67.

Crabtree, J. (2010) 'David Cameron's Battle to Connect', *Wired.co.uk,* 24 March 2010, available online at http://www.wired.co.uk/magazine/archive/2010/04/features/david-camerons-battle-to-connect (accessed 5 April 2010).

Crewe, I. (1981a) 'Electoral Participation', in D. Butler, H. R. Penniman and A. Ranney (eds), *Democracy at the Polls* (Washington, DC: American Enterprise Institute), 216–63.

Crewe, I. (1981b) 'Why the Conservatives Won', in H. Penniman (ed.), *Britain at the Polls 1979* (Washington, DC: American Enterprise Institute), 263–305.

Crewe, I. (1984) 'The Electorate: Partisan Dealignment Ten Years On', in H. Berrington (ed.), *Change in British Politics* (London: Frank Cass), 183–215.

Crewe, I. (1985a) 'Great Britain', in I. Crewe and D. Denver (eds), *Electoral Change in Western Democracies* (London: Croom Helm), 100–50.

Crewe, I. (1985b) 'How to Win a Landslide Without Really Trying', in A. Ranney (ed.), *Britain at the Polls 1983* (Washington, DC: American Enterprise Institute), 155–96.

Crewe, I. (1986) 'On the Death and Resurrection of Class Voting: Some Comments on *How Britain Votes'*, *Political Studies,* 35, 620–38.

Crewe, I. (1988) 'Has the Electorate become Thatcherite?', in R. Skidelsky (ed.), *Thatcherism* (Oxford: Basil Blackwell), 25–49.

Crewe, I. (1992a) 'A Nation of Liars? Opinion Polls and the 1992 Election', *Parliamentary Affairs,* 45, 475–95.

Crewe, I. (1992b) 'The 1987 General Election', in D. Denver and G. Hands (eds), *Issues and Controversies in British Electoral Behaviour* (Hemel Hempstead: Harvester Wheatsheaf), 343–54.

Crewe, I. (1997) 'The Opinion Polls: Confidence Restored?', in P. Norris and N. Gavin (eds), *Britain Votes 1997* (Oxford: Oxford University Press), 61–77.

Crewe, I. (2001) 'The Opinion Polls: Still Biased to Labour', in P. Norris (ed.), *Britain Votes 2001* (Oxford: Oxford University Press), 86–101.

Crewe, I. (2002) 'A New Political Hegemony', in A. King (ed.), *Britain at the Polls 2001* (New York: Chatham House), 207–32.

Crewe, I. (2005) 'The Opinion Polls: The Election They Got (Almost) Right', in P. Norris and C. Wlezien (eds.), *Britain Votes 2005* (Oxford: Oxford University Press), 28–42.

Crewe, I. and King, A. (1994) 'Did Major win? Did Kinnock lose? Leadership effects in the 1992 election', in A. Heath, R. Jowell and J. Curtice with B. Taylor (eds), *Labour's Last Chance? The 1992 Election and Beyond* (Aldershot: Dartmouth), 125–47.

Crewe, I. and Payne, C. (1971) 'Analysing the Census Data', in D. Butler and M. Pinto-Duschinsky, *The British General Election of 1970* (London: Macmillan), 416–36.

Crewe, I. and Thomson, K. (1999) 'Party Loyalties: Dealignment or Realignment', in G. Evans and P. Norris (eds), *Critical Elections: British Parties and Voters in Long-Term Perspective* (London: Sage), 64–86.

Crewe, I., Fox, T. and Alt, J. (1977) 'Non-voting in British General Elections 1966–October 1974', in C. Crouch (ed.), *British Political Sociology Yearbook,* Vol. 3 (London: Croom Helm), 38–109.

Crewe, I., Fox, A. and Day, N. (1995) *The British Electorate 1963–1992* (Cambridge: Cambridge University Press).

Crewe, I., Sarlvik, B. and Alt, J. (1977) 'Partisan Dealignment in Britain 1964–1974', *British Journal of Political Science,* 7, 129–90.

Curtice, J. (1992) 'The Hidden Surprise: The British Electoral System in 1992', *Parliamentary Affairs,* 45, 466–74.

Curtice, J. (2001) 'The Electoral System', in P. Norris (ed.), *Britain Votes 2001* (Oxford: Oxford University Press), 239–50.

Curtice, J. (2004) 'Proportional Representation in Scotland: Public Reaction and Voter Behaviour', *Representation,* 40, 329–41.

Curtice, J. Fisher, S. and Ford, R. (2010) 'The British General Election of 2010: The Results Analysed', Paper presented at the Annual Meeting of the American Political Science Association, Washington, DC, 2–5 September.

Curtice, J. and Semetko, H. (1994) 'Does it Matter What the Papers Say?', in A. Heath, R. Jowell and J. Curtice (eds), *Labour's Last Chance: The 1992 Election and Beyond* (Aldershot: Dartmouth), 43–63.

Curtice, J. and Steed, M. (1982) 'Electoral Choice and the Production of Governments: The Changing Operation of the Electoral System in the UK since 1955', *British Journal of Political Science,* 12, 249–98.

Curtice, J. and Steed, M. (1986) 'Proportionality and Exaggeration in the British Electoral System', *Electoral Studies,* 5, 209–28.

Curtice, J. and Steed, M. (1988) 'Analysis', in D. Butler and D. Kavanagh, *The British General Election of 1987* (London: Macmillan), 316–62.

Curtice, J. and Steed, M. (1992) 'The Results Analysed', in D. Butler and D. Kavanagh, *The British General Election of 1992* (London: Macmillan), 322–62.

Curtice, J. and Steed, M. (1997) 'The Results Analysed', in D. Butler and D. Kavanagh, *The British General Election of 1997* (London: Macmillan), 293–325.

Curtice, J. and Steed, M. (2000) 'And Now for the Commons? Lessons from Britain's First Experience with Proportional Representation', *British Elections and Parties Review,* 10, 193–215.

Curtice, J. and Steed, M. (2001) 'An Analysis of the Results', in D. Butler and D. Kavanagh, *The British General Election of 2001* (Basingstoke: Palgrave Macmillan), 304–38.

Curtice, J., Fisher, S. and Steed, M. (2005) 'The Results Analysed', in D. Kavanagh and D. Butler, *The British General Election of 2005* (Basingstoke: Palgrave Macmillan), 235–59.

Curtice, J., Seyd, B., Park, A. and Thomson, K. (2000) *Wise After the Event? Attitudes to Voting Reform following the 1999 Scottish and Welsh Elections* (London: Constitution Unit).

Dalton, R. (1984) 'Cognitive Mobilization and Partisan Dealignment in Advanced Industrial Democracies', *Journal of Politics*, 46, 264–84.

Deacon, D. and Wring, D. (2002) 'Partisan Dealignment and the British Press', in J. Bartle, R. Mortimore and S. Atkinson (eds), *Political Communications: The General Election of 2001* (London: Frank Cass).

Deacon, D., Golding, P. and Billig, M. (1998) 'Between Fear and Loathing: National Press Coverage of the 1997 British General Election', *British Elections and Parties Review*, 8, 135–49.

Denver, D. (1994) *Elections and Voting Behaviour in Britain*, 2nd edn (Hemel Hempstead: Harvester Wheatsheaf).

Denver, D. (1998a) 'The British Electorate in the 1990s', in H. Berrington (ed.), *Britain in the Nineties: The Politics of Paradox* (London: Frank Cass), 197–217.

Denver, D. (1998b) 'The Government That Could Do No Right', in A. King (ed.), *New Labour Triumphs: Britain at the Polls* (New York: Chatham House), 15–48.

Denver, D. (2001) 'The Liberal Democrat Campaign', in P. Norris (ed.), *Britain Votes 2001* (Oxford: Oxford University Press), 86–101.

Denver, D. (2005) 'Valence Politics: How Britain Votes Now', *British Journal of Politics and International Relations*, 7, 292–9.

Denver, D. and Halfacree, K. (1992a) 'Inter-constituency Migration and Party Support in Britain', *Political Studies*, 40, 571–80.

Denver, D. and Halfacree, K. (1992b) 'Inter-constituency Migration and Turnout at the British General Election of 1983', *British Journal of Political Science*, 22, 248–54.

Denver, D. and Hands, G. (1974) 'Marginality and Turnout in British General Elections', *British Journal of Political Science*, 4, 17–35.

Denver, D. and Hands, G. (1985) 'Marginality and Turnout in British General Elections in the 1970s', *British Journal of Political Science*, 15, 381–8.

Denver, D. and Hands, G. (1990) 'Issues, Principles or Ideology? How Young Voters Decide', *Electoral Studies*, 9, 19–36.

Denver, D. and Hands, G. (eds) (1992) *Issues and Controversies in British Electoral Behaviour* (Hemel Hempstead: Harvester Wheatsheaf).

Denver, D. and Hands, G. (1997a) *Modern Constituency Electioneering* (London: Frank Cass).

Denver, D. and Hands, G. (1997b) 'Turnout', in P. Norris and N. Gavin (eds), *Britain Votes 1997* (Oxford: Oxford University Press), 212–24.

Denver, D. and Hands, G. (2004) 'Exploring Variations in Turnout: Constituencies and Wards in the Scottish Parliament Elections of 1999 and 2003', *British Journal of Politics and International Relations*, 6, 527–42.

Denver, D., Hands, G. and MacAllister, I. (2003) 'Constituency Marginality and Turnout in Britain Revisited', *British Elections and Parties Review*, 13, 174–94.

Denver, D., Hands, G. and MacAllister, I. (2004) 'The Electoral Impact of Constituency Campaigning in Britain, 1992–2001', *Political Studies*, 52, 289–306.

Denver, D., Hands, G., Fisher, J. and MacAllister, I. (2002) 'Constituency Campaigning in 2001: The Effectiveness of Targeting', in J. Bartle, R. Mortimore and S. Atkinson (eds), *Political Communications: The General Election of 2001* (London: Frank Cass), 158–80.

Denver, D., Hands, G., Fisher, J. and MacAllister, I. (2003) 'Constituency Campaigning in Britain 1992–2001: Centralization and Modernization', *Party Politics, 9*, 541–59.

Downs, A. (1957) *An Economic Theory of Democracy* (New York: Harper).

Dunleavy, P. (1979) 'The Urban Basis of Political Alignment: Social Class, Domestic Property Ownership and State Intervention in Consumption Processes', *British Journal of Political Science, 9*, 409–43.

Dunleavy, P. (1980) 'The Political Implications of Sectoral Cleavages and the Growth of State Employment', *Political Studies, 28*, 364–83 and 527–49.

Dunleavy, P. (1987) 'Class Dealignment in Britain Revisited', *West European Politics, 10*, 400–19.

Dunleavy, P. and Margetts, H. (1999) 'Reforming the Westminster Electoral System: Evaluating the Jenkins Commission Proposals', *British Elections and Parties Review, 9*, 46–71.

Dunleavy, P., Margetts, H. and Bastow, S. (2001) 'Freed from Constraint: Political Alignments in the 2000 London Elections', Paper presented at the PSA annual conference, Manchester.

Edgeworth, F. (1905) 'The Law of Error', *Transactions of the Cambridge Philosophical Society, 20*, 35–65 and 113–44.

Electoral Commission (2001a) *Campaign Expenditure for Great Britain Parties,* Electoral Commission Website.

Electoral Commission (2001b) *Election 2001, The Official Results* (London: Politico's).

Electoral Commission (2003) *Party Political Broadcasting: Report and Recommendations* (London: Electoral Commission).

Electoral Commission (2005) *Register of Campaign Expenditure,* Electoral Commission website.

Electoral Commission (2010) *UK General Election 2010 Campaign Spending Report* (London: The Electoral Commission).

Electoral Studies (2000) Special Issue on 'Economics and Elections', 19 (2/3).

Evans, G. (1993) 'The Decline of Class Divisions in Britain? Class and ideological preferences in the 1960s and the 1980s', *British Journal of Sociology* 44, 449–71.

Evans, G. (1999) *The End of Class Voting: Class Voting in Comparative Perspective* (Oxford: Oxford University Press).

Evans, G. (2000) 'The Continued Significance of Class Voting', *Annual Review of Political Science, 3*, 401–17.

Evans, G. and Andersen, R. (2005) 'The Impact of Party Leaders: How Blair Lost Labour Votes', in P. Norris and C. Wlezien (eds), *Britain Votes 2005* (Oxford: Oxford University Press), 162–80.

Evans, G. and Norris, P. (eds) (1999) *Critical Elections* (London: Sage).

Evans, G., Heath, A. and Payne, C. (1999) 'Class: Labour as a Catch-All Party?', in G. Evans and P. Norris (eds), *Critical Elections: British Parties and Voters in Long-Term Perspective* (London: Sage), 87–101.

Evans, G. and Tilley, J. (forthcoming), 'How Parties Shape Class Politics: Explaining the Decline of the Class Basis of Party Support', *British Journal of Political Science*, in press.

Fallon, I. and Worcester, R. (1992) 'The Use of Panel Studies in British General Elections', Paper presented at EPOP/Political Communications conference, University of Essex, September 1992.

Farrell, D. (2001) *Electoral Systems: A Comparative Introduction* (Basingstoke: Palgrave Macmillan).

Farrell, D., McAllister, I. and Broughton, D. (1995) 'The Changing British Voter Revisited: Patterns of Election Campaign Volatility since 1964', in D. Broughton, D. Farrell, D. Denver and C. Rallings (eds), *British Elections and Parties Yearbook 1994* (London: Frank Cass), 110–27.

Festinger, L. (1962) *A Theory of Cognitive Dissonance* (London: Tavistock).

Field, W. (1997) *Regional Dynamics: The Basis of Electoral Support in Britain* (London: Frank Cass).

Fieldhouse, E. and Cutts, D. (2007) *Electoral participation in Britain's South Asian communities* (York: Joseph Roundtree Foundation).

Fieldhouse, E. and Cutts, D. (2008) 'Diversity, Density and Turnout: The Effect of Neighbourhood Ethno-religious Composition on Voter Turnout in Britain', *Political Geography,* 27, 530–48.

Fiorina, M. (1981) *Retrospective Voting in American National Elections* (New Haven, CT: Yale University Press).

Fisher, J. (2001) 'Campaign Finance', in P. Norris (ed.), *Britain Votes 2001* (Oxford: Oxford University Press), 125–36.

Fisher, J. and Denver, D. (2008) 'From Foot-slogging to Call Centres and Direct Mail: A Framework for Analyzing the Development of District-level Campaigning', *European Journal of Political Research,* 47, 794–826.

Fisher, J. and Denver, D. (2009) 'Evaluating the Electoral Effects of Traditional and Modern Modes of Constituency Campaigning in Britain, 1992–2005', *Parliamentary Affairs,* 62, 196–210.

Fisher, J., Cutts, D., and Fieldhouse, E. (2010) 'Constituency Campaigning in the 2010 British General Election', Paper presented at the annual meeting of the Elections, Public Opinion and Parties (EPOP) specialist group of the Political Studies Association, University of Essex, September.

Fisher, J., Denver, D., Fieldhouse, E., Cutts, D. and Russell, A. (2006) 'Constituency Campaigning in 2005: Ever More Centralization?', in D. Wring, J. Green, R. Mortimore and S. Atkinson (eds), *Political Communications: The British General Election of 2005* (Basingstoke: Palgrave Macmillan).

Foley, M. (2000) *The British Presidency* (Manchester: Manchester University Press).

Franklin, M. (1985) *The Decline of Class Voting in Britain* (Oxford: Oxford University Press).

Franklin, M. (1996) 'Electoral Participation', in L. LeDuc, R. Niemi and P. Norris (eds), *Comparing Democracies: Elections and Voting in Global Perspective* (London: Sage), 216–35.

Franklin, M. (2002) 'The Dynamics of Electoral Participation', in L. LeDuc, R. Niemi and P. Norris (eds), *Comparing Democracies 2: New Challenges in the Study of Elections and Voting* (London: Sage), 148–68.

Franklin, M. and Hughes, C. (1999) 'Dynamic Representation in Britain', in G. Evans and P. Norris (eds), *Critical Elections: British Parties and Voters in Long-Term Perspective* (London: Sage), 240–58.

Galbraith, J. and Rae, N. (1989) 'A Test of the Importance of Tactical Voting: Great Britain 1987', *British Journal of Political Science,* 19, 126–36.

Gallup, *Political Index.*

Gallup, *Political and Economic Index.*

Gavin, N. and Sanders, D. (1997) 'The Economy and Voting', in P. Norris and N. Gavin (eds), *Britain Votes 1997* (Oxford: Oxford University Press), 123–32.

Geddes, A. and Tonge, J. (eds) (2002) *Labour's Second Landslide* (Manchester: Manchester University Press).

Geddes, A. and Tonge, J. (eds) (2005) *Britain Decides: The UK General Election 2005* (Basingstoke: Palgrave Macmillan).

Gibson, R. K., Williamson, A. and Ward, S. (2010) *The Internet and the 2010 Election: Putting the Small 'p' Back in Politics?* London: Hansard Society.

Goldthorpe, J. H., Lockwood, D., Bechhofer, F. and Platt, J. (1968) *The Affluent Worker* (Cambridge: Cambridge University Press).

Goodhart, C. and Bhansali, R. (1970) 'Political Economy', *Political Studies,* 18, 43–106.

Hain, P. (1998) *Proportional Misrepresentation* (Aldershot: Gower).

Harris, R. (2001) 'The Left Blinds Itself to the Truth about bin Laden', *Daily Telegraph,* 18 December 2001.

Harrop, M. (1986) 'Press Coverage of Post War British Elections', in I. Crewe and M. Harrop (eds), *Political Communications: The General Election Campaign of 1983* (Cambridge: Cambridge University Press).

Harrop, M. and Scammell, M. (1992) 'A Tabloid War', in D. Butler and D. Kavanagh, *The British General Election of 1992* (London: Macmillan), 180–210.

Harrop, M., Heath, A. and Openshaw, S. (1992) 'Does Neighbourhood Influence Voting Behaviour – and Why?', in I. Crewe, P. Norris, D. Denver and D. Broughton (eds), *British Elections and Parties Yearbook 1991* (Hemel Hempstead: Harvester Wheatsheaf), 103– 20.

Hart, J. (1992) *Proportional Representation: Critics of the British Electoral System 1820–1945* (Oxford: Clarendon Press).

Heath, A. and Taylor, B. (1999) 'New Sources of Abstention?', in G. Evans and P. Norris (eds), *Critical Elections* (London: Sage), 164–80.

Heath, A., Jowell, R. and Curtice, J. (1985) *How Britain Votes* (Oxford: Pergamon Press).

Heath, A., Jowell, R. and Curtice, J. (2001) *The Rise of New Labour: Party Policies and Voter Choices* (Oxford: Oxford University Press).

Heath, A., Jowell, R., Curtice, J., Evans, G., Field, J. and Witherspoon, S. (1991) *Understanding Political Change* (Oxford: Pergamon Press).

Heath, A., Jowell, R., Curtice, J. with B. Taylor (eds) (1994) *Labour's Last Chance? The 1992 Election and Beyond* (Aldershot: Dartmouth).

Heath, O. and Johns, R. (2010) 'Measuring Political Behaviour', in M. Bulmer, J. Gibbs and L. Hyman (eds), *Social Measurement through Social Surveys* (Aldershot: Ashgate), 47–68.

Independent, The (2010) 'Vote for a Change. Real Change.', 2 May 2010, available online at http://www.independent.co.uk/opinion/leading-articles/ leading-article-vote-for-change-real-change-1960288.html (accessed 10 January 2011).

Ipsos MORI (2010). 'Ipsos MORI – Final Election Poll', available online at: http://www.ipsos-mori.com/researchpublications/researcharchive/ poll.aspx? oItemId=2607 (accessed 16 September 2010).

Jenkins, R. (1998) *Report of the Independent Commission on the Voting System* (London: The Stationery Office).

Johnston, R. and Pattie, C. (2001) 'It's the Economy, Stupid – But Which Economy? Geographical scales, retrospective economic evaluations and voting at the 1997 British general election', *Regional Studies,* 35, 309–20.

Johnston, R., Pattie, C. and Allsop, J. (1988) A *Nation Dividing* (London: Longman).

Johnston, R., Pattie, C. and Rossiter, D. (2005) 'The Election Results in the UK Regions' in P. Norris and C. Wlezien (eds), *Britain Votes 2005* (Oxford: Oxford University Press), 130–45.

Johnston, R., Rossiter, D. and Pattie, R. (2006) 'Disproportionality and Bias in the Results of the 2005 General Election: Evaluating the Electoral System's Impact', *Journal of Elections, Public Opinion and Parties,* 16 (1), 37–54.

Johnston, R., Pattie, C., Dorling, D. and Rossiter, D. (2001) *From Votes to Seats: The Operation of the UK Electoral System since 1945* (Manchester: Manchester University Press).

Johnston, R., Pattie, C., Dorling, D., MacAllister, I., Tunstall, H. and Rossiter, D. (2000) 'The Neighbourhood Effect and Voting in England and Wales: Real or Imagined?', in *British Elections and Parties Review,* 10, 47–63.

Johnston, R., Pattie, C., Dorling, D., Rossiter, D., Tunstall, H. and MacAllister, I. (1998) 'New Labour Landslide – Same Old Electoral Geography?', *British Elections and Parties Review,* 8, 35–64.

Kavanagh, D. (1995) *Election Campaigning: The New Marketing of Politics* (Oxford: Basil Blackwell).

Kavanagh, D. and Butler, D. (2005) *The British General Election of 2005* (Basingstoke: Palgrave Macmillan).

Kavanagh, D. and Cowley, P. (2010) *The British General Election of 2010* (Basingstoke: Palgrave Macmillan).

King, A. (1975) 'Overload: Problems of Governing in the 1970s', *Political Studies,* 23, 284–96.

King, A. (2002a) 'Do Leaders' Personalities Really Matter?' in A. King (ed.) *Leaders' Personalities and the Outcomes of Democratic Elections* (Oxford: Oxford University Press), 1–43.

King, A. (ed.) (2002b) *Britain at the Polls 2001* (New York: Chatham House).

King, A. (2006) 'Why Labour Won', in J. Bartle and A. King (eds) *Britain at the Polls 2005* (Washington, DC: CQ Press), 151–84.

King, A. and Wybrow, R. (2001) *British Political Opinion 1937–2000* (London: Politico's).

Kirchheimer, O. (1966) 'The Transformation of the Western European Party Systems', in J. LaPalombara and M. Weiner (eds) *Political Parties and Political Development* (Princeton, NJ: Princeton University Press), 177–200.

Klingemann, H.-D., Volkens, A., Bara, J., Budge, I. and McDonald, M. (2006) *Mapping Policy Preferences II: Estimates for Parties, Electors, and Governments in Eastern Europe, European Union and OECD 1990–2003* (Oxford: Oxford University Press).

Lazarsfeld, P., Berelson, B. and Gaudet, H. (1968) *The People's Choice,* 3rd edn; first published 1944 (New York: Columbia University Press).

Lijphart, A. (1994) *Electoral Systems and Party Systems* (Oxford: Oxford University Press).

Lipset, S. M. and Rokkan, S. (1967) *Party Systems and Voter Alignments* (New York: Free Press).

Margetts, H., van Heerde, J. and Dunleavy, P. (2005) 'Explaining Voters' Choices in London Elections 2004', Paper presented at the PSA annual conference, Leeds.

McAllister, I. and Studlar, D. (1992) 'Region and Voting in Britain: Territorial Polarization or Artifact', *American Journal of Political Science*, 36, 168–99.

McCallum, R. B. and Readman, A. (1947) *The British General Election of 1945* (Oxford: Oxford University Press).

McFarlane, A. (2010) 'Will Tactical Voting Swing 2010 General Election?' BBC News Online, available at http://news.bbc.co.uk/1/hi/uk_politics/election_2010/8612463.stm (accessed 2 April 2011).

McKenzie, R. and Silver, A. (1968) *Angels in Marble* (London: Heinemann).

McLean, I. (1982) *Dealing in Votes* (London: Martin Robertson).

Mill, J. S. (1963) *Considerations on Representative Government*, World Classics edn (Oxford: Oxford University Press).

Miller, W. (1977) *Electoral Dynamics in Britain since 1918* (London: Macmillan).

Miller, W. (1978) 'Social Class and Party Choice in England: A New Analysis', *British Journal of Political Science*, 8, 257–84.

Miller, W. (1979) 'Class, Region and Strata at the British General Election of 1979', *Parliamentary Affairs*, 32, 376–82.

Miller, W. (1981) *The End of British Politics* (Oxford: Clarendon Press).

Miller, W. (1991) *Media and Voters* (Oxford: Clarendon Press).

Miller, W. and Mackie, M. (1973) 'The Electoral Cycle and the Asymmetry of Government and Opposition Popularity', *Political Studies*, 21, 263–79.

Miller, W., Tagg, S. and Britto, K. (1986) 'Partisanship and Party Preference in Government and Opposition: The Mid-term Perspective', *Electoral Studies*, 5, 31–46.

Miller, W., Clarke, H., Harrop, M., Leduc, L. and Whiteley, P. (1990) *How Voters Change* (Oxford: Clarendon Press).

Milne, R. S. and Mackenzie, H. C. (1954) *Straight Fight* (London: Hansard Society).

Milne, R. S. and Mackenzie, H. C. (1958) *Marginal Seat* (London: Hansard Society).

Moon, N. (1999) *Opinion Polls: History, Theory and Practice* (Manchester: Manchester University Press).

Mughan, A. (1993) 'Party Leaders and Presidentialism in the 1992 Election: A Post-war Perspective', in D. Denver, P. Norris, D. Broughton and C. Rallings (eds), *British Elections and Parties Yearbook 1993* (London: Frank Cass), 193–204.

Newton, K. (1993) 'Economic Voting in the 1992 General Election', in D. Denver, P. Norris, D. Broughton and C. Rallings (eds), *British Elections and Parties Yearbook 1993* (Hemel Hempstead: Harvester Wheatsheaf), 158–76.

Newton, K. and Brynin, M. (2001) 'The National Press and Party Voting in the UK', *Political Studies*, 49, 265–85.

Nicholas, H. G. (1951) *The British General Election of 1950* (London: Macmillan).

Niemi, R., Whitten, G. and Franklin, M. (1992) 'Constituency Characteristics,

Individual Characteristics and Tactical Voting in the 1987 British General Election', *British Journal of Political Science,* 22, 229–54.

Nordlinger, E. (1967) *Working-Class Tories* (London: Macgibbon & Kee).

Norpoth, H. (1992) *Confidence Regained: Economics, Mrs. Thatcher and the British Voter* (Ann Arbor, MI: University of Michigan Press).

Norris, P. (1987) 'Four Weeks of Sound and Fury? ... The 1987 British Election Campaign', *Parliamentary Affairs,* 40, 458–67.

Norris, P. (1990) *British By-elections* (Oxford: Clarendon Press).

Norris, P. (1997a) *Electoral Change in Britain since 1945* (Oxford: Basil Blackwell).

Norris, P. (1997b) 'Political Communications', in P. Dunleavy, A. Gamble, I. Holliday and G. Peele (eds), *Developments in British Politics* 5 (London: Macmillan), 75–88.

Norris, P. (ed.) (2001) *Britain Votes 2001* (Oxford: Oxford University Press).

Norris, P. and Wlezien, C. (eds) (2005) *Britain Votes 2005* (Oxford: Oxford University Press).

Norris, P., Curtice, J., Sanders, D., Scammell, M. and Semetko, H. (1999) *On Message: Communicating the Campaign* (London: Sage).

Norton, P. (2002) 'The Conservative Party: Is There Anyone Out There?', in A. King (ed.), *Britain at the Polls 2001* (New York: Chatham House), 68–94.

O'Leary, C. (1962) *The Elimination of Corrupt Practices in British Elections 1868–1911* (Oxford: Clarendon Press).

Ofcom (2010) 'UK Adults' Media Literacy', Research Paper 17 May, available online http://stakeholders.ofcom.org.uk/market-data-research/media-literacy/medlitpub/medlitpubrss/adultmedialitreport/ (accessed 4 October 2011).

Palmer, H. (1995) 'Effects of Authoritarian and Libertarian Values on Conservative and Labour Party Support in Great Britain', *European Journal of Political Research,* 27, 273–92.

Paterson, L., Brown, A., Curtice, J., Hinds, K., McCrone, D., Park, A., Sproston, K. and Surridge, P. (2001) *New Scotland, New Politics?* (Edinburgh: Polygon).

Pattie, C. and Johnston, R. (1998) 'Voter Turnout at the British General Election of 1992: Rational Choice, Social Standing or Political Efficacy?', *European Journal of Political Research,* 33, 263–83.

Pattie, C. and Johnston, R. (1999) 'Context, Conversation and Conviction: Social Networks and Voting at the 1992 British General Election', *Political Studies,* 47, 877–99.

Pattie, C. and Johnston, R. (2001) 'Talk as a Political Context: Conversation and Electoral Change in British Elections, 1992–1997', *Electoral Studies,* 20, 17–40.

Pattie, C., Johnston, R. and Fieldhouse, E. (1993) 'Plus ca change? The Changing Electoral Geography of Great Britain, 1979–92', in D. Denver, P. Norris, D. Broughton and C. Rallings (eds), *British Elections and Parties Yearbook 1993* (Hemel Hempstead: Harvester Wheatsheaf), 85–99.

Pattie, C., Johnston, R. and Fieldhouse, E. (1995) 'Winning the Local Vote: The Effectiveness of Constituency Campaign Spending in Great Britain, 1983–1992', *American Political Science Review,* 89, 969–83.

Pattie, C., Denver, D., Johns, R. and Mitchell, J. (2011) 'Raising the Tone? The

Impact of "Positive" and "Negative" Campaigning on Voting in the 2007 Scottish Parliament Election', *Electoral Studies*, 30 (2), 333–43.

Pedersen, M. N. (1979) 'The Dynamics of European Party Systems: Changing Patterns of Electoral Volatility', *European Journal of Political Research*, 7, 1–26.

Pulzer, P. G. (1967) *Political Representation and Elections in Britain* (London: George Allen & Unwin).

Quinn, T. (2006) 'Tony Blair's Second Term' in J. Bartle and A. King (eds.) *Britain at the Polls 2005* (Washington DC: CQ Press).

Rallings, C. and Thrasher, M. (1990) 'Turnout in Local Elections: An aggregate data analysis with electoral and contextual data', *Electoral Studies*, 9, 79–90.

Rallings, C. and Thrasher, M. (2000) *British Electoral Facts 1832–1999* (Aldershot: Ashgate).

Rallings, C. and Thrasher, M. (2005) *Election 2005: The Official Results* (Plymouth: Local Government Chronicle).

Reif, K. H. and Schmitt, H. (1980) 'Nine Second-Order Elections', *European Journal of Political Research,* 8, 3–45 and 145–62.

Rose, D. and Sullivan, O. (1996) *Introducing Data Analysis for Social Scientists,* 2nd edn (Buckingham: Open University Press).

Rose, R. (1974) 'Britain: Simple Abstractions and Complex Realities', in R. Rose (ed.), *Electoral Behaviour* (New York: Free Press).

Rose, R. and McAllister, I. (1986) *Voters Begin to Choose* (London: Sage).

Rose, R. and McAllister, I. (1990) *The Loyalties of Voters* (London: Sage).

Rosenbaum, M. (1997) *From Soapbox to Soundbite: Party Political Campaigning in Britain since 1945* (London: Macmillan).

Saggar, S. (1998) *The General Election 1997: Ethnic Minorities and Electoral Politics* (London: Commission for Racial Equality).

Sanders, D. (1991) 'Government Popularity and the Next General Election', *Political Quarterly,* 62, 235–61.

Sanders, D. (1992) 'Why the Conservatives Won – Again', in A. King (ed.), *Britain at the Polls 1992* (New York: Chatham House), 171–222.

Sanders, D. (1993) 'Forecasting the 1992 British General Election Outcome: The Performance of an Economic Model', in D. Denver, P. Norris, D. Broughton and C. Rallings (eds), *British Elections and Parties Yearbook 1993* (Hemel Hempstead: Harvester Wheatsheaf), 100–15.

Sanders, D. (1995) 'It's the Economy, Stupid: The Economy and Support for the Conservative Party, 1979–1994', *Talking Politics,* 7, 158–67.

Sanders, D. (1999) 'The Impact of Left–Right Ideology', in G. Evans and P. Norris (eds) *Critical Elections* (London: Sage), 181–206.

Sanders, D. (2005) 'The Political Economy of UK Party Support, 1997–2004: Forecasts for the 2005 General Election', *Journal of Elections, Public Opinion and Parties,* 15, 47–71.

Sanders, D., Burton, J. and Kneeshaw, J. (2002) 'Identifying the True Identifiers: A Question Wording Experiment', *Party Politics*, 8, 193–205.

Sanders, D., Ward, H. and Marsh, D. (1987) 'Government Popularity and the Falklands War: A Reassessment', *British Journal of Political Science,* 17, 281–313.

Sanders, D., Clarke, H., Stewart, M. and Whiteley, P. (2001) 'The Economy and Voting', in P. Norris (ed.), *Britain Votes 2001* (Oxford: Oxford University Press), 223–38.

Sarlvik, B. and Crewe, I. (1983) *Decade of Dealignment* (Cambridge: Cambridge University Press).

Scammell, M. (1995) *Designer Politics: How Elections are Won* (London: Macmillan).

Scammell, M. and Harrop, M. (1997) 'The Press', in D. Butler and D. Kavanagh, *The British General Election of 1997* (London: Macmillan), 156–85.

Seymour-Ure, C. (2002) 'New Labour and the Media', in A. King (ed.), *Britain at the Polls 2001* (New York: Chatham House), 117–42.

Shaw, E. (1994) *The Labour Party since 1979* (London: Routledge).

Steed, M. (1986) 'The Core-Periphery Dimension of British Politics', *Political Geography Quarterly,* 5, 91–103.

Stokes, D. (1963) 'Spatial Models of Party Competition', *American Political Science Review,* 57, 368–77.

Stokes, D. (1992) 'Valence Politics', in D. Kavanagh (ed.), *Electoral Politics* (Oxford: Clarendon Press).

Swaddle, K. and Heath, A. (1989) 'Official and Reported Turnout in the British General Election of 1987', *British Journal of Political Science,* 19, 537–51.

Teer, F. and Spence, J.D. (1973) *Political Opinion Polls* (London: Hutchinson).

Thrasher, M. (2010) 'Written Evidence Submitted by Michael Thrasher on the Parliamentary Voting System and Constituencies Bill (PVSCB 11)', available online at http://www.publications.parliament.uk/pa/cm201011/cmselect/cmpolcon/437/437we13.htm (accessed 15 May 2011).

Trenaman, J. and McQuail, D. (1961) *Television and the Political Image* (London: Methuen).

Trilling, R. (1976) *Party Image and Electoral Behavior* (New York: Wiley).

Wallas, G. (1910) *Human Nature in Politics* (London: Constable).

Whiteley, P. (1986) 'The Accuracy and Influence of the Polls in the 1983 General Election', in I. Crewe and M. Harrop (eds), *Political Communications: The 1983 Election Campaign* (Cambridge: Cambridge University Press), 312–24.

Whiteley, P. and Seyd, P. (1994) 'Local Party Campaigning and Voting Behaviour in Britain', *Journal of Politics,* 56, 242–51.

Williamson, A. (2010) 'Inside the Digital Campaign', in R. Gibson, A. Williamson and S. Ward, *The Internet and the 2010 Election: Putting the Small 'p' Back in Politics?* (London: Hansard Society).

Wintour, P. (2010) 'Labour: Voters' "Submerged Optimism" will Stop Tory Win', *The Guardian* 19 February 2010, available online at: http://www.guardian.co.uk/politics/2010/feb/19/labour-voters-optimism-tory-election (accessed 19 February 2010)

Worcester, R. and Mortimore, R. (1999) *Explaining Labour's Landslide* (London: Politico's).

Worcester, R. and Mortimore, R. (2001) *Explaining Labour's Second Landslide* (London: Politico's).

Worcester, R., Mortimore, R. and Baines, P. (2005) *Explaining Labour's Landslip: The 2005 General Election* (London: Methuen).

Wring, D., Mortimore, R. and Atkinson, S. (eds) (2011) *Political Communication in Britain* (Basingstoke: Palgrave Macmillan).

Name Index

Subject Index